Montessori, Dewey,

and

Capitalism

MONTESSORI, DEWEY, AND CAPITALISM

EDUCATIONAL THEORY FOR A
FREE MARKET IN EDUCATION

JERRY KIRKPATRICK

TLJ BOOKS
CLAREMONT, CALIFORNIA

Publisher's Cataloging-in-Publication Data

Kirkpatrick, Jerry.
   Montessori, Dewey, and Capitalism : educational theory for a
free market in education / Jerry Kirkpatrick.

   p. cm.
   Includes bibliographical references and index.

   ISBN 978-0-9787803-2-6 (hardcover)
   ISBN 978-0-9787803-3-3 (pbk.)

1. Montessori method of education. 2. Dewey, John, 1859–1952.
3. Education—Economic aspects—United States. 4. Education
and state—United States. 5. Free enterprise. 6. Educational change.
7. Education—Social aspects—United States. I. Title.

LC66 .K71 2008
379.7321—dc22   2007904768

Library of Congress Catalog Card Number: 2007904768

TLJ Books, P. O. Box 1165, Claremont, CA 91711
http://www.tljbooks.com

Printed in the United States of America

To Thea

Contents

Preface

This book presents a philosophy of education that requires capitalism for its full realization.

Laissez-faire capitalism is the social system in which all means of production, including roads, schools, and hospitals, are privately owned and operated. The only function of government is to protect individual rights, not to run or regulate businesses, including those in the field of education. I assume that this system is morally and economically unassailable.

My initial ambition was to project the mechanism by which a free market in education might operate, if such were to exist. Today, of course, we have nothing that remotely resembles competitive free markets in education.

By "free market in education" I mean the complete separation of education and state, in the same way and for the same reasons that we now have the complete separation of church and state. All formal schooling would be provided by profit-making entrepreneurs competing with one another for the same parent-student dollar, and the government, whether federal, state, or local, would be completely out of the education business. My aim, therefore, was to describe in broad strokes what a truly free—politically free—educational system would be like. Only by holding a clear vision of the goal, so my assumption stated, can one define the steps required to establish a free market in education. And that would require a thorough understanding of its nature.

By "mechanism" of a free market in education I mean the specific structure of the educational market. How would a free market in education differ from that of the state controlled system we now have? Would there be evaluative grades, examinations, and degrees? What different kinds of educational goods and services would be marketed? And how would such educational businesses operate in terms of aims, teaching methodology, curriculum, and management? In other words, what would a free market in education be like in practice? These are some of the questions I had planned to attempt to answer.

The present work has not strayed too far from this original goal, especially in chapter 5, but in the course of my research I discovered that my interests were more fundamental than the concrete projection and description initially conceived. My reading of history, the history of education, and, especially, the history of educational thought led me to realize that no philosophy of education existed explicitly advocating capitalism for its implementation. John Dewey and his progressive colleagues and predecessors unambiguously advocated the state as the proper provider of education, but advocates of capitalism for the most part argue that the state should get out of education and leave the issue at that. Some of the latter, and I fall into this group, have harshly criticized progressive education and have generally assumed that a form of traditional education would be prominent in a capitalist system; such an education, it was assumed, would be better under capitalistic entrepreneurship than under past and present state control. I no longer hold this assumption, for the following reasons.

My long-time admiration of Maria Montessori was shaken somewhat when I read that she considered herself to be a progressive educator. My criticism of Dewey turned to a guarded admiration after I read several of his major works on both education and philosophy.[1] My reading of the history of educational thought then put Montessori and Dewey together as the culmination of a trend that has been evolving since at least the Enlightenment. This trend urges educators to respect the child as a unique individual. It argues that tender guidance, not coercion and control, will embolden children to seek the knowledge, values, and skills they need to grow and become independent. The attitude

---

[1] Filtered interpretations provided by commentators, followers, and critics are never trustworthy sources of information, especially for writers whose ideas develop in complex historical contexts and, like Dewey's, are sometimes couched in difficult-to-understand styles.

of forcing children to bow to the will of adults, says this trend, along with, more generally, a pervasive insensitivity toward the young, kills the energy and curiosity that otherwise would naturally flourish.

In this trend, however, I noticed a significant problem, especially as it was put into practice in the twentieth century. Progressive educators attempted to respect the uniqueness of individual children by dispensing with coercion in the classroom. At the same time, they coerced the delivery of the classroom itself. They coerced the funds to pay for education by forcibly expropriating money from some parents for the benefit of the children of others. And they compelled all children to fill the seats of the coercively provided classrooms. When I recognized this inconsistency in the policies of the progressives, I realized that there existed a philosophy of education for a free market in education, one that emphasized individual uniqueness and independence but was confusingly commingled with the philosophy of socialism. From this point on I focused my research on development of the purpose, method, and content of education that would imply capitalism. The correct connection between society and child-centered learning is not "democracy and education," as Dewey's major educational work is titled—democracy for Dewey and his progressive colleagues being euphemism for unlimited majority rule that supports interventionist economics (if not Fabian socialism) and socialized education.

The correct connection is capitalism and education.

Acknowledgments

My interest in education began early, so I have numerous acknowledgments. My parents' approach to child-rearing was old-school authoritarianism that I vigorously contested, sometimes to my detriment. However, my mother would often talk about her seven years, in rural western Kansas, as teacher in a one-room schoolhouse. Were it not for these stories, I probably would not have become a teacher. My father's education stopped at high school and his (very early) morning job was to clerk in the local post office. In the afternoon, when I was about twelve, he decided that the half acre behind our home could be divided and two houses could be put there. Against the protests of my mother, he proceeded single-handedly to build two houses. And sometimes I helped him as day laborer. Although he was skilled in household repair and modest renovation, his only education for this task was to buy a book on how to build a house and to follow its recommendations precisely. From this example of my father's determined and unpretentious personality, I learned, first, that credentials and formal schooling do not dictate ability or qualification and, second, that if I wanted to know how to do something, or, more simply, to know, I should first buy a book. (Today, I first search the Internet.)

My two older brothers, by their examples, showed me the way to higher education, so much so that I began reading their college catalogues in the sixth grade. My awareness of the difference between public and private education came when I entered a private school for my last two years of high school (paid for in part with proceeds from the sale of my father's first completed house). In public-school tenth grade, I attended an honors English class and earned gentlemanly A's and B's. In private school, junior-year English, Miss Kleinschmit, who frequently urged her students to "beware the cult of mediocrity," gave me a D-, mostly for my inability to write a coherent sentence. Lest I join the ranks of the mediocre, Miss Kleinschmit encouraged me to take remedial composition classes, including hers taught at the sophomore level. I did remediation and it is to Miss Kleinschmit that I today owe my ability to write and probably my success in college at a time when compositional skills were still somewhat valued. To the private school experience, I owe my initial awareness that private schools are better at educating than their state-run counterparts.

In college one professor considerably influenced my subsequent teaching style by demonstrating in action the value of the lecture. His method convinced me that highly complex concepts can be explained successfully to anyone. Jacques Barzun's *Teacher in America*, which I read in college, finally convinced me that I would enjoy teaching as a profession. My philosophical and economic indebtedness, as will be evident in the pages of this book, is to Ayn Rand and Ludwig von Mises, respectively. My personal and professional indebtedness goes to George Reisman, for being a model of what it means to be a scholar and teacher, particularly in economics; to Edith Packer, for her knowledge of and teaching about psychology; and to my wife, Linda Reardan, for her personal support for this project and for the many hours of discussion we have had on philosophy and education. These three friends over the years have also shown me what it means to possess independence, integrity, and courage. And last, but not least, I am deeply indebted to the one person who has taught my wife and me more about education than we could ever have imagined: our daughter, Thea, to whom this book has been dedicated.

MONTESSORI, DEWEY,

AND

CAPITALISM

1

Capitalism and Education

In the university of Oxford, the greater part of the public professors have, for these many years, given up altogether even the pretence of teaching.

The discipline of the colleges and universities is in general contrived, not for the benefits of the students, but for the interest, or more properly speaking, for the ease of the masters. Its object is, in all cases, to maintain the authority of the master, and whether he neglects or performs his duty, to oblige the students, in all cases to behave to him as if he performed it with the greatest diligence and ability.

—Adam Smith[1]

THE PURPOSE OF EDUCATION is to prepare the young for adult life as independent human beings.

One form of education is parenting, and a major purpose of parenting is to teach children to become independent by the time they reach adulthood. The process of parenting gradually shifts from total care for wholly dependent infants to decreasing care for increasingly independent children and adolescents. By the time children reach adulthood, they should be able to minister to all of their needs, physical and mental, without aid from the parents. In a division-of-labor society, formal education assists parents in this progression toward independence.

---

[1] *An Inquiry into the Nature and Causes of the Wealth of Nations* (1776); repr., 2 vols. in one, ed. Edwin Cannan (Chicago: University Chicago Press, 1976), vol. 2, 284, 287.

The concept of independence, however, means more than providing one's own food, shelter, and clothing. It means independent judgment, a first-hand perception and evaluation of the facts of one's world—and oneself—unbiased by the judgments of parents, friends, workgroups, clubs, television reporters, political parties, or governments. It means the confident self-assertiveness to look out at the world, to process what is seen, and to act without also first having to look over one's shoulder to seek approval. Independent judgment requires a fund of knowledge, values, and skills from which to make intelligent decisions and to take intelligent actions. It requires the skill of reasoning to arrive at objective conclusions by adhering to the laws of logic. More importantly, it requires integrity and courage to act on those conclusions. Formal education, therefore, is not just cognitive; it is also normative, psychological, and behavioral.

Thinking and acting intelligently, and with integrity and courage, is not automatic or flawless. Children and adolescents must be taught how to do so, but they must also be allowed to make mistakes without threat of punishment. That is, they must be free to grow on their own without interference from authoritarian parents or teachers; the proper relationship of adult to child or adolescent is one of nurture, not coercion or neglect. When the children and adolescents become adults in society, they must also be allowed to make mistakes without threat of punishment, but because there is no societal parent, they must be allowed to correct the mistakes themselves and to do so without interference from other adults, especially those who work in the government. That is, as adults they must be politically free to grow on their own, testing their conclusions in the marketplace of ideas and pursuing their own values in the marketplace of goods and services. An education that aims at independence in adulthood is one that requires freedom in the home, in the classroom, and in society.

The purpose of formal education is to prepare the young for adult life as independently thinking and acting individuals in a capitalist society.

THE PHILOSOPHY OF EDUCATION

No philosophy of education exists, however, that explicitly requires capitalism for its implementation. Contemporary theories, including those formulated since the Enlightenment, either advocate the state as provider of education or do not discuss who is to provide the education. John Dewey's theory of undivided interest exemplifies the former, Maria Montessori's theory of concentrated attention the latter.[2] Some contemporary writers, usually economists, do advocate free markets in education, but often do not promote a particular philosophy of education; their contention is to "let the market decide" when it comes to determining the proper theory of education. Sometimes they denounce the theories of the progressive educators and assert that a free market would gravitate toward a better theory, such as Montessori's, ignoring or ignorant of the fact that Montessori herself was a progressive educator. In any event, the economists do not tie their arguments for free markets in education to a specific philosophy of education.

This book presents a philosophy of education that unites a theory of concentrated attention and independent judgment with free-market capitalism. It argues, in part, that since the Renaissance and, especially, the Enlightenment, the trend in educational philosophy has been gradually to recognize the freedom, creative power, and value of the individual mind. The book's theme is that the distinctive nature of human consciousness—namely, that it is volitional and conceptual, yet natural—requires uninterrupted concentration and autonomy, or reason and freedom, in education. This means nurturing the young, not coercing or neglecting them. It means encouraging the development of an intensive and sustained interest or purpose in life along with the ability to exercise independent judgment. It means finally that only a competitive marketplace of private, for-profit educational service businesses in a system of laissez-faire capitalism can fulfill these requirements.

Philosophy of education is a derivative science that rests on psychology, economics, and philosophy; it consists of three interrelated areas: purpose, method, and content. The purpose or aim of education describes the kind of adult or end result that the educational system is to produce. For example, in ancient Greece and Rome, the purpose of education was to train good (moral) men who were skilled at public speaking, civic or state life being the ultimate achievement of a male person in classical civilization; in the medieval world, the aim of education was to train clerics for the church.

---

[2] Although her theory does not discuss who the provider of education should be, Montessori did make these two comments: "The state must never abandon the child" and "This means that society's first step must be to allocate a higher proportion of its wealth to education." Maria Montessori, *The Absorbent Mind*, trans. Claude A. Claremont (1949; repr., New York: Henry Holt and Company, 1995), 14.

By implication, the purpose of education indicates which persons are entitled to an education. Everyone? Or certain privileged classes, races, or genders? Only in the last two hundred and fifty years, with the rise of a commitment to universal education, has the question of which persons not been an issue for the philosophy of education. Prior to the Enlightenment, education was restricted to a small percentage of the earth's population—usually sons of aristocrats. While education to this day has not become truly universal worldwide, the premise remains unquestioned in the developed world. Every human being morally deserves to be given an opportunity for education. Thus, the purpose component of a theory of education rests on the branch of philosophy known as ethics.

Exactly how the education is to be delivered—in organizational structure and in teacher-student contact—is the issue of method. Whether the church, state, or private enterprise is to provide the education and whether it is to be provided as formal schooling or by private tutors is the organizational question of method. In the classical world, the state played only a minor role in the delivery of education, not becoming involved in a significant way until the latter part of the Roman Empire. For nearly a thousand years, private tutors and entrepreneurial teachers were the means of educational delivery. It would be anachronistic, however, to assert that the ancient world practiced capitalism in education.[3] In the medieval world, the church provided the education.

Teacher-student contact specifies the activities performed by each in the teaching and learning process. It is here in recent decades that some

---

[3] The Roman Empire did enjoy an extensive division of labor and significant inter-regional trade during the second century AD, based on the rule of law and respect of private property for certain classes, but this was not capitalism. Rome was a militaristic society and its roads were built to transport armies, not goods for trade with the populace. Trade and productive labor were performed by slaves, foreigners, or members of the lower classes. Rondo Cameron, *A Concise Economic History of the World* (New York and Oxford: Oxford University Press, 1989), 37–41. Broad scale respect for every individual's rights, including property rights, is the essential requirement of capitalism. Rights were a product of the Enlightenment. Cf. Ludwig von Mises, *Human Action*, 3rd rev. ed. (Chicago: Henry Regnery Company, 1966), 767–69; Andrew J. Coulson, *Market Education: The Unknown History* (New Brunswick, NJ: Transaction Publishers, 1999), 37–58. Indeed, fee-paid teachers in the ancient world, along with anyone else who had to make a living through commercial transactions, were despised. "'He's either dead or else he's teaching somewhere,' some wag says about someone who is missing." H. I. Marrou, *A History of Education in Antiquity*, trans. George Lamb (New York: Sheed & Ward, 1956), 204.

of the bitterest debates in the philosophy of education have occurred. Is lecturing the correct method of teaching or the group discussion? What is the value of memorization and recitation, if any? Which is the best method of teaching reading: phonics or whole word? And what is the place of physical punishment? In the ancient world, where books were rare and expensive, the instructor lectured and children memorized, recited, and repeated. If the children made mistakes, they were beaten, sometimes quite harshly. This method continued, essentially unchanged, throughout the Middle Ages.

Method of education rests on the philosophic branches of metaphysics, epistemology, and politics. Politics (or social philosophy and, by extension, economics) determines the organizational structure of an educational system because politics determines the types of institutions a society will ultimately support. A socialist or interventionist political philosophy calls for state-run education, a church-dominated society calls for church-run schools, and a capitalist theory calls for a free market in education. Metaphysics in conjunction with psychology (specifically, philosophical psychology) provides the theory of human nature and of the human being's place in the universe on which to base a theory of the proper method of education. Epistemology (and the philosophy of mind) provides the theory of knowledge and mind on which the specific teaching and learning methods are based.

The content of education derives from the culture in which the education occurs and refers most particularly to curriculum. Wide latitude, however, exists among different theories as to how much of or in what way the culture is to be transferred to the young. In ancient Greece and Rome, the content was essentially reading, writing, and speaking. In the absence of the zero, arithmetic was difficult to learn. Students read the literature of the epic poets and playwrights of their time period and practiced public speaking based on the best orations of the day. In the Middle Ages, students studied the Bible and, sometimes, a sanitized ancient literature. Not until two hundred years after the scientific revolution of the seventeenth century did science find its way into the curriculum of most modern European and American schools. Today, progressive education downplays the significance of content, emphasizing the skill of thinking as more important than any particular content.

Philosophies of education present distinct views of children. In the ancient world, children were seen as ignorant beings who must memorize, recite, and repeat in order to acquire the culture, and be beaten if they failed to do so. In the Middle Ages children were seen as evil small adults—few differences between adulthood and childhood were recognized or respected at that time—who must passively absorb the authority-based rules of the church and be severely punished if they misbehaved or failed to learn their lessons.[4] This view of children as evil small adults persists to this day—albeit in less extreme form than occurred in the Middle Ages—in what is often labeled "traditional" or "conservative" educational theory.

The theory presented in this book holds a different view of children. It sees them as energetic beings that possess a seemingly unstoppable drive for maturity, an unquenchable thirst for knowledge, and an insatiable curiosity, all of which, unfortunately, are too often crushed by autocratic adults. It sees them as beings that possess a volitional consciousness but the development of their minds and free will is a nurturing process that must occur in distinct stages progressing to adulthood. The aim of education is psychological as well as intellectual independence. Psychologically independent children—and subsequent adults—pursue their values with neither timidity nor aggression, but with confident self-assertion, free of the anxiety that drives others to pursue defense values and other defensive maneuvers to compensate for their lack of self-esteem. Intellectually independent children become self-aware adults who possess the ability to think conceptually and to feel their true emotions without the fear of interference from either internal or external censors.

The method of education advocated in this book is that of a free market of educational entrepreneurs who guide and stimulate children to learn further. The children, however, must choose their particular learning activities within a range of options that are provided by the teacher. The content of education is the essentials of the culture's accumulated knowledge and the values and appropriate skills required to pursue a career and personal life in a capitalist society.

---

[4] Children were seen as evil because of the doctrine of original sin. They were viewed as small adults because, in the Middle Ages, there was no concept of childhood as we understand it today, namely as a stage of development that requires protection and guidance. Children then were exposed to everything adult, ranging from coarse language and jokes to sexual behavior. Marriage occurred at thirteen or fourteen and in school no differentiation was made among ages or backgrounds. Exact age often was not known, for in a time of short life spans, keeping track of one's age did not seem relevant. Philippe Ariès, *Centuries of Childhood: A Social History of Family Life*, trans. Robert Baldick (New York: Vintage Books, 1962).

UNSOLVED PROBLEMS OF MODERN EDUCATION

A number of problems in modern education remain unsolved. They can be summarized in a single statement: How to provide *mass, in-depth, economical* education that *cultivates individual differences* and produces *independence*.

Of these five problems, only mass education has been achieved with any certainty. In-depth education is precisely what many critics today claim has not been achieved. Economical education in the form of "free" public schools is euphemism when the actual tax costs per child are calculated; it is also euphemism to assert that public schools have been free of political interference. A longtime goal of progressive education has been the cultivation of individual differences but such an attainment has been elusive. And the fostering of independence in children also has not been achieved; rather, dependence on a variety of persons and institutions has been imbued in children by our bureaucratic educational system.

Each of these points requires elaboration.

Mass education today means universal, popular education. This means that all children, whatever their station in life, as opposed to a small upper-class elite, are entitled to an education. Mass education has been achieved today, to the extent that it has been achieved, through compulsion. Guided by the premise that democracy requires an educated populace and that the free market allegedly cannot provide mass education on a fair and economical basis, compulsory, universal education has been advocated since the eighteenth century.

In-depth education refers to more than fragments of information, smatterings of conventional values, or crude familiarity with technique. It means the acquisition of detail in a particular subject that is organized into essential categories. It means the absorption and integration of values that are truly one's own. It means the ability to perform certain tasks, including mental tasks, with confidence and effectiveness. In-depth education consists of knowledge, values, and skills that, once acquired, are retained and readily recalled for competent use. It is mastery learning, in the sense that all students should possess the same accomplished level of knowledge, values, and skills appropriate to age and interests.[5] It is not the kind of C- or D-level education

---

[5] The concept of mastery learning was introduced in the 1920's as part of the Winnetka Plan in the public schools of Winnetka, Illinois. The child was to achieve one hundred percent mastery of the essentials of a learning module before

common today that says "I did Plato last year" or "I kinda know when the American Civil War was fought" or worst of all: "I kinda know how to multiply eight times nine" (using a calculator).

Economical education refers to the price parents must pay to buy a year's worth of education for their child. It is true that government-provided schooling has furnished this education to parents either "free" or at nominal cost. When tax expenditure per child, however, is calculated, when schooling expenditures are compared to the rate at which consumer prices have increased in past years, and when for-profit private schooling becomes competitive in quality—and almost in pricing—with the public schools, the boast of having achieved economical education becomes laughable.[6] Justice is an issue that also must be raised here, for some people are being coerced into paying for the education of others. The problem of how to provide an economical education that does not infringe on the rights of others has not been solved and the epithet of a "free" education also carries with it the premise that such an education is absent political influence. This premise has been challenged in recent decades; today, there is little pretense about the politicization of government-run education.[7]

Individual differences refers to the different abilities, paces of learning, and interests that we all possess and exhibit. The private tutorial is the teaching method that best caters to these differences; the class-

---

moving on to the next one. Arthur Zilversmit, *Changing Schools: Progressive Education Theory and Practice, 1930–1960* (Chicago: University of Chicago Press, 1993), 40–43. The current system of evaluating students on a five-point scale (from A to F) will never achieve mastery learning.

[6] Tax expenditure per child, kindergarten through 12th grade, in 2004–05 averaged $8701, excluding capital outlay. In contrast, non-sectarian, privately owned elementary schools can be found in southern California charging as little as $7000 for ten month's worth of education, and that amount must cover capital expenditures. From 1982–83 to 2002–03, expenditures per child for K–12 schooling increased from $2736 to $8044; the increase exceeded the rate of rising consumer prices by nearly 70 percent per year. National Center for Education Statistics (NCES), "Common Core of Data," Table 3, http://nces.ed.gov/pubs2007/expenditures/tables.asp and NCES, "Digest of Education Statistics: 2005" Table 162, http://nces.ed.gov/programs/digest/d05/tables_2.asp.

[7] Charles Leslie Glenn, Jr., *The Myth of the Common School* (Amherst, MA: University of Massachusetts Press, 1987). The usual dictionary definition of "common school" is "free, public elementary school." Historically, however, "common" meant, and still means, common values, imposed by the government usually to erase differences among immigrants. See Lawrence A. Cremin, *Popular Education and Its Discontents* (New York: Harper & Row, 1989), 85–125, for a discussion of the politicization of public education.

room lecture does not. Child-centered learning has long been one of the themes of progressive education, meaning that the child and his or her uniqueness, not the subject matter or teacher, are what are focused on. Success in catering to individual differences while at the same time providing in-depth learning is one of the major challenges to modern education—and progressive education has achieved neither. Throughout recent history, educators have swung back and forth between the two poles of sameness or standardization (the traditionalists) versus tailoring to the individual child (the progressives). The task is to combine the two.

On a superficial level, universal, popular education does produce a kind a physical independence, in the sense that high school and college graduates can find work and support themselves throughout their lives. Full-scale psychological and intellectual independence, however, has not been achieved. In fact, the present educational system of government-provided schooling generates dependence by breeding a bureaucratic mentality. When a product is provided by the government, in accordance with strict rules and a budget, as opposed to in accordance with the needs of the market and the requirements of profit, customers become passive and cynical about the quality of service to be expected. They become resigned to their inability to fight city hall and they become dependent on city hall to provide certain services, never considering that there might be other options. The extreme of this dependency could be seen in the fear that some Russian citizens experienced with the collapse of the Soviet Union. Bureaucratic education breeds dependence; free-market education would breed independence.

THE THEORY OF CONCENTRATED ATTENTION AND CAPITALISM

The purpose of this book is to present a theory of education that will most effectively achieve the transition from helpless infant to mature, independent adult, while providing the maximum of knowledge, values, skills, and confidence required to flourish in a modern, free society. The means to the end of independence is the power of concentrated attention, that is, the ability of children, as they mature, to focus their minds uninterruptedly for increasingly longer periods of time and with greater intensity. The value to mature adults of concentrated attention is the ability to set and pursue long-range goals, the significance of which is the achievement of a purpose in life. This is exhibited as a productive career.

Many adults, however, have not achieved the power of concentrated attention, as shown by their lack of purpose in life, their short-range planning, and their psychological dependence on a variety of people and institutions. The premise of this book is that concentrated attention must be developed in the young from the earliest time in order properly to nourish the child toward independence.

Montessori and Dewey

The notion of concentrated attention is not new—Maria Montessori first used the phrase in 1917 in her book *Spontaneous Activity in Education*.[8] Montessori's concept, however, does not differ in essence from John Dewey's theory of undivided interest.[9] Indeed, the idea has been evolving in educational theory and practice since the seventeenth century, as will be highlighted in the next chapter.

Montessori and Dewey agree in essentials on how concentrated attention and undivided interest are to be achieved in the process of formal schooling: the instructor provides materials and guidance to the children who then choose, in Dewey's terms, which to experience or, in Montessori's terms, which to work with. A carefully structured setting, consisting of learning materials, gently directs the children, within a range of options, to develop their powers of directed focus. Thus, in the jargon of experimental science, the dependent variable (or criterion) of educational success is concentrated attention or undivided interest; the independent (or predictor) variables are materials in a structured setting that teach the knowledge, values, and skills the children will need as mature adults.[10]

Montessori identified the fundamental fact that underlies her method by observing the behavior of a three-year-old girl. The little

---

[8] Maria Montessori, *Spontaneous Activity in Education,* trans. Florence Simmonds (1917; repr., Cambridge, MA: Robert Bentley, 1971).

[9] John Dewey, *Interest and Effort in Education* (Boston: Houghton Mifflin Co., 1913). Dewey's first treatment of this topic appeared in Dewey, "Interest in Relation to the Training of the Will," in *Second Supplement of the Herbart Year Book for 1895* (1896; reprinted in John J. McDermott, ed., *The Philosophy of John Dewey: Two Volumes in One*, Chicago: University of Chicago Press, 1981), 421–42.

[10] For more on the similarities between Montessori and Dewey, see Eleanor Nicholson, "An Analysis of Dewey and Montessori—Philosophers with Many Similar Concepts." *The Constructive Triangle* 6 (1979): 12–21, and Janet Kierstead, "Montessori and Dewey: The Best from Both," in M. P. Douglass, ed., *Claremont Reading Conference, 45th Yearbook* (Claremont, CA: Claremont Graduate School, 1981), 88–95.

girl, she reports, was "deeply absorbed in a set of solid insets, removing the [differently sized] wooden cylinders from their respective holes and replacing them. The expression on the child's face was one of such *concentrated attention* that it seemed to me an extraordinary manifestation; up to this time none of the children had ever shown such fixity of interest in an object; and my belief in the characteristic instability of attention in young children, who flit incessantly from one thing to another, made me peculiarly alive to the phenomenon." The child continued to work with the insets for forty-four repetitions, during which time Montessori "picked up the little arm-chair in which [the girl] was seated, and placed chair and child upon the table."[11] The child's concentration was unbroken, despite singing by other children nearby.

In subsequent experiments Montessori observed: "Each time that such a polarization of attention took place, the child began to be completely transformed, to become calmer, more intelligent, more expansive."[12] The child's separate energies, in other words, began to function together in a purposeful way. The polarization of attention, then, became Montessori's standard by which teaching activities and materials were judged: to the extent that activities and materials produced a polarization of attention and repetition of actions related to the sustained attention, to that extent the activities and materials were judged appropriate for use in her schools.

This concentration of attention, Montessori noted, varies with the age of the child. The three-year-old concentrates for thirty minutes at a time, but the six-year-old may concentrate for two hours without interruption or fatigue, and the still older child may work on a single project, with many repetitions, for seven or eight days.[13] By extension, we may say that an adult will have learned to concentrate for perhaps weeks, months, or even years at a time on a single project.

Dewey's doctrine of undivided interest holds that genuine interest is the identification of self with the object or end that one is pursuing. Anything that stands between the self of the child and the object to be learned divides the child's attention and thereby leads to a "disintegration of character, intellectually and morally." In traditional education, the tasks given to children are so uninteresting that their minds focus initially on what is required to complete the tasks, and to please

---

[11] Montessori, *Spontaneous Activity*, 67, 68. Emphasis added.

[12] Ibid., 68.

[13] Ibid., 80, 109.

the instructors; then, the children immediately switch to thoughts or imaginations that are more pleasing. Attention, focus, and interest are split between schoolwork that the children do not like and daydreams that please them much better. Their energies are dissipated and dependence is bred.[14]

"Genuine interest," says Dewey, "is the accompaniment of the identification, through action, of the self with some object or idea, because of the necessity of that object or idea for the maintenance of a self-initiated activity." Or, as he also puts it: "interest means a unified activity."[15] When we are interested in something, there is no separation between the means and end of the activity; each step of the way toward the end is seen by the genuinely interested person as part of the end or, as it were, as a fragment of the end. When schoolwork is forced on children without their choice or cooperation in the selection of tasks, no relationship can be seen between the tasks that the instructors want performed and the selves of the children; the end is to please the instructors, the means is to perform the tasks. Interest has been transformed into an external system of rewards and punishment.

For Montessori, concentrated attention is encouraged by what she calls the "prepared environment." This includes the classroom itself—the way it is designed and set up—and the "didactic materials" with which the children work; the instructor gives lessons on the materials and guides the children to the materials' most effective use. The function of the theoretician in education is to determine the elements of the prepared environment that will produce concentrated attention and independence. The task of the environment is to nourish the children and to define the limits of their liberty—which is to say that the children are not let loose to do literally anything they please, but to experience those activities that have been demonstrated to advance their development. Children choose, within a range of options, those tasks that will both interest and educate them.[16]

Similarly, Dewey states that the job of the instructor is to discover the kinds of experiences that will stimulate and sustain genuine interest and then make those experiences available to the children. Interestingly, Dewey is not a foe of subject matter, as critics—and supporters—frequently portray him. "The important question," he states, "is what

---

[14] Dewey, *Interest and Effort*, 7, 91.

[15] Ibid., 14, 15.

[16] Montessori, *Spontaneous Activity*, 71.

specific subject-matter is so connected with the growth of the child's existing concrete capabilities to give it a moving force."[17] The goal of education for Dewey is growth of the individual child. Thus, Dewey offers an objective standard by which to judge the selection of experiences, activities, materials, and books.

Contrary to the way he has been remembered, John Dewey is neither an opponent of subject matter nor a proponent of method over content. Method, Dewey says, is the ordering of subject matter for its most effective use. "Never is method something outside of the material." He refers to knowledge or information as the necessary "working capital" with which thinking conducts its business. "The problem of teaching is to keep the experience of the student moving in the direction of what the expert already knows."[18] Dewey, indeed, in one of his last writings on education, was highly critical of his progressive colleagues who were "contemptuous of the organization of facts and ideas."[19] "Good teaching," he states, "is teaching that appeals to established powers while it includes such new material as will demand their redirection for a new end, this redirection requiring thought—intelligent effort."[20]

The primary difference between the Montessorian and Deweyan approaches to education is that Montessori was a practitioner who developed many specific concrete activities to be used in her schools. Dewey was a practitioner for a short time, but spent most of his career writing on philosophical topics, which sometimes included educational theory. Montessori emphasized repetition of the action that causes polarization of attention; Dewey did not. Indeed, Dewey, commenting on Montessori's system, cautioned that her "additional technical knowledge" could, if not watched carefully, degenerate into "isolated mechanical exercises," a dangerous tendency, he pointed out, that is "attendant upon the spread of every definitely formulated system."[21]

---

[17] Dewey, *Interest and Effort*, 62.

[18] John Dewey, *Democracy in Education: An Introduction to the Philosophy of Education* (New York: Free Press, 1916), 165, 158, 184.

[19] Dewey, *Experience and Education* (1938; repr., New York: Collier Books, 1963), 82.

[20] Dewey, *Interest and Effort*, 58.

[21] Ibid., 74. And "isolated mechanical exercises" is what one will find today in some, perhaps many, schools with Montessori's name on them. Training in any method does not guarantee that the student and soon-to-be teacher will fully absorb the technique taught and then be able to apply it in new situations. In education (and parenting) a few classes on how to be less autocratic will not erase the authoritarian tendencies that were imbued in most in childhood.

In Dewey's case, the abstruseness of his writing style contributed, at least in part, to causing followers who were charged with putting his ideas into practice to do so, ironically, without much of what he would have called "intelligent effort." This lack of "intelligent effort" by educators, in turn, led to decades of less-than-satisfactory experiments in the public school system.[22]

The Contradiction in Progressive Education

Montessori's explicitly stated goal of education is independence. Dewey's goal is growth of the individual organism in society. While Montessori does not deny the significance of the social, such as cooperative learning activities, Dewey goes so far as to assert that the school should be an instrument of social policy and a means of social change. In the tradition of social liberalism, Dewey emphatically advocates the state as the only proper institution to own and operate the schools.

Social liberalism—or progressive liberalism, as it is more familiarly known—evolved in the late nineteenth century, emphasizing that self-realization or self-actualization of the individual human mind is the essence of liberty, that reason, not religious scripture, is the source of morality, and that science and technology, not capitalism, are the source of modern material civilization. Hearkening back to its origins in the Enlightenment, social liberalism advocates that the mind must be free to develop on its own without interference—mainly from the church, but also from the government; this placed emphasis on the freedom of speech and press, the separation of church and state, and a strong undercurrent of secular naturalism. As social liberalism continued to evolve in the latter part of the nineteenth century, big business was added to its list of threats to liberty.[23]

Several policies followed from this conception of liberalism. Physical wants must be satisfied first; thus, social legislation was justified to put victims, real or imagined, on a level playing field, to uphold the

---

[22] See, for example, Diane Ravitch, *Left Back: A Century of Failed School Reforms* (New York: Simon & Schuster, 2000).

[23] T. H. Green, "Lectures on the Principles of Political Obligation," in *Lectures on the Principles of Political Obligation and Other Writings*, ed. Paul Harris and John Morrow (Cambridge: Cambridge University Press, 1986), 13–193; originally published posthumously in 1895. L. T. Hobhouse, *Liberalism* (1911; repr., Westport, CT: Greenwood Press, 1964). Frederick Copleston, *A History of Philosophy*, vol. 8, *Bentham to Russell* (Garden City, NY: Doubleday, Image Books, 1985), 171–78. John Dewey, *Liberalism and Social Action* (New York: G. P. Putnam's Sons, 1935).

value of equality. Slavery, of course, had to be abolished. The alleged privileged classism of the industrial capitalists had to be opposed and regulated. And most significantly, the lasting power and stability of a democratic society required state-run education. For the social liberal, education is necessary primarily to remove religious prejudice and to encourage personal enhancement. Secondarily, especially in the United States, education is required to provide common values to immigrants and lower classes, that is, to "Americanize" them. Thus, a proper function of government, according to the social liberal, is to provide an education to all. Further, because a minimal literacy is required to maintain a democratic society, education to a certain level of attainment must be compulsory.

Dewey and his followers in the progressive education movement never questioned the idea of state-provided, compulsory education. This idea, of course, pre-dates Dewey in the United States by many decades and originated in the Enlightenment just prior to and at the time of the French Revolution.[24] The notion, however, of a state-provided progressive education contains a glaring contradiction to its theoretical premise of concentrated attention and undivided interest; there also are contradictions in the social liberal's conceptions of liberty and equality, especially as they apply to education.

The notion of a self-directed, mentally active education—one that encourages personal enhancement by providing a nurturing environment for the free pursuit of interests—is completely nullified by having such an education provided by the state. The environment is one of coercion because the state holds the legal monopoly on the use of physical force. Any activity the state administers, and this includes education, is backed by its police powers. The notion that the coercive powers of the state can provide a free, self-directed, nourishing education is tantamount to saying kidnappers can provide love and care to their victims. Superficially, the love and care, as well as a free, self-directed, nourishing education, may appear to be present, but freedom and coercion are opposites and any attempt to merge the two is a contradiction; the outcome will be failure,

---

[24] James Bowen, *A History of Western Education*, vol. 3, *The Modern West* (New York: St. Martin's Press, 1981), 242–81. "National" education at the time of the French Revolution meant, and today in many countries still means, using the national government to educate children so they will exhibit a specific, secular nationality. "Americanization" in the United States falls into this tradition, although the school system was never fully controlled at the national level.

perhaps tragedy. That such an education should be compulsory is just one additional contradiction.

Ideas that contain contradictions cannot succeed when put into practice; sooner or later, they will fail. The notion that humans can fly by flapping their arms while jumping off a cliff is a crude example in which failure is immediate. The notion that socialism can succeed without resort to market prices, however, is more sophisticated; it required many decades to reveal its failings. Nonetheless, socialism's inevitable collapse was predicted in 1920 by economist Ludwig von Mises, who argued that socialism lacked a means of economic calculation and thereby a method of allocating resources to their most productive uses.[25] Socialized education also lacks a means of economic calculation, especially cost control, as seen annually by the expenditures and tuitions that far outrun increases in consumer prices and, generally, by its enormous waste of resources. In a free market, real prices decline while innovation flourishes; in a free market in education, the quality of service over time would improve while the real cost to students and parents would fall.

As an experiment in freedom at the point of a gun, progressive education has run its course. Failed learning is rampant, as evidenced by the extensive remediation required for first-year college students and the inability of college seniors to compute decimals using a calculator. Authoritarian demands for obedience continue to be heard from teachers and administrators alike, nearly all of whom today claim to be progressives; this, of course, stems from the bureaucratic and authoritarian nature of state-provided education, as well as from the ingrained, unchanged attitude that young people should slavishly obey the dictates of adults. Progressive education has failed because it said to the young, "You choose what you want to learn," then figuratively and literally slapped their hands when bureaucratic rules were not followed. There is no better way to silence a mind than by sending these confusing signals.

As a political monopoly and massive bureaucracy, state-provided education works solely for the comfort of those who run the system—the teachers and administrators—at the expense of those they allegedly serve—the students and parents. The point here is not that the ideas per se

---

[25] Ludwig von Mises, "Economic Calculation in the Socialist Commonwealth," (1920); reprinted in F. A. Hayek, ed., *Collectivist Economic Planning: Critical Studies on the Possibilities of Socialism* (Clifton, NJ: Augustus M. Kelley, 1975).

of progressive education are false or corrupt, but that the essence and spirit of them clash with their means of implementation. Rigid and regimented—that is, traditional—education can and is provided successfully by the coercive powers of the state, successfully at least in the sense that A students seem to learn what is taught. Japan today and the United States prior to the introduction of progressive ideas are good examples. But just as an authoritarian state can boast about its lawful, orderly society, at the price of freedom, so also can traditional, bureaucratic education boast about its knowledgeable students, at the price of timidity, rebelliousness, dependence, and, above all, the repression of interests.

The Contradictions in Social Liberalism

The social liberal argues that liberty is the absence of interference by the church, government, or business and that equality is equality of opportunity. Education supposedly unites both because freedom to develop the human mind requires education and equality demands that everyone be given the same opportunity for education. Thus, the government provides education for all and, to insure that everyone has the same opportunity, the education is made compulsory. This line of reasoning, however, is filled with contradictions.

Economist Mises has referred to the social version of liberalism, alternatively, as "moderate socialism" or as "partly socialist and partly interventionist."[26] And so it is. The problem with the traditional version of liberalism, that is, classical or market liberalism, is that it has never had an unambiguous criterion by which to distinguish acceptable from unacceptable social behavior. The novelist-philosopher Ayn Rand has offered a precise formulation, namely that no one—individual or government—may initiate the use of physical force against others and that the only proper use of force is in retaliation against those who initiate its use. Except in emergency situations, the retaliatory use of force is delegated to the government.[27] At the political level, this criterion means that all acts resulting from the mutual consent of adults—whether

---

[26] Ludwig von Mises, *Liberalism: A Socio-Economic Exposition*, trans. Ralph Raico (Kansas City: Sheed Andrews & McMeel, 1978), 197, 199. Originally published in German in 1927.

[27] Ayn Rand, *The Virtue of Selfishness: A New Concept of Egoism* (New York: New American Library, 1964), 31. The social liberal's counterpart to this principle is: all products and acts that are intrinsically harmful must be regulated or banned. Debate centers on what constitutes intrinsic harm, but it could in fact be anything.

moral or immoral—must be legal. At the fundamental level of ethics, it means that each person's life is an end in itself, not a means to the ends of others. Direct or indirect initiation of physical force is the only way in which human rights are violated.[28]

This criterion, then, sustains the essence of liberty as the power of self-realization—because each person is an end in him- or herself. Freedom is the power of each individual to develop his or her mind and to act without interference from others. Big businesses, contrary to what the social liberals imply, do not initiate physical force against competitors, consumers, or workers and, consequently, do not deprive them of their freedom. The power of big business is economic, not political, and it derives from repeated successes in the marketplace of satisfying customers better than the competition.[29] In the nineteenth century, some industrialists did act like privileged royalty and farmers and laborers did seem to be victims of these "privileged classes," but market entrepreneurs—that is, those who held no privileges from the government—did not acquire their wealth unjustly by denying anyone's liberty. Political entrepreneurs, on the other hand, who did hold governmental privileges, did cause harm.[30]

Rand's criterion also clarifies the meaning of equality. By being an end in him- or herself, each individual possesses the same rights—in any social context, including before the law. Equality does not mean the same ability, the same wealth and income, or the same opportunities. Equality of opportunity is a confused concept that on the surface may sound appealing, because it proposes to give everyone the same chance of success in society by giving each person the same "opportunities," for example, education. On examination, however, the concept is just a more general term for the equality of wealth and income, which is another name for the redistribution of wealth. This is because

---

[28] Fraud is an indirect initiation of physical force.

[29] On the distinction between economic and political power, see Ayn Rand, "America's Persecuted Minority: Big Business," in *Capitalism: The Unknown Ideal* (New York: New American Library, 1966), 39. Cf. Franz Oppenheimer, *The State*, trans. John M. Gitterman (1914; repr., New York: Free-Life Editions, 1975), 12–15.

[30] See Burton Folsom, Jr., *Entrepreneurs vs. the State: A New Look at the Rise of Big Business in America, 1840–1920* (Reston, VA: Young America's Foundation, 1987). James J. Hill of the Great Northern Railroad represents the former; Leland Stanford and the "Big Four," who ran the Central Pacific, represent the latter. There are many other market entrepreneurs who do not deserve to be called "robber barons" and many political entrepreneurs who deserve the label.

the same chance of success in society, according to advocates of the equality-of-opportunity doctrine, requires not just the same education, but also the same (or equivalent) income, food, shelter, clothing, car, and so on. Genuine equality, however, means each individual possesses the *same freedom to take action* without fear or threat of harm from others. It means the freedom to see and seize opportunities, not to be given them.[31]

Market—Not Social—Liberalism

The theory of concentrated attention and independent judgment calls for the elimination of coercion in education. When the state takes money from some citizens in order to educate the children of others, force is initiated and some citizens benefit at the expense of others; those taxed are treated as means to the ends of those educated by the state. Indeed, the notion of a state-provided education deserves to be labeled *illiberal* because it promotes and maintains the very thing liberalism in the Enlightenment, and later, fought to eliminate, namely privilege. As Mises defines it, "Privilege is an institutional arrangement favoring some individuals or a certain group at the expense of the rest."[32] Compulsory education is blatantly illiberal, because it makes children wards of the state. The theory of concentrated attention requires market liberalism, or capitalism.[33] Indeed, at the risk of oversimplification, one might say that the fundamental premises of progressive education, as they have evolved since the Enlightenment, *require laissez-faire capitalism.*

Market and social liberalism share certain premises: self-realization of the individual human mind as the essence of liberty, which demands the freedom of speech and press; strong value placed on reason, science, and technology as the source of modern material civilization; and the complete separation of church and state, with an emphasis on secular naturalism, including the naturalization of consciousness.

---

[31] George Reisman, *Capitalism: A Treatise on Economics* (Ottawa, IL: Jameson Books, 1996), 337–43.

[32] Mises, *Liberalism*, 29.

[33] The term "market liberalism" was suggested, as an updated name for classical liberalism and counter to the more awkward "libertarianism," in David Boaz and Edward H. Crane, eds., *Market Liberalism: A Paradigm for the 21st Century* (Washington, DC: Cato Institute, 1993), 8–9. Today, libertarianism seems to have come into the vernacular.

Market liberalism, however, holds that genuine freedom requires the complete separation of business and state, in the same way and for the same reasons as the complete separation of church and state. It holds that consistent respect for individual rights, especially property rights, leads to private ownership of the means of production, which, in turn, leads to laissez-faire capitalism. Laissez-faire also means the complete separation of education and state.

Social liberals are mistaken. Reason, science, and technology did not by themselves create modern, material civilization. Freedom to enjoy the fruits of one's labor and to trade with others without interference from the government is the cause of material progress. This freedom, which necessitates an uncompromised recognition of property rights, led to the extensive division of labor we have today, in which each individual, especially each market entrepreneur, is able to use reason, science, and technology to his or her most productive and profitable ends. Without capitalism, reason, science, and technology at the end of the eighteenth century would have remained, respectively, little more than a mental exercise, a curiosity, and a hobby. Instead, capitalism unleashed their creative and productive powers. Socialism destroys all such powers.

Religious conservatives are equally mistaken. They feign a belief in capitalism but do not hesitate to advocate governmental coercion to control everyone's personal life, especially the bodies of women. They seek to regulate speech and press to sanitize it of "unworthy" language; they even explicitly seek to regulate business—we have antitrust laws, after all, thanks to the conservatives. They aim to annul the Enlightenment's accomplishment of separating church and state. And above all, they want the state (or church) to provide education in order to control what is taught; they, of course, adamantly advocate traditional and coercive methods of education.[34] In this sense conservatives are pre-Enlightenment, for they value neither reason nor freedom in social life in general or in education in specific. They are, in fact, enemies of both capitalism and the theory of concentrated attention.[35]

---

[34] For example, one conservative-leaning talk-show host in Los Angeles boasted about how, when he was smacked by his teacher at school, his father would then smack him again when he got home, on the assumption that if the teacher hit him, he must have done something wrong. The host complained about how parents today would have sued the school. The litigiousness of today's society aside, the host heartily approved of the premises of corporal punishment and obedience to authority.

[35] The difference between today's social liberals and conservatives, says Ayn Rand, is that they each want to control what they consider important and leave

Market liberalism holds that genuine freedom must be pushed to its rational limit: the complete separation, not just of church and state, but also of business and state and, most importantly, of education and state. The theory of concentrated attention—as a truly progressive education—requires these separations. Only then can there be an unhampered moral, psychological, economic, and political progress.

free what they despise. The former want to control the material world (business), the latter the spiritual (speech, press, education, morality); the former want to leave the spiritual world free, the latter the material. There is overlap between the two, but the contrast is apt. They both, of course, share the morality of altruism, which enables them to call for sacrifices in the areas they want to control. Ayn Rand, "Censorship: Local and Express," in *Philosophy: Who Needs It* (New York: Bobbs-Merrill, 1982), 228.

2

Historical Origins

> None of the things [children] are to learn should ever be made
> a burden to them or imposed on them as a *task*. Whatever is so
> proposed presently becomes irksome: the mind takes an aversion
> to it, though before it were a thing of delight or indifference.
>
> —John Locke[1]

> In fact, self and interest are two names for the same fact; the
> kind and amount of interest actively taken in a thing reveals
> and measures the quality of selfhood which exists. Bear in
> mind that interest means the active or moving *identity* of the
> self with a certain object....
>
> —John Dewey[2]

ALTHOUGH SUGGESTION of the theory of concentrated attention can
be found in antiquity, most of the notion's development has occurred
since the Enlightenment.

From ancient Greece to the present, traditional education has operated, and continues to operate, essentially on the premise of coercion.
Fear is the motivator and a passive and sometimes rebellious child is
the result. The core idea behind the theory of concentrated attention,

---

[1] *Some Thoughts Concerning Education*, eds. Ruth W. Grant and Nathan Tarcov
(1690; repr., Indianapolis: Hackett Publishing, 1996), 51 (§ 73). Emphasis in original.

[2] *Democracy and Education* (New York: The Free Press, 1916), 352. Emphasis in
original.

on the other hand, is the doctrine of interest. At its broadest level, this notion says that interest—student desire and choice, rather than coercion—is the most effective motivator of learning. Student needs and wants, not teacher dictates, are the proper guides to education.

In the traditional view, children are expected to face the front of the classroom, put folded hands on desktop, and be totally obedient to the teacher. If they fail to recite a memorized lesson accurately, they are punished, sometimes physically. Children are given little or no choice about what they will learn, how they will learn it, or when they will learn it. In the Middle Ages, the notion of original sin added an extra ferocity to the coercion and punishment, a ferocity that is still with us today.[3] Until quite late, perhaps the sixteenth century, children were routinely grouped together regardless of age, stage of development, or pace of learning.[4] In traditional education, children's needs and wants are irrelevant.

Against this backdrop of traditional education, the present chapter outlines the evolution of the theory of concentrated attention.

PLATO AND QUINTILIAN

In ancient Greece and Rome, Plato and Quintilian provide the first suggestions of the theory of concentrated attention.

Plato (c. 428–c. 348 BC) is an unlikely source, given his totalitarian theory of society, and indeed his statement of the idea does seem out of context with his overall political philosophy. In the *Republic*, after stating that subjects such as arithmetic and geometry should be introduced in childhood, Plato says that these should not be introduced "in the guise of compulsory instruction, because for the free man there should be no element of slavery in learning. Enforced exercise does no harm to the body, but enforced learning will not stay in the mind. So avoid compulsion, and let your children's lessons take the form of

---

[3] In countries where corporal punishment is no longer allowed, teachers can still use verbal intimidation and humiliation for similar effect. As of 2007, only seventeen countries worldwide have abolished corporal punishment of children, and only twenty-seven of the fifty American states have banned its use in schools. Global Initiative to End All Corporal Punishment of Children, "End All Corporal Punishment of Children," http://endcorporalpunishment.org/pages/frame.html.

[4] Broad differentiations into primary, secondary, and higher education were made as early as Hellenistic Greece. Within each level, however, no further divisions were made.

play."[5] Plato here is arguing that if knowledge is to be retained, learning must be an enjoyable process, not a chore. And it is compulsion that destroys the desire to learn.[6]

In the *Laws*, Plato defends the value of play in education, but undercuts it by demanding that education be compulsory. His totalitarianism also destroys any chance of freedom in education. Compulsion is justified "on the ground that the child is even more the property of the state than of his parents. And, mind you, my law will apply in all respects to girls as much as to boys."[7] Plato, at least, was the first philosopher of education to recognize the educational needs of women—by dictating that girls and boys both should be slaves of the state!

Aristotle (384–322 BC) points out the importance of pleasure in the performance of an activity, but does not promote this idea in his educational theory.[8] In his theory of self-actualization, Aristotle can be said to have implicitly laid the foundations of the organic metaphor—the notion that the child is an unfolding flower that must be left free to blossom. The next education writer of significance who provides indications of the theory of concentrated attention is Quintilian (AD c. 35–c. 96). Writing on the education of an orator in the early Roman Empire, Quintilian probably represents the best of the ancient world. Isocrates (436–338 BC) before him, as well as Cato the elder (234–149 BC) and Cicero (106–43 BC), all describe the aim of education as the development of a moral man who speaks well, and Quintilian does not disagree with them.[9] He does, however, offer

---

[5] Plato *Republic* 7.536d. *The Republic of Plato*, trans. Francis MacDonald Cornford (New York: Oxford University Press, 1941), 258.

[6] A few lines later, we are reminded just how warlike Plato's society was: "You remember, too, our children were to be taken to the wars on horseback to watch the fighting, and, when it was safe, brought close up like young hounds to be given a taste of blood." Ibid.

[7] Plato *Laws* 7.804d. *The Collected Dialogues of Plato Including the Letters*, eds. Edith Hamilton and Huntington Cairns (Princeton, NJ: Princeton University Press, 1961), 1376.

[8] "If a man finds writing or doing sums unpleasant and painful, he does not write, or does not do sums, because the activity is painful." Aristotle *Nicomachean Ethics* 10.5.1175b15. *The Basic Works of Aristotle*, ed. Richard McKeon (New York: Random House, 1941), 1101.

[9] The moral "man" was decidedly a male person, not a generic human being. Some girls in the ancient world did receive an education, at the primary level, but it was rare. William Boyd, *The History of Western Education*, 6th ed. (London: Adam and Charles Black, 1952), 15, 62, 66.

additional insights that are relevant to the theory of concentrated attention.[10]

Developing Plato's embryonic thought, Quintilian emphasizes the need for relaxation and play in the educational process. "Thus pupils refreshed and restored by recreation bring more energy to their studies and a keener mind whereas the mind as a rule refuses tasks imposed by harsh compulsion."[11] Indeed, Quintilian was one of the first education writers to oppose corporal punishment, because of the shame and humiliation it causes. Careful supervision, he says, is what is needed to effect learning, not physical punishment. Teachers, he concludes, must find ways to motivate students to learn.[12]

Quintilian further acknowledges that effective education requires adaptation to age and ability. For example, lessons in the early years are given in the form of play, emulation, and competition. Quintilian opposes the ancient world practice of teaching the names and order of letters before the children can recognize them. Thus, he first suggests giving carved ivory letters of the alphabet to the children to play with. Then, he suggests giving them cut-out letters on a board so they may trace the letters with their styluses; this provides motor training for the hand that will be needed subsequently to learn how to write, a technique not used again until Montessori. Quintilian also sees no reason why children should not be taught basic skills at home before the traditional school-entering age of seven, an idea that foreshadows the modern preschool.[13]

Quintilian was the first education writer to focus on the individual student; consequently, his theory can be described as child-centered. The child-centeredness stems probably from his many years' experience as a teacher, rather than from philosophical commitment. Like many rhetoricians in the ancient world, Quintilian frowned upon philosophy as hopelessly impractical. William Smail summarizes Quintilian's achievements by highlighting two qualities that any good instructor should possess: "His success as a teacher was mainly due to the sweet

---

[10] These insights may have represented widespread educational practice in the first century AD. Method of teaching in the Roman Empire is said to have been essentially Hellenistic. H. I. Marrou, *A History of Education in Antiquity*, trans. George Lamb (New York: Sheed & Ward, 1956), 375.

[11] Quintilian *Institutio Oratoria* 1.3.9. *Quintilian on Education*, trans. William M. Smail (New York: Teachers College Press, 1938), 31.

[12] Ibid., 1.3.14, 32–33.

[13] Ibid., 1.1.15–27, 14–18.

reasonableness of his nature and his untiring devotion to the welfare of his pupils."[14] What was unusual about Quintilian was that these two qualities were not possessed by many teachers in the ancient world.

THE JESUITS

For the next fifteen hundred years no educational theory appears that reflects ideas related to the theory of concentrated attention.

Educational practice throughout the Middle Ages was thoroughly traditional, with original sin added to it to make the treatment of students especially harsh. Teachers assumed that children were evil and likely to do evil things before they walked into the classroom. Thus, Charlemagne, leader of the Carolingian renaissance during the late eighth and early ninth centuries, is said to have "personally whipped a boy who made a mistake in Latin grammar."[15] It was indeed not a good time to be a slow or ungifted student. Stories from the medieval years also tell of boys between six and ten being "imprisoned on frosty nights," left "naked in an unheated cellar," flogged daily "until the blood flowed," and "suspended for hours in a well."[16]

By the late Middle Ages and early Renaissance, however, progress in educational practice was occurring. During the fourteenth century, students for the first time were organized into eight grades, to allow for different abilities and paces of learning. Books became easier to read, as the florid medieval manuscript style was replaced by modern book design, standardized with wide margins and spacing between lines. In the fifteenth century, the first use of individual exercise books occurred in Europe, although the practice apparently originated in Constantinople. Moveable type, of course, and the development of Roman typeface culminated in the pocket-sized book that made the diffusion of learning unstoppable.[17]

The Middle Ages produced little in the way of educational theory. Quintilian's work was lost throughout the entire period, an incomplete

---

[14] Ibid., xlvii.

[15] Morris Bishop, *The Middle Ages* (1968; repr., Boston: Houghton Mifflin, 1987), 27.

[16] James Bowen, *A History of Western Education*, vol. 2, *Civilization of Europe* (New York: St. Martin's Press, 1975), 231. Bowen's examples are from R. R. Bolgar, *The Classical Heritage and Its Beneficiaries* (Cambridge: The University Press, 1954), 257, 429n3. Presumably, not every day was this brutal, but the examples give a flavor of the times.

[17] Bowen, *Civilization of Europe*, 174, 190, 223, 257–59.

manuscript not rediscovered until the 1350's. The full text was found in 1416. After their reintroduction, Quintilian's ideas immediately influenced a number of Renaissance writers, including Vergerio (1349–1420) and Thomas Elyot (c. 1490–1546). Vergerio argued that quick and slow children may be equally intelligent and that knowledge must be organized into smaller units so that the slower child may more readily grasp the material.[18] Elyot introduced the organic metaphor into modern thought.[19] The aim of education for Renaissance writers was to produce a Christian gentleman or, as it has also been described, to instill in the student a lettered piety—"lettered" meaning a knowledge of the Greek and Latin languages and literature, "piety" meaning a knowledge and practice of the tenets of Christianity.

And lettered piety was the goal of Jesuit educational theory, the next doctrine that contains seeds of the theory of concentrated attention.[20] In fact, Jesuit theory is believed to be a systematization of Renaissance educational practice.[21] For example, the prelection, an extended lesson assignment, and concertation, a contest among students, are adaptations of methods used in the universities.[22] As a result, Jesuit theory and practice is viewed today as fundamentally traditional, as indeed it is. Like Plato's theory, Jesuit educational doctrine is an unlikely source of the theory of concentrated attention. Nonetheless, the Jesuits did make a few innovations.

The Society of Jesus, founded by Ignatius Loyola (1491–1556) in 1539, placed profound emphasis on education. It was the first organization to train teachers and to provide teachers with a thoroughly detailed how-to manual, the *Ratio Studiorum* or Plan of Studies, which was adopted in 1599. In catering to student needs, Jesuit education divided schooling into at least thirteen grades, to enable all levels of ability and

---

[18] Ibid., 216–18.

[19] Ibid., 399.

[20] See Allan P. Farrell, *The Jesuit Code of Liberal Education: Development and Scope of the Ratio Studiorum* (Milwaukee, WI: The Bruce Publishing Co., 1938), especially p. 408, for a discussion of how the aims of twentieth-century Jesuit education in the United States did not differ much from those of the sixteenth century.

[21] The direct influence on the Jesuits was the University of Paris, while a significant influence on the medieval universities was Quintilian. Allan P. Farrell, *The Jesuit Ratio Studiorum of 1599*, trans. Allan P. Farrell (Washington, DC: Conference of the Major Superiors of Jesuits, 1970), ix-x.

[22] Bowen, *Civilization of Europe*, Ibid., 430–31.

paces of learning to be recognized.[23] Slower students repeated courses as needed; faster students were promoted to the next level. Teachers were encouraged to learn the everyday common language and to remain fifteen minutes after a lecture to answer student questions—both practices uncommon in the sixteenth century. Supervision and governing by love, rather than by compulsion and punishment, were the recommended means of correcting student errors; corporal punishment, specifically, if needed at all, was to be disassociated from teaching.[24]

The Jesuits suggested for the first time that natural science be included in the curriculum—insofar as science supported and enhanced Christian theology. Later revisions of Jesuit doctrine provided for the teaching of modern literature in the vernacular, that is, in the local dialect of the common people, rather than in the more formal medieval Latin; mathematics and the methods of the natural sciences were included in these revisions.[25] The techniques of emulation and competition—the contests, for example, in which one group of students seeks to find and correct the errors of another group—are much criticized today by the progressives, but must be mentioned as an important concern by the Jesuits for motivation. The premises of traditional education ignore positive motivation altogether; the Jesuits recognized its importance. Further, the subjects that the Jesuits taught during this time period were presented in-depth and in succession, rather than simultaneously as they are today; this can be viewed as a primitive approach to concentrated attention, because the purpose was to have students focus on and learn well one subject at a time.[26]

As traditional as Jesuit doctrine may seem, it does have its elements of modernity.

COMENIUS, LOCKE, AND ROUSSEAU

The development of the theory of concentrated attention begins in earnest with the work of Comenius, Locke, and Rousseau. Comenius states the basic premise of adapting instruction to the child, not the child to instruction. Locke refutes original sin and emphasizes the

---

[23] Ibid., 425.

[24] Robert R. Rusk, *The Doctrines of the Great Educators*, 2nd ed. (London: Macmillan and Company, 1954), 72, 76, 84–85.

[25] Ibid., 72, 83.

[26] Ibid., 77–80.

primacy of nurture. And Rousseau develops the notion of the organic child who must be left free to unfold.

The modern idea of universal education—which includes the education of girls—was first expressed by Martin Luther and promoted widely throughout the Protestant Reformation. If each individual can access God directly, rather than through the intermediary of a priest, said the Protestants, then this access will be improved by a vernacular Bible and universal education.[27] John Amos Comenius (1592–1670), Czech education reformer and Protestant minister, furthered the notion of universal education with a fully developed plan for learning from preschool to university. In addition, as a follower of Francis Bacon, he strongly rejected the scholastic, rationalistic approach to education and advocated empiricism. It is here that Comenius' contributions to the development of concentrated attention can be observed.

The guiding premise of Comenius was always to follow nature, for "nature," he says, "observes a suitable time. For example: a bird that wishes to multiply its species does not set about it in winter, when everything is stiff with cold, nor in summer, when everything is parched and withered by the heat."[28] A suitable time, therefore, must also be observed in children in order successfully to teach them; children develop in distinct stages, so some basic knowledge, values, and skills must be taught before other more difficult material. The vernacular language, in particular, must be taught before Latin. "To attempt to teach a foreign language before the mother-tongue has been learned," says Comenius, "is as irrational as to teach a boy to ride before he can walk."[29]

Comenius was first to probe the subject of developmental stages and to apply the notion to writing textbooks. He argued that knowledge must be properly ordered from the easier and more concrete to the more difficult and abstract. Practicing what he preached, he proceeded to write graded textbooks for children to use at different ages.[30] His crowning achievement, a work that continued to be published and used for two centuries, was *Orbis Sensualium Pictus* or The Visible World in

---

[27] The education, according to Luther and his Protestant followers, should also be compulsory.

[28] John Amos Comenius, *The Great Didactic*, 1632; trans. M. W. Keatinge (New York: Russell & Russell, 1910), 112–13. Emphasis of the first sentence in the original was omitted for ease of reading.

[29] Ibid., 267.

[30] James Bowen, *A History of Western Education*, vol. 3, *The Modern West* (New York: St. Martin's Press, 1981), 102–04.

Pictures, published in 1658. This was the world's first illustrated picture book. Printed side by side beneath each picture is a description of the illustration in both Latin and a vernacular language.[31] The principle ultimately is Aristotle's, by way of Bacon: if there is nothing in the mind that first did not come through the senses, then sensual, concrete objects are what first must be shown to children so they may acquire knowledge in a properly ordered manner. In *The Great Didactic* Comenius boldly asserts that examples must "come before rules."[32]

In addition to the premise that instruction should be adapted to the child, Comenius anticipated the doctrine of interest. He argues: "The desire to know and to learn should be excited in boys in every possible manner" and: "Every study should be commenced in such a manner as to awaken a real liking for it on the part of the scholars...."[33] Reflecting the thought of the Jesuits, Comenius suggested that emulation and competition be used to stimulate interest. Corporal punishment and interest being opposed to one another, he argued that the former must never be used on children who fail to learn, because it is the teacher who is at fault, not the children.[34] A "musician," he says, "does not strike his lyre a blow with his fist or with a stick, nor does he throw it against the wall, because it produces a discordant sound; but, setting to work on scientific principles, he tunes it and gets it into order."[35] So also should teachers set to work on scientific principles to tune their students and to get them into order.

A significant advance in educational thought occurred when John Locke (1632–1704) rejected the doctrine of innate ideas, the notion that we are born already possessing certain concepts and principles, including moral principles; our minds at birth, says Locke, are tabula rasa. In the same vein, Locke demolishes the doctrine of original sin, major underlying premise of traditional education for over a thousand years. The child's mind, he says, is like a sheet of "white paper or wax to be

---

[31] Ibid. John Amos Comenius, *Orbis Sensualium Pictus, English and Latin* (1659; repr., London: Oxford University Press, 1968). The first vernacular language was German, but in addition to English, other editions included French, Italian, and Polish, among others.

[32] Comenius, *Great Didactic*, 116.

[33] Ibid., 130, 146.

[34] Ibid., 139.

[35] Ibid., 250.

molded and fashioned as one pleases."[36] Thus, Locke adopts the view known as the primacy of nurture, often illustrated by this statement: "I think I may say that of all the men we meet with, nine parts of ten are what they are, good or evil, useful or not, by their education. 'Tis that which makes the great difference in mankind."[37]

Locke's approach to education is aristocratic and favored home tutoring to group teaching. In this way, though, Locke emphasizes the importance of catering to individual differences, which last is inevitably compromised in a group setting. He opposes teaching Latin or Greek in the early years, arguing that if any foreign language is to be taught to an Englishman, it should be French, and the language should be taught directly through conversation, rather than through the bookish and punitive methods of the Scholastics.[38] Indeed, reading in the vernacular should be taught as soon as possible after the child learns to talk.[39]

Since it is not possible to learn all knowledge in existence, Locke promotes the frequency-of-use principle as guide to selecting subjects of study. He states, "And since it cannot be hoped [the pupil] should have time and strength to learn all things, most pains should be taken about that which is most necessary, and that principally looked after which will be of most frequent use to him in the world."[40] Here we have one of the first modern statements of learning for practical, consequential reasons, rather than for its own sake. Locke even suggests that young gentlemen learn two or three manual trades as a hobby, especially bookkeeping, which is essential to managing an estate.

Locke rejects the notion that learning must be drudgery and advocates play and recreation as an essential part of the process. Forcing a boy to learn at one particular moment when he is not ready, says Locke, simply creates an aversion to learning. "He that loves reading, writing, music, etc. finds yet in himself certain seasons wherein those

---

[36] Locke, *Thoughts*, 161 (§ 216).

[37] Ibid., 10 (§ 1). In the eighteenth century, Locke's ideas were pushed to their ultimate extremes of environmental determinism and materialism. His explicit statements, however, need not be taken to such extremes.

[38] Ibid., 120 (§ 162). "Children learn to dance and fence without whipping," says Locke elsewhere (61, § 86). They even learn French, Italian, arithmetic, and drawing without need of the rod. The cause of the child's resistance to learning Latin and Greek, says Locke, must lie in the nature of the subjects and the methods of teaching.

[39] Ibid., 113 (§ 148).

[40] Ibid., 70–71 (§ 94).

things have no relish to him; and if at that time he forces himself to it, he only pothers and wearies himself to no purpose. So it is with children."[41] Thus, the tutor must observe the child carefully and wait for the critical moment in which to begin a particular subject.

"The great skill of a teacher is to get and keep the attention of his scholar," says Locke. Whatever teachers offer to pupils, anticipating the theory of concentrated attention, it must be "as grateful and agreeable as possible." Harsh statements and corporal punishment are not the way to a child's mind. As Locke puts it: "Passionate words or blows from the tutor fill the child's mind with terror and affrightment, which immediately takes it up and leaves no room for other impressions." And, anticipating Dewey's theory of undivided interest, he states: "'Tis impossible children should learn anything whilst their thoughts are possessed and disturbed with any passion, especially fear, which makes the strongest impression on their yet tender and weak spirits."[42]

According to one writer, the significance of Locke's ideas lies "not so much in [his] rejection of innate ideas as in [his] rejection of original sin."[43] Historian Peter Gay picks up on this assessment and argues that the eighteenth century's rejection of original sin combined with the Enlightenment's "recovery of nerve" to create a "pedagogical optimism" never before enjoyed.[44] Locke's ideas indeed made possible the educational thought of Rousseau.

Jean-Jacques Rousseau (1712–1778) revolutionized educational thought by encouraging adults to see the child *as a child*, not as a miniature adult. As Rousseau puts it in his preface to *Émile*: "The wisest writers devote themselves to what a man ought to know, without asking what a child is capable of learning. They are always looking for the man in the child, without considering what he is before he becomes a man."[45]

---

[41] Ibid., 51 (§ 74).

[42] Ibid., 124–25 (§ 167).

[43] J. A. Passmore, "The Malleability of Man in Eighteenth-Century Thought," in Earl R. Wasserman, ed., *Aspects of the Eighteenth Century* (Baltimore: Johns-Hopkins Press, 1965), 22.

[44] Peter Gay, *The Enlightenment*, vol. 2, *The Science of Freedom* (New York: Alfred A. Knopf, 1969), 511–12. Gay uses the phrase "recovery of nerve" as the opposite of Gilbert Murray's "failure of nerve." Murray used his phrase to describe the rise of asceticism, mysticism, and pessimism in ancient Greek culture's decline; generally, it was a loss of self-confidence and hope. See Gilbert Murray, *Five Stages of Greek Religion* (Garden City, NY: Doubleday & Co., 1955) 119.

[45] Jean-Jacques Rousseau, *Émile*, trans. Barbara Foxley (London: J. M. Dent & Sons, 1911), 1.

Or, to state it differently: just as it is not precisely correct to refer to a tadpole as a miniature frog, so also it is not appropriate to describe a child as a small and ignorant adult who needs to be stuffed with what the adult knows. As the tadpole and frog are functionally different organisms possessing unique needs, so also are the child and adult human being.[46]

Rousseau's two main educational influences are Plato and Locke; the integration of the two in Rousseau provides the foundations of modern progressive education. Of Plato's *Republic*, Rousseau says, "It is the finest treatise on education ever written."[47] Thus, in his *Considerations on the Government of Poland*, Rousseau advocates a strong, publicly financed national—as in nationalistic—educational system.[48] Consistent with his Protestant background, Rousseau advocates universal, compulsory education. Critics have sometimes overlooked this aspect of his views, emphasizing Rousseau's "back to nature" appeals in *Émile*. Rousseau, however, is a man of the Enlightenment who advocates the necessity of a strong national education.

According to Peter Gay, the key to understanding Rousseau is to appreciate that he is "not wholly in the Enlightenment, but he [is] of it."[49] Essentially, Rousseau is a Protestant living in Catholic France, caught between the secularism of the philosophes and the intolerance of the church. Thus, he opposes the rationalistic, mechanistic materialism of the scientific revolution that was spreading rapidly throughout the Enlightenment and stresses the cognitive value of emotions, as well as the presence in humans of a self-determined will and spirit—influential ideas that eventually spawned the romantic revolt against the Enlightenment. In his political writings, notably the *Social Contract*, Rousseau introduced his own form of intolerance, namely that personal desires must be subordinated to the General Will, which is universal law or moral principle that has been handed down by God.

Though a Protestant, Rousseau is still a man of the Enlightenment, which means that he is strongly influenced by Locke, especially Locke's

---

[46] The analogy to a tadpole and frog is from Jean Piaget, *Science of Education and the Psychology of the Child*, trans. Derek Coltman (New York: Orion Press, 1970), 153, 159–60. The primary task of early education, as Piaget sees it, is to *form* the mind, not to furnish it.

[47] Rousseau, *Émile*, 8.

[48] Jean-Jacques Rousseau, *Considerations on the Government of Poland*, trans. Willmoore Kendall (Minneapolis: Minneapolis Book Store, 1947).

[49] Gay, *Science of Freedom*, 529.

rejection of original sin.[50] Rousseau extends this notion further to assert that humans are born good, which makes them equal at birth, but are corrupted by society. Since we cannot go back to nature—and Rousseau does not advocate such an idea—the aim of education is to prepare children for living in the uncorrupted society of the Social Contract, where all citizens subordinate their wills to the General Will.

In early education, the goal is to develop the original, uncorrupted nature of the child. Children, says Rousseau, must be allowed to unfold or develop their latent powers naturally. They must be freed of the constraints of the bookish, scholastic education prevalent at the time—that is, they must be left free to use their senses, to enjoy first hand the experiences of nature, and to discover knowledge on their own without having it told to them by someone else. Rousseau states, referring to the imaginary pupil, Émile:

> Put the problems before him and let him solve them himself. Let him know nothing because you have told him, but because he has learnt it for himself. Let him not be taught science, let him discover it. If ever you substitute authority for reason he will cease to reason; he will be a mere plaything of other people's thoughts.[51]

Here is the first statement of modern educational theory.

A few pages later, referring to the stage of early adolescence and anticipating the theory of concentrated attention, Rousseau continues:

> It is not your business to teach him the various sciences, but to give him a taste for them and methods of learning them when this taste is more mature. That is assuredly a fundamental principle of all good education.
>
> This is also the time to train him gradually to prolonged attention to a given object; but this attention should never be the result of constraint, but of interest or desire....[52]

Acknowledging that children progress through distinct stages of development before they reach maturity, Rousseau argues that each stage requires a different approach to education. Not until the last stage—

---

[50] "Let us lay it down as an incontrovertible rule that the first impulses of nature are always right; there is no original sin in the human heart...." Rousseau, *Émile*, 56.

[51] Ibid., 131.

[52] Ibid., 134–35.

later adolescence, or about age fifteen—do children begin to learn from others through instruction and reading.

Throughout this education, one guiding premise stands out. "Present interest," says Rousseau, "that is the motive power, the only motive power that takes us far and safely."[53] Stimulate a desire to learn in children and no other method or gimmick will be required. Critics of Rousseau have made much of his "negative" or "natural" education, especially his desire to put off learning to read or reason until adolescence, but the value in Rousseau's theory as it relates to the theory of concentrated attention is his insistence on knowing the child before attempting to teach. And knowing the child means freeing the child from the rationalistic constraints of traditional education. It is this point that has influenced nearly all subsequent education writers, including Montessori, earning Rousseau the appellation "father of modern education."

PESTALOZZI, HERBART, AND FROEBEL

Rousseau's influence was immediate and extensive. In the late eighteenth and early nineteenth centuries, three education writers studied the psychology of the child and consequently further developed the foundations of modern education, especially the theory of concentrated attention. Pestalozzi emphasized the inductive approach to learning through his "object lesson." Herbart stressed conceptualization in learning, but not in the rationalistic manner of the Scholastics; he also formally proposed for the first time the doctrine of interest as essential motivator of student learning. And Froebel, father of the kindergarten, extended the doctrine of interest to the doctrine of play. All three endorsed the organic metaphor, viewing the child as a bud that must be allowed to unfold and blossom.

Johann Heinrich Pestalozzi (1746–1827), a practitioner who operated several schools in Switzerland, modeled his approach to education on the ideas of Rousseau. He assumed, as did Rousseau, that the child is born good and that education must follow the child's nature. He also emphasized catering to the uniqueness of each child, acknowledging that there are differences from one individual to the next and that each child develops through distinct stages to adulthood. Unlike Rousseau, he sought a means of educating all children, including the poor and orphaned. Drawing on the organic metaphor, he states that the child is "endowed with all

---

[53] Ibid., 81.

the faculties of human nature, but none of them developed: *a bud not yet opened*. When the bud uncloses, every one of the leaves unfolds, not one remains behind. Such must be the process of education."[54] Because of his efforts, Pestalozzi is credited with laying the foundation for modern public schools that are open to everyone.[55]

The question for Pestalozzi is, what are the faculties of human nature and how should education be adapted to them? Since human faculties are sense-based, all knowledge comes through the senses. Pestalozzi's approach to education therefore is inductive, broken into steps that match the process by which we acquire knowledge. Vague sense impressions confront us initially, he says, but gradually we find distinct impressions standing out from the others; as the impressions grow clearer, they eventually become definite ideas. Through the process of *Anschauung*—direct or personal experience of facts—we are able to make sense out of these vague impressions and begin to know the essential nature of things.[56] As William Boyd puts it, "A lesson in which the child sees, handles or otherwise makes direct acquaintance with an object is an *Anschauung* lesson." Thus, geography is better learned by seeing rivers and mountains first hand than by reading about them in a book.[57] Comenius provided objects to the child by way of pictures; Pestalozzi argues that the objects themselves should be brought to the child (or the child should be taken to the objects).

In English Pestalozzi's *Anschauung* became well known as the "object lesson," after the much reprinted text *Lessons on Objects* by Henry and Elizabeth Mayo. The point of *Anschauung* is that learning must be grounded in concrete facts in order for the child to acquire clear and definite ideas. The teacher who possesses already definite ideas must carefully divide them into their fundamental components, then order and illustrate them with concrete objects in order to give the child an *Anschauung* lesson. Reading, observes Pestalozzi, presupposes speaking,

---

[54] Johann Heinrich Pestalozzi, *Letters on Early Education, Addressed to J. P. Greaves, Esq.* (London: Sherwood, Gilbert, and Piper, 1827), 7. Emphasis in original.

[55] Rusk, *Great Educators*, 187.

[56] *Anschauung* is sometimes translated as intuition, but in Pestalozzi's context it means any of the following: "immediate awareness, direct acquaintance, direct appreciation, concrete experience, personal contact, first-hand impressions, face-to-face knowledge, the direct impact of things and persons." Rusk, *Great Educators*, 193. "Sense-impression" is also a common translation; Pestalozzi refers to his method as the "ABC of *Anschauung*," or the ABC of Sense-Impression.

[57] Boyd, *History of Western Education*, 324.

writing presupposes drawing, and arithmetic presupposes objects that can be added and subtracted. The path to teaching reading is through the sounds of letters, vowels, and syllables—Pestalozzi thus developed a phonics-based method of teaching reading.[58] For writing, the child is taught first to draw lines and curves, foreshadowing Montessori's approach to teaching writing. For arithmetic, concrete objects are used to illustrate why nine plus seven equals sixteen.

On teaching arithmetic, Pestalozzi states:

> The elements of number, or preparatory exercises of Calculation, should always be taught by submitting to the eye of the child certain objects representing the units. A child can conceive the idea of two balls, two roses, two books; but it cannot conceive the idea of "Two" in the abstract. How would you make the child understand that two and two make four, unless you show it to him first in reality? To begin by abstract notions is absurd and detrimental, instead of being conducive. The result is, at best, that the child can do the things by rote without understanding it; a fact which does not reflect on the child but on the teacher, who knows not a higher character of instruction than mere mechanical training.[59]

Thus, instruction, in Boyd's summation, must "follow the order of the mind's growth," which means that a correct order of learning must be developed.[60]

As the result of one of his early experiments, Pestalozzi noted that his method "quickly developed in the children a sense of capacities hitherto unknown. They realized their own power and the tediousness of the ordinary school tone vanished like a ghost. They wanted to learn, they found they could do it, they persevered, they succeeded, and they laughed. Their tone was not that of learners. It was the tone of unknown capacities roused from sleep."[61] This empowerment of children by matching educational materials to their ages and abilities foreshadows Montessori's "discoveries of the child," which

---

[58] Blaise Pascal (1623–1662) was first to devise a phonemic alphabet that enabled children to learn the sounds of the letters first, before learning their names. Ibid., 260. Blending the sounds of consonants with those of the vowels is the essence of the phonics method of learning to read.

[59] Pestalozzi, *Letters on Early Education*, 135.

[60] Boyd, *History of Western Education*, 326.

[61] Johann Heinrich Pestalozzi, *How Gertrude Teaches Her Children: An Attempt to Help Mothers to Teach Their Own Children*, trans. Lucy E. Holland & Frances C. Turner (Syracuse, NY: C. W. Bardeen, 1898), 43–44.

occurred by unleashing the child's natural drives through concentrated attention.

Johann Friedrich Herbart (1776–1841), professional philosopher and successor to Kant at the University of Königsberg, was influenced by Pestalozzi but went well beyond Pestalozzi's *Anschauung*. Indeed, Herbart was first to develop the philosophy of education—or "pedagogics," as he called it—into a distinct science. In psychology, he coined the phrase "threshold of consciousness" and was one of the first to acknowledge the existence of a dynamic conscious and subconscious mind.[62] Applying psychology to education, Herbart was among the first to describe learning as a conceptual process that consists of distinct steps; failure to follow the steps correctly or at all, he said, would produce blocks or inhibitions in learning. A modest practitioner—not unlike Dewey—Herbart founded a demonstration school in Königsberg with which to test and implement his educational ideas; the school eventually became an institution for training teachers.[63]

"Pedagogics as a science," according to Herbart, "is based on ethics and psychology. The former points out the goal of education; the latter the way, the means, and the obstacles."[64] The aim of education is to instill virtue, and because virtue requires a many-sided interest, effective teaching means stimulating interest. "Mere information," says Herbart, "does not suffice; for this we think of as a supply or store of facts, which a person might possess or lack, and still remain the same being. But he who lays hold of his information and reaches out for more, takes an interest in it."[65] Herbart, then, for the first time in the history of educational ideas, fully elaborates the doctrine of interest; to stimulate interest a specific technique of teaching is called for and Herbart proceeds to provide one. First, the concept of interest.

States Herbart, "Interest means self-activity" and self-activity takes place when ideas arise spontaneously in the child's mind. This means essentially that the ideas are generated internally by the child's own choice, not forced in by an external agent.[66]

---

[62] Robert I. Watson, *The Great Psychologists*, 4th ed. (New York: J. B. Lippincott, 1978), 233–35.

[63] Boyd, *History of Western Education*, 340.

[64] Johann Friedrich Herbart, *Outlines of Educational Doctrine*, trans. Alexis F. Lange (New York: Macmillan, 1901), 2.

[65] Ibid., 44.

[66] Ibid., 60.

In the typical recitation, Herbart points out, where the child is merely reproducing material previously memorized, the activity is imposed from outside by the instructor. "It is the teacher's business, while giving instruction, to observe whether the ideas of his pupils rise spontaneously or not. If they do, the pupils are said to be attentive; the lesson has won their interest." Interest determines attention and attention for Herbart means "readiness to form new ideas." "Apperceiving activity" cultivates both interest and attention.[67]

Apperception is the process of acquiring and understanding new ideas in the context of one's already existing knowledge. When a child, for example, who has seen many real horses suddenly recognizes a horse in a picture book, apperception has occurred. An older student who, while working hard on a mathematics assignment, just as suddenly sees the solution to the problem has also experienced apperception. Apperception is a kind of bursting forth of subconscious material that unites "with whatever [new, but] similar elements present themselves. Now this apperceiving activity," says Herbart, "must be exercised constantly in all instruction."[68] Self-activity, in other words, and therefore interest and attention, result from apperceiving activity.

To promote apperceiving activity in children Herbart proposes a specific technique of teaching that consists of four steps: clearness, association, system, and method.[69] Clearness means that new material should be presented to children broken into small, easily digestible chunks so the children may fully understand the new before continuing. Association means that new material must be related to the current knowledge and context of the children; to improve association Herbart encourages informal conversations with the children to draw out what they already know in relation to the new material. System means generalization, that is, the identification of relevant principles that cause or explain the new material; this step enables children to organize the new ideas in their minds for best retention. Finally, method means application of the new material in assigned exercises, performed by the children. Herbart cautions against the mechanical use of these steps,

---

[67] Ibid., 62–63.

[68] Ibid., 67.

[69] Ibid., 53–57.

noting that they must be adapted to different subjects and to different ages.[70]

The goal of furthering a many-sided interest is what today would be called a well-rounded education. It means that a single-sided interest is too narrow a preparation for success in later life. For Herbart, single-sided interest tended toward selfishness (as the concept does in the minds of numerous advocates of well-roundedness today). Since Herbart's primary aim in education was to instill virtue, his concept of a many-sided interest was important as a counter to egoism (as it is in the minds of numerous advocates of well-roundedness today). Specifically, what Herbart considered necessary for a many-sided curriculum were the subjects of history and natural science. In short, he advocated a standard liberal education, which included the study of Latin and Greek languages and literature.[71]

Friedrich Froebel (1782–1852) used Pestalozzi's educational findings as part of an elaborate metaphysics (based on German idealism) and applied the metaphysics to education to develop what he eventually called the kindergarten. The aim of education, according to Froebel, is to acquire knowledge of the eternal law of unity of all things and to find one's place within this unity. The theory of education is "the system of directions, derived from the knowledge and study of that law" that will guide "thinking, intelligent beings in the apprehension of their life-work." Practice is "the self-active application of this knowledge in the direct development and cultivation of rational beings toward the attainment of their destiny."[72] Behind the abstruse language, this is an early statement of the link between education and productive work.

Froebel pushes the organic metaphor to its limit. He states, "We grant space and time to young plants and animals because we know that, in accordance with the laws that live in them, they will develop properly and grow well; young animals and plants are given rest, and arbitrary interference with their growth is avoided, because it is known that the opposite practice would disturb their pure unfolding and sound development; but the young human being is looked upon as a piece of wax,

---

[70] Mechanical use of the Herbartian steps is precisely what happened in practice in late nineteenth and early twentieth century American education. This, of course, gave the progressives much to criticize and label as "traditional."

[71] Herbart, *Outlines*, 80.

[72] Friedrich Froebel, *The Education of Man*, trans. W. N. Hailmann (New York: D. Appleton and Company, 1895), 4.

a lump of clay, which man can mold into what he pleases." Modifying Locke's premise of tabula rasa, Froebel argues that while children do not possess innate ideas, they do—like plants and animals—possess innate capacities that must be allowed to develop. Interference with this development, through an "interfering education," can only "annihilate, hinder, and destroy."[73]

Following Rousseau, Froebel recognizes four stages of development: infancy, childhood, boyhood, and youth. He is most remembered for his discussion of childhood, which he considered to be the most important of the four. The most significant activity at the stage of childhood is play. According to Froebel, play is not a purposeless activity.

> [It] is the highest phase of child-development—of human development at this period; for it is self-active representation of the inner.... A child that plays thoroughly, with self-active determination, perseveringly until physical fatigue forbids, will surely be a thorough, determined man.... Play, at this time is not trivial, it is highly serious and of deep significance.... The plays of childhood are the germinal leaves of all later life; for the whole man is developed and shown in these, in his tenderest dispositions, in his innermost tendencies.[74]

Play lays the foundation for work, the most significant activity of later life. Thus, the seriousness and concentration of the child who engages in play must not be interrupted, lest the child's development be thwarted.

To enhance development, Froebel created a number of objects, called "gifts," to be given to children throughout the stage of childhood. The first was a wooden or woolen ball, the second a sphere, a cube, and a cylinder, all made of wood. The third was a wooden cube, divided into eight smaller cubes. And so on. The gifts were symbolic of his metaphysics, as well as illustrative of geometrical figures, and

---

[73] Ibid., 8–9. Agreeing with Rousseau, Froebel holds that "surely, the nature of man is in itself good." Ibid., 120. It should be noted here that post-Darwinian biology and modern psychology do not refute Locke's notion of tabula rasa; innate capacities are not the same as innate ideas. Capacities need to be allowed to develop without interference, but it also does matter which content is taught to the young. Describing the Chinese as animals, as the Japanese did in their schools in the 1930's, and the Jews as vermin, as the Nazis did in their schools, for example, and urging jihad against the infidel Americans are content of education that will leave an indelible mark on unformed minds.

[74] Ibid., 54–55. Italics were omitted from a portion of this quotation.

have been controversial.[75] Nonetheless, the pattern of giving materials to children to play with that at the same time are educative was taken up with enthusiasm by Montessori. Froebel also created materials and activities, called "occupations," to be given and performed throughout the stage of boyhood. The purpose of such occupations as sewing, paper weaving, and building a hut—activities that foreshadow the Dewey school—was to develop manual skills and to stimulate work. Froebel's distinction between play and work also foreshadows Dewey's: "What formerly the child did only for the sake of the activity, the boy now does for the sake of the result or product of his activity."[76] Froebel further introduced into his schools activities such as drawing and gardening, as well as instruction in religion, language, mathematics, and natural science.

Froebel coined the term "kindergarten" late in life when he realized that something was needed to differentiate his schools of natural growth from the traditional German "state-machines" that were "cutting out and shaping" children as if in a factory.[77] Even the word "school" sounded too negative and coercive for Froebel, so he came up with a long German word that literally meant "a place where small children can be fully engaged [in creative activity]." This was too long and clumsy, so he shortened it to kindergarten, a garden for children.[78] Today, the kindergarten has been relegated to preschool, but for Froebel it *was* school.

DEWEY AND MONTESSORI

With Dewey and Montessori, this historical sketch arrives finally at the modern foundations of the theory of concentrated attention. Dewey and Montessori, as has been suggested in previous pages, each had their own influences and catalysts. For Dewey, springboards for the devel-

---

[75] See William Heard Kilpatrick, *Froebel's Kindergarten Principles Critically Examined* (New York: The Macmillan Co., 1916). Kilpatrick acknowledged that "Froebel's endeavor" was "one of the most original and most valuable suggestions yet made for the education of the child." Ibid., 145. As an empiricist, though, Kilpatrick thoroughly criticized the patent unreality of Froebel's metaphysical symbolism. "The ball," says Kilpatrick, "will never be thought of [by the child] in connection with unity, nor the cube with multiplicity." Ibid., 200.

[76] Froebel, *Education of Man*, 99. Italics omitted. For Dewey's distinction between play and work, see below, p. 61.

[77] Quoted in Bowen, *Modern West*, 336.

[78] Bowen, *Modern West*, 340.

opment of his ideas were the American Herbartians. For Montessori, her immediate influences, in addition to the several education writers discussed above, were the French physicians Itard and Séguin.

John Dewey (1859–1952) began writing on education in the 1890's during the American Herbartian movement. Herbart's ideas were not widely accepted in his lifetime, but were revived in the late nineteenth century by the German educators Ziller, Stoy, and Rein.[79] Dispensing with Herbart's metaphysics, Tuiskon Ziller (1817–1882) accepted Herbart's principles of teaching, developed pedagogy as an applied science, or "pedagogical technology," as it might be called, and used the principles to train future teachers. Karl Volkmar Stoy (1815–1885) and Wilhelm Rein (1847–1929) continued this tradition.

Rein expanded Herbart's four formal steps of instruction into five and renamed all but one of them, making the steps more descriptive of the teaching process and therefore more readily grasped by and taught to prospective teachers. Herbart's first step, clarity, was divided into two by Rein and named "preparation" and "presentation." Herbart's second step, association, remained the same in Rein's scheme. System was renamed "generalization" and method became "application." These five steps of lesson planning then became the model of teacher education and, consequently, of teaching. Charles de Garmo and Charles and Frank McMurry spawned the Herbartian movement by bringing the ideas to the United States in the 1890's.[80] *The Method of the Recitation* by the McMurrys was a delineation of the five steps to be used by prospective teachers; the work was hailed as a demonstration of scientific pedagogy.[81]

Dewey's response to Herbartianism was to present his own five steps of a complete act of thought and to develop a doctrine of interest. Dewey's five steps consist of the following: "(i) a felt difficulty;

---

[79] Ibid., 348–51. At this point it should be mentioned that although he advocated a free market in education, Herbert Spencer (1820–1903) did not provide original contributions to the theory of concentrated attention. His educational ideas essentially follow Pestalozzi. See *Education: Intellectual, Moral and Physical* (New York: D. Appleton and Company, 1896). And his arguments for a free market in education are the practical ones that economists who write on education today recite. See *The Man Versus the State* (1884; repr., Indianapolis: Liberty Classics, 1981), 226–43. He does make the important point that compulsory education violates the right of free speech. Ibid., 240–41.

[80] Bowen, *Modern West*, 366–74.

[81] Charles and Frank McMurry, *The Method of the Recitation* (New York: Macmillan, 1897).

(ii) its location and definition; (iii) suggestion of possible solution; (iv) development by reasoning of the bearings of the suggestion; (v) further observation and experiment leading to its acceptance or rejection; that is, the conclusion of belief or disbelief."[82] This process is said to be a generalization of scientific method, the problem-identification and hypothesis-testing procedure used by experimental scientists. Dewey, however, did not like such labels. Today, we understand the process as problem-solving thinking.

Dewey acknowledges "obvious resemblances" between the Herbartians' five steps and his, specifically the movement from inductive to deductive reasoning. The primary difference, according to Dewey, is that the Herbartian procedure lacks a difficulty or problem as "origin and stimulus of the whole process." Thus, Dewey concludes that the Herbartian method seems to deal with "thought simply as an incident in the process of acquiring information, instead of treating the latter as an incident in the process of developing thought."[83] He also argues that the Herbartian steps should not be followed rigidly; although excellent for a teacher to follow when preparing a recitation, they "should not prescribe the actual course of teaching."[84] Flexibility, he says, is the key to the correct implementation of any formal steps of instruction.

For the Herbartians interest is self-initiated activity that is stimulated by the five steps of effective teaching. For Dewey, undivided interest in which the self is identified with the object or end being pursued is stimulated by Dewey's five steps of a complete act of thought. "The problem of instruction," states Dewey, "is thus that of finding material which will engage a person in specific activities having an aim or purpose of moment or interest to him, and dealing with things not as gymnastic appliances but as conditions for the attainment of ends."[85] It

---

[82] John Dewey, *How We Think* (1910; repr., Buffalo, NY: Prometheus Books, 1991), 72. This process is described by Dewey in various works, sometimes in slightly different formulations. For example, see Dewey, *Democracy and Education*, 150.

[83] Dewey, *How We Think*, 203–04.

[84] Ibid., 204. For Dewey, recitation is a "place and time for stimulating and directing reflection," not for reproducing memorized lessons. However, Dewey regards the reproduction of "memorized matter" to be an "indispensable incident" in "cultivating a thoughtful attitude." Ibid., 201–02. This is another point, in addition to those mentioned in chapter 1, that is often not remembered about Dewey—namely that, along with valuing subject matter and not putting method over content, he *values memorization*.

[85] Dewey, *Democracy and Education*, 132.

is the teacher's responsibility to develop these materials and experiences and to match them to the child's age and interests. Following Froebel, the activities of the younger child (under seven years old, usually) are called play; for the older child, they are called work.[86] Both activities, for Dewey, are occupations.

The difference between play and work, according to Dewey, is a matter of degree, not kind; essentially, the distinction is based on time-span. While playing with a toy boat, for example, the means and end are simultaneous; the enjoyment felt during the activity is an end in itself, with no further end to pursue other than the enjoyment of playing with the boat. Making a boat, on the other hand, requires one or more steps that constitute a means to the end of playing boat. Thus, making a boat is work and this requires forethought and patience. Younger children do not foresee an end beyond the activity of playing boat; older children project and hold the specific results of their actions—the finished boats—while exerting time and effort to find materials with which to make the boats.[87]

In a proper school the teacher provides occupations to engage the student's interest. Occupation, for Dewey, is "a mode of activity on the part of the child which reproduces, or runs parallel to, some form of work carried on in social life."[88] That is, the school should be a microcosm of the larger society into which the child will eventually move. Education, therefore, is not a preparation for later life; it is an adaptation of life to the needs and interests of the child in the present.[89] Thus, the Dewey School at the University of Chicago from 1896

---

[86] John Dewey, *The School and Society* (1900; repr., Chicago: University of Chicago Press, 1990), 145.

[87] Dewey, *Democracy and Education*, 203. The distinction, Dewey points out, is based on psychology, not economics, so work here does not refer to paid labor. Younger children, Dewey also points out, can be said to engage in work as well as play—because of the intensity and seriousness with which they concentrate on their activities.

[88] Dewey, *School and Society*, 132.

[89] "Education is life, not a preparation for life" is a well-worn slogan of the progressives that in fact is equivocal. Progressive education is a preparation for what comes after the education, presumably later life. The phrase originated as a contrast to the traditionalists' demands for sterile memorization of subject matter; like a squirrel storing nuts for the winter, children store knowledge until they become adults. The progressives said, "Bring life to the classroom—to stimulate interest and to promote growth." Thus, children in the progressive classroom learn about life first-hand, rather than having to wait until they leave school.

to 1904 taught children from the ages of four to thirteen by means of such practical occupations as woodworking, gardening, weaving and sewing, and cooking.[90]

These occupations were not exercises in manual training to prepare the child for later skilled work; rather, they were vehicles by which the traditional subject matter of reading, writing, arithmetic, science, geography, and history were taught. The purpose of the occupations was to maintain interest through problem solving thinking, of the kind the original explorers, scientists, and pioneers might have had to perform, thereby moving the child's mind from the concrete problem of building, say, a small playhouse to the more abstract issues of number, measurement, and arithmetic. Gradually, the child moves into the more traditional areas of subject matter and eventually to the level of learning from traditional textbooks.

Dewey, it must be emphasized once again, did not abandon subject matter nor did he disvalue learning from textbooks. His ideas are merely the culmination of the modern trend away from abstract, rationalistic book learning in the child's early years to learning from concrete, problem-solving experience. Dewey's long-term plan for his school at the University of Chicago was stated quite explicitly. In a report to the President of the University of Chicago, he said that the goals of the school were to identify the child's interests so as to select appropriate subject matter and methods, to organize subject matter for each year, to gradually separate "the subject matter into its more specialized phases," i.e., to separate "history from science, biological science from physical science, etc.," and "to provide demand and opportunity for the continuous introduction of symbols in reading, writing, and number, and the necessity for an increased use of books as auxiliaries."[91]

Indeed, Dewey was highly critical of his progressive colleagues for not developing a proper subject matter. When progressive teachers failed to provide guidance or goals to their students, Dewey responded pointedly: "Now such a method is really stupid. For it attempts the impossible, which is always stupid; and it misconceives the conditions

---

[90] For a detailed discussion and history of the Dewey School, see Katherine Camp Mayhew and Anna Camp Edwards, *The Dewey School: The Laboratory School of the University of Chicago 1896–1903* (New York: D. Appleton-Century Company, 1936).

[91] John Dewey, *The President's Report: July, 1898–July, 1899* (1900; reprinted in John Dewey, *The Middle Works, 1899–1924*, vol. 1, *1899–1901*, ed. Jo Ann Boydston (Carbondale, IL: Southern Illinois University Press, 1976), 318.

of independent thinking. There are a multitude of ways of reacting to surrounding conditions, and without some guidance from experience these reactions are almost sure to be casual, sporadic and ultimately fatiguing, accompanied by nervous strain." As carpenters guide their apprentices, says Dewey, so must teachers their elementary school pupils.[92]

More specifically, Dewey's fundamental criticism of educational reforms that were often made in his name focused on the educators' failure to develop a progressively organized subject matter appropriate for age and maturity of the children being taught. Traditional educators, said Dewey, tended to emphasize the external conditions of learning, such as subject matter, at the expense of the internal needs for growth, but the progressives were committing the opposite error. "The organized subject-matter of the adult and the specialist cannot provide the starting point" of education, says Dewey, but it does provide the goal. And it is toward this goal that subject matter—in the form of occupations for younger children and books and other aids to investigation for older ones—must be organized and directed. "The problem of teaching," to repeat a quotation from chapter 1, "is to keep the experience of the student moving in the direction of what the expert already knows."[93]

And it is a mistake to assume that Dewey thought the methods used in elementary school should continue to be used in the higher grades, on through to university. Undivided interest for Dewey matures with age and experience. It may require the occupations of weaving or gardening in the earlier years, but as children grow older the materials to give them a growth experience may include a map of England or a book on ancient Greece. Certainly, at the university level, Dewey did

---

[92] John Dewey, "Individuality and Experience," (1926; reprinted in John Dewey et al., *Art and Education*, The Barnes Foundation Press, 1929), 180. Another analogy Dewey uses is that of mother to infant: "The wise mother takes account of the needs of the infant but not in a way which dispenses with her own responsibility for regulating the objective conditions under which the needs are satisfied. And if she is a wise mother in this respect, she draws upon past experiences of experts as well as her own for the light that these shed upon what experiences are in general most conducive to the normal development of infants." John Dewey, *Experience and Education* (1938; repr., New York: Collier Books, 1963), 41–42.

[93] Dewey, *Experience and Education*, 86, 42, 83. Dewey, *Democracy and Education*, 184. Dewey also suggests that the unruliness and ill-mannered behavior found in progressive classrooms is caused by the educators' lack of subject-matter planning. Dewey, *Experience and Education*, 56–57.

not imagine that elementary level occupations would be used. At the graduate level of education, Dewey the teacher insisted on verbatim recall of the words of philosophers under study.[94]

"The ideal aim of education," says Dewey, "is creation of [the] power of self-control," achieved by instilling in children knowledge, character, and skill. The means to this end is a progressively organized subject matter that allows the children an undivided interest for as long as they need to effect their own growth.[95]

In contrast to Dewey the professional philosopher, Maria Montessori (1870–1952) was trained in Italy as a physician and became an innovator in educational theory and practice by working first with mentally retarded children in Rome, then with normal but indigent children in one of Rome's slums. Her general influences were Comenius, Locke, Rousseau, Pestalozzi, and Froebel, as well as Aristotle by way of her Thomistic background. Her immediate influences were the physicians Jean-Marc-Gaspard Itard (1775–1838) and Edouard Séguin (1812–1880). Their techniques of working with deaf and retarded children through motor and sensory training led to the development of her unique method of early childhood education.[96]

For Montessori the goal of education is independence and independence is achieved through freedom and work—freedom for the organism to unfold on its own and work to advance the organism's growth and development.[97] The aim of traditional education in contrast, according to Montessori, is obedience and conformity to the will of adults; in such a system the children are treated like slaves and the result is psychological scars and dependence.[98] Indeed, Montessori described children in the traditional classroom as "beautiful butter-

---

[94] Walter B. Veazie, "John Dewey and the Revival of Greek Philosophy," in *University of Colorado Studies, Series in Philosophy*, No. 2, 1961, 1–2.

[95] Dewey, *Experience and Education*, 64. John Dewey, "Progressive Education and the Science of Education," *Progressive Education*, July-August-September 1928, 204.

[96] Bowen, *Modern West*, 394–97. Montessori, it should be pointed out, was the first female physician in Italy.

[97] Maria Montessori, *The Montessori Method*, trans. Anne E. George (1912; repr., New York: Schocken Books, 1964), 95–96. Maria Montessori, *The Absorbent Mind*, trans. Claude A. Claremont (1949; repr., New York: Henry Holt & Company, 1995), 89–90.

[98] Maria Montessori, *Spontaneous Activity in Education*, trans. Florence Simmonds (Frederick A. Stokes, 1917; reprint, Cambridge, MA: Robert Bentley, 1971), 20, 29.

flies, mounted by means of pins, their outspread wings motionless."[99] Her response was to let the butterflies fly.

Fully endorsing the organic metaphor, Montessori argues that "education is not something which the teacher does"; to be more precise, it "is a natural process which develops spontaneously in the human being. It is not acquired by listening to words, but in virtue of experiences in which the child acts on his environment. The teacher's task is not to talk, but to prepare and arrange a series of motives for cultural activity in a special environment made for the child."[100] Between birth and the age of six, says Montessori, children possess powerful learning capabilities that parents and teachers should take heed not to disturb or interrupt. Rather, parents and teachers should assist the development of children by providing them carefully prepared environments. This will enable them to acquire the ability to concentrate for long periods of time, which, as a result, will enable them to become calm and psychologically confident. They will learn the perseverance needed to succeed in the world as an adult.

The "absorbent mind" is the term Montessori used to describe the ability of young children to soak up everything in their environment. Montessori used the term "absorbent" deliberately and distinguished it from the kind of learning older children and adults exhibit. Acquisition of language is one illustration of the contrast between these two types of learning. The mother tongue is "absorbed" with relative ease by three-year-olds, but a second language acquired by older children and adults is learned laboriously and, usually, not very well. It is not just language, however, says Montessori, that young children absorb. Their manners and customs of birthplace, their sense of home or family culture in which they are reared, and even their posture, bearing, and gait are all absorbed in those early years in the same way that language is. The child, says Montessori, "incarnates in himself all of the world about him that his eyes see and his ears hear." And these experiences "are not just remembered; they form part of his soul."[101] They stay with the child throughout life.

It is this absorbency in early childhood that Montessori insists must be carefully nurtured, by leaving children free to explore their environment without interruption. (Of course, they need to be protected from

[99] Montessori, *Montessori Method*, 14.

[100] Montessori, *Absorbent Mind*, 8.

[101] Ibid, 62–65, 181, 189.

harm. Freedom, for Montessori, does not mean license.) If a parent takes a two-year-old for a walk and the child wants to examine a street sign for several minutes, the parent should not yank the toddler's arm and drag the child away. This is an authoritarian adult forcing a child to conform to the needs of the adult, rather than the adult trying to tune into and nurture the needs of the child. The child in this example, quite simply, has never seen a street sign before and wants to examine it carefully. The reason adults think children cannot concentrate for long periods of time, says Montessori, is that adults never give them a chance to concentrate—because adults are constantly interrupting the children and making them do what the adults want them to do.

Freedom to absorb and work with what is in the child's environment leads to concentrated attention. In the classroom of the Montessori preschool (ages three to six, usually), the environment consists of a variety of experimentally tested "didactic materials," such as the knobbed cylinders of different diameters that must be matched to appropriate holes in a block of wood and the sandpaper letters that begin to accommodate the child to the shapes of letters and the motions that will be required for writing; the child is free to choose, with the guidance of the teacher, which materials to work with at any given time.[102] "Experimentally tested" here means materials that have repeatedly led to concentrated attention have been retained; those that did not have been discarded.[103] Teachers are not lecturers in the traditional mold; rather, they facilitate learning experiences, by paying attention to the child's needs, giving lessons on and noting progress in the use of the graded materials, and suggesting new materials, appropriate to age and stage of development, to work with.

Montessori calls the specific form of concentrated attention that children exhibit in her schools "work," not only because of the diligent and sustained, almost adult-like effort displayed by the children, but

---

[102] The work of Séguin in particular influenced Montessori to develop this "didactic materials" approach to education. Montessori, *Montessori Method*, 28–47. The sandpaper letters are reminiscent of Quintilian's carved ivory letters. Montessori children learn to write before they learn to read; both activities usually begin to occur in the fourth year.

[103] Interestingly, toys were a casualty of this testing. Montessori discovered that young children value learning over playing games when she put the names of toys on cards and told the children they could play with the toys if they found the correct item. This was to be a reading game, but the children did not want to play with the toys, once retrieved; instead, they wanted more cards with words on them so they could test their reading abilities by finding the correct toy. Ibid, 298–301.

also because their work does in fact have an ultimate aim, a goal beyond the immediate object, for example, of inserting different-sized cylinders into the correct holes. That aim is the growth and development of independence. For adults, work usually involves an external end, such as putting sand into a wheel barrow in order to build a sidewalk or to fill up a hole. For children, putting sand in a wheel barrow is often the immediate end, because the barrow, once filled, is promptly emptied and then refilled! But the child's ultimate aim is internal—namely to grow—because repeated fillings of the barrow lead to the psychological conclusion, "I can do it." Thus, "what we mean by education is to help the child's developing life." Montessori concludes, "we can only rejoice each time [the child] shows us that he has reached a new level of independence."[104]

An important discovery of Montessori's is that certain psychological problems disappear when children are allowed to pursue their own interests in a prepared environment that stimulates concentrated attention. This is her concept of "normalization." Deviations or defects of character, as Montessori refers to these problems caused by interfering adults, such as rowdiness, possessiveness, and indolent passivity, vanish when the child becomes interested in a didactic material and begins to concentrate on it. After a short time, anxiety is replaced by inner calm and purposefulness. Outwardly, patience and a respect for others develops, because such a child learns to appreciate the absorption of others in these materials and is now willing to wait until a desired material is free. Confidence and self-esteem are the results of the normalizing process of concentrated attention.[105]

---

[104] Ibid, 88–89. E. M. Standing, *Maria Montessori: Her Life and Work* (1957; repr., New York: Plume/Penguin, 1984), 142–43. The wheel barrow example is from Standing. Note that Montessori's concept of work is consistent with Dewey's, as is her emphasis on growth.

[105] Montessori, *Absorbent Mind*, 201–07, 223. Maria Montessori, *The Secret of Childhood*, trans. M. Joseph Castelloe (1936; repr., New York: Ballantine Books, 1972), 154–76. Notably, Montessori considers adults, specifically, parents, to be the cause of many of these problems that are eliminated by freedom and work. See Donna Bryant Goertz in *Children Who Are Not Yet Peaceful: Preventing Exclusion in the Early Elementary Classroom* (Berkeley, CA: Frog, Ltd., 2001) for examples of how she used Montessori's principles to normalize elementary-aged, so-called problem children. Many of these children came to her on medication. With understanding and interest-guided concentration, they left at peace with themselves and others. Medication, says Goertz, has become the new spanking.

While the early years of a child's life reflect the task of absorbing the environment, according to Montessori, the later years—from age six on—call for the acquisition of culture.[106] Thus, Montessori developed didactic materials for the elementary child, from age six to twelve, continuing with the premises of free choice of materials to work with, as guided by the teacher, and concentrated attention.[107] Beyond age twelve, Montessori's ideas on education for the adolescent and young adult, that is, for secondary and higher education, are brief and undeveloped.[108]

Suffice it to say that Montessori's theory of concentrated attention is the most developed of the child-friendly ideas on education that have been evolving over the last 2500 years.[109] With the historical sketch of the theory of concentrated attention now complete, we must move on to a more thorough look at the theory's foundations.

---

[106] Maria Montessori, *To Educate the Human Potential* (1948; repr., Oxford: Clio Press, 1989), 3.

[107] Maria Montessori, *The Montessori Elementary Material*, trans. Arthur Livingston (1917; repr., Cambridge, MA: Robert Bentley, Inc., 1971).

[108] See Maria Montessori, *From Childhood to Adolescence* (1948; repr., New York: Schocken Books, 1976), 97–135. Also, see below chap. 5, p. 178.

[109] William Heard Kilpatrick, professor at Teacher's College, Columbia University, from 1909–38, wrote a scathing critique of Montessori's method in 1914, effectively killing its acceptance in American education schools. He argued, in essence, that her approach was too individualistic, which it was in the face of the social liberal tide then consuming twentieth century America, and too conceptual, which it also was in the face of the behaviorist psychology of Edward L. Thorndike that came to dominate education schools. William Heard Kilpatrick, *The Montessori System Examined* (Boston: Houghton Mifflin Company, 1914). Kilpatrick avidly taught a blend of Dewey and Thorndike.

3

Foundations

Thus the process of forming and applying concepts contains the essential pattern of two fundamental methods of cognition: *induction* and *deduction*.

The process of observing the facts of reality and of integrating them into concepts is, in essence, a process of induction. The process of subsuming new instances under a known concept is, in essence, a process of deduction.

—Ayn Rand[1]

SUCCESS IN HUMAN LIFE requires the expert use of consciousness to guide one's choices and actions.

At root, therefore, education is intellectual, meaning that the knowledge, values, and skills acquired in school consist primarily in the accumulation of concepts and principles and in the application of these concepts and principles to concrete situations. "Intellectual" here does not mean that learning is an end-in-itself disconnected from practical action. It means that abstractions and, especially, their use in everyday life are prerequisites to living a happy, independent life in a free society; it means that mind and body are one integrated unit, but that bodily action is controlled and directed by the mind. Thus, the pursuit of a productive career requires long-range thinking, intense focus, and sustained effort, all driven by an ability to think conceptually

---

[1] *Introduction to Objectivist Epistemology*, expanded 2nd ed. (New York: NAL Books, 1990), 28. Emphasis in original.

about the world in which one lives and the ability both to adapt to that world and to change it.

The philosophical and psychological foundations of the theory of concentrated attention encompass a spectrum of ideas that include the nature of consciousness, the functions of consciousness in the acquisition and use of knowledge, the role of consciousness in guiding actions, and the relationship between one's consciousness-guided actions and those of others in personal and social situations. These foundations embrace the fields of metaphysics, epistemology, psychology, ethics, and political philosophy. It is to these topics that we now turn, beginning with the technical philosophical doctrine of intrinsicism and its effects on the understanding of consciousness as an active entity that possesses volition.

INTRINSICISM REJECTED

No doctrine has dominated philosophy and the philosophy of education as has the doctrine of intrinsicism. In philosophy, the doctrine underlies the view that consciousness is essentially passive and therefore has no nature; as consequence, it underlies determinism, the view that human beings do not possess freedom of the will. Historically, intrinsicism made possible the doctrine of original sin and all of the harsh consequences that followed from that theory. Because of its influence in philosophy, the doctrine of intrinsicism in education made possible the traditional view that justifies the teaching principles of coercion and obedience, thus denying validity to the needs and wants of the child. Because of its enormous influence in the history of philosophy and education, intrinsicism must now be examined and refuted to justify the correct premises underlying the theory of concentrated attention.

The Doctrine and Its By-Products

The term "intrinsicism" was coined by Ayn Rand,[2] but the concept has been known as a distinct doctrine in philosophy, if only as a glimmer, for over a century. Kierkegaard's despair over the death of God, which refers to contemporary culture's dismissal of the relevance of God and religion to life, and Nietzsche's lack of despair were mod-

---

[2] Ibid., 52–54, 79; Ayn Rand, *Capitalism: The Unknown Ideal* (New York: New American Library, 1966), 14–19.

ern philosophy's first awareness that there might be alternatives to the "intrinsically eternal" truths of religion. In today's context intrinsicism and religion, especially the more fundamentalist and orthodox branches of religion, may be thought of as highly similar, although the two are not identical. Intrinsicism is broader than religion and its origin is to be found in ancient Greek thought. It is the philosophical doctrine that essences and values exist in reality as archetypes and are directly grasped by the human mind.

The basic form of intrinsicism is Plato's, which holds that essences and values exist in another realm of reality. Aristotle rejected Plato's division of reality and placed these objects of knowledge in the common-sense world of everyday life. Essences, in Aristotle's view, are like nuggets of ore embedded in sedimentary rock, that is, "tableness," the essence of "table," is embedded in every concrete table we observe in the world. (Values, for Aristotle, did not so exist, but later theorists did see them as intrinsic.) Hegelian idealism can even be said to constitute a form of intrinsicism inasmuch as essences and values, for Hegel, are independent of individual minds, albeit a historical or developing part of the Absolute Mind. According to intrinsicism, the human mind is passive and has no nature of its own; its function is to mirror the objects of reality as accurately as possible.

The doctrine is called "intrinsicism" because essences and values are believed to inhere intrinsically in (or beyond) nature; they are fixed and eternal, and they cannot be altered by the human mind. Aristotle's common-sense version of intrinsicism is the one most today still accept. We "just see" or grasp the form (or essence) of tableness in the particular tables that we observe; that is, our minds separate the form from the matter or "stuff" of the table. Knowing is the process of grasping essences. Similarly, we just see or grasp that telling a lie to friends, employers, or spouses is not good. The implied educational theory is that children must learn how to "just see" these essences and values; if they do not, then they must be doing something wrong and must be corrected, often harshly through physical punishment. (Politically, intrinsicism implies far worse: those who do not see what is right must be coerced to act correctly or even be liquidated.)

Recently identified as a distinct doctrine, intrinsicism for centuries has been known as, and today is still confused with, objectivism, but in fact the former is a special case of the latter.[3] Objectivism holds that the objects of knowledge exist independently of the mind's act of knowing them and may be known by and related to individuals as values in a non-arbitrary way. These objects include the ordinary objects of perception, such as the computer on which I am writing this book, as well as our own inner thoughts and emotions, which constitute the objective reality of the science of psychology.[4] Only in the special case of intrinsicism are the objects of knowledge seen as archetypal essences and values.[5] The opposite of intrinsicism is subjectivism, the view that essences and values are entirely dependent on the contents of consciousness and, as a result, have no connection to or basis in reality.

Intrinsicism, while an advance over the mythopoeism of Mesopotamian and Egyptian cultures, has troubled western philosophy for 2500 years. Richard Rorty, referring to intrinsicism (with a slightly different emphasis) as the mirror-of-nature theory of the mind, calls the doctrine the "original sin of epistemology."[6] Similarly, John Dewey asserts that humankind's desire for permanence—of the kind allegedly found in essences and values embedded in reality—has led to the "absurd search for an intellectual philosopher's stone" wherein the permanent becomes converted into the "intrin-

---

[3] I am using the term "objectivism" as it has historically been used in philosophy. It should not be confused with the name Rand gave to her philosophy, "Objectivism," spelled with the upper case "O." Rand claims to have based her philosophical essays on the historical term, and I think she succeeded, although occasionally her writing is tinged with remnants of intrinsicism.

[4] In a different usage, of course, thoughts and emotions are "in the mind" and are therefore subjective. Ontological objectivism means that there exists a world external to and separate from the knower. For the psychologist, the external world is the content of other people's consciousness, and, from an epistemologically unbiased perspective, the content of his or her own consciousness. Epistemological objectivism means that there exists a valid method of knowing the objects of reality, whether those objects be material or mental. On the dichotomy between primary and secondary qualities, which allegedly causes serious problems for objectivism, see Rand, *Objectivist Epistemology*, 279–82. "Everything we perceive is perceived by some means," says Rand, but this does not make the world or our knowledge of it, subjective, ideal, or unknowable. Ibid., 281.

[5] This point must be emphasized because the phrase "object of knowledge" is ambiguous. To the intrinsicist, the object of knowledge is not the table, chair, or couch that we perceive, but the essences "tableness," "chairness," and "couchness."

[6] Richard Rorty, *Philosophy and the Mirror of Nature* (Princeton, NJ: Princeton University Press, 1979), 12–13, 60.

sically eternal."[7] The early work of Wittgenstein and Heidegger, according to Rorty, that is, the picture theory of meaning and the philosophical categories, respectively, are two additional examples of what Rorty refers to as the mirror theory and what I am referring to as intrinsicism.[8]

As a day-to-day sense of life or world view, intrinsicism has permeated western culture from ancient Greece to the present. In the Greco-Roman world, knowledge was believed to be acquired through intuition by opening one's eyes and looking out at the world; Greeks and Romans subscribed to the what-you-see-is-what-you-get perceptual theory of naive realism. Their primitive science emphasized intuition, deduction, and a crude trial and error rather than induction and experimentation. Their purpose in life was to discover their fate and act accordingly; for moral guidance, Greeks and Romans consulted oracles. If illicit behavior was discovered in the course of one's life, then that behavior must immediately be righted, as Oedipus righted his by gouging out his eyes.

The modern world's view of intrinsicism is more complicated, because modernity for the past several centuries has been attempting to remove itself from intrinsicism's grasp. From Descartes to Hegel, philosophers continued to search for, but failed to find, the "ultimate stuff" of reality—substance, things-in-themselves, intrinsic essences and values. Instead, they tended to conclude that the intrinsic is a "something, I know not what," an "unknowable noumenon," or ideas in the mind of the Absolute. Even linguistic analysts can be said to be searching for intrinsic meaning.

At the level of the average person, intrinsicism is held as a common-sense Aristotelianism, yet the average person in this post-Darwinian

---

[7] John Dewey, *Experience and Nature*, 2nd ed. (Chicago: Open Court, 1929), 26. Cf. Dewey's discussion of the spectator theory of knowledge in John Dewey, *The Quest for Certainty*, 1929; reprinted in *The Later Works, 1925–1953*, vol. 4, 1929: *The Quest for Certainty*, ed. Jo Ann Boydston (Carbondale and Edwardsville: Southern Illinois University Press, 1984). When the spectator theory of knowledge is understood as Dewey's version of intrinsicism, his attacks on the theory can be seen as polemics against a corrupt version of objectivism. Dewey's critics, many of whom are rooted in the idealist tradition and are therefore intrinsicists, have never grasped or appreciated his usage of the term "spectator." They accuse Dewey of being a subjectivist, when in fact he puts forth an essentially objectivist view.

[8] Rorty, *Mirror of Nature*, 5. I reject Rorty's skepticism, as I do Kierkegaard's despair. What is needed today is not skepticism or despair but a theory of objectivism without intrinsicism.

age knows that there are no fixed, eternal species put on earth by God and that nothing is fixed and eternal in the way it was once thought to be. Since the Enlightenment, intellectuals and average persons alike have known, if only in a rudimentary manner, that knowledge is manufactured by the mind out of the raw materials of reality, especially through the methods of experimental science, and that one's moral purpose in life is to seek happiness on earth, by being the controller of one's own fate. Average persons today, however, and probably many intellectuals, are confused; they long for the days of stable knowledge and values, knowing that such immutability is not possible, and crave for something more than the subjectivism and relativism that is currently being offered.

Intrinsicism exerted its greatest influence in the Middle Ages and developed at that time the formidable form that is now being fought off by modernity. It incorporated two related but independent doctrines, both of which have profoundly shaped the traditional view of education: rationalism and dogmatism. In the Middle Ages intrinsicism looked like this: knowledge was acquired through revelation from God, often after long study of approved authorities. It was God who put the essences and values in the world, but we, by studying St. Augustine, Plotinus, and Plato, as well as the Scriptures, must apply considerable effort to grasp the essences and values. Our moral purpose in life, people believed, was to discover one's original sin, then act in such ways as to achieve redemption. Realistically, this meant obeying the authority of the church.

Once the essences and values have been grasped, consequences may be deduced. In the High Middle Ages, specifically the twelfth and thirteenth centuries, medieval Scholastics formalized the method that today is known as rationalism. This doctrine consists of syllogistic reasoning from approved authoritative premises to a new and consistent conclusion. The conclusions sometimes were not practical or logical in an empirical sense, because practicality was not Scholasticism's aim.[9]

---

[9] A preoccupation with deductive reasoning may result in a lack of concern for truth; this means that the distinction in logic between validity and truth must always be kept clearly in mind. For example, the following syllogism is valid, in its formal structure, but its premises and conclusion are false (because angels do not exist): all angels have wings; Gabriel is an angel; therefore, Gabriel has wings. Alternatively, a syllogism may be valid and produce a true conclusion even though the premises are false: all bananas are animals; all trout are bananas; therefore, all trout are animals. Rationalists are totally captivated by the process of deductive

Scholasticism sought to clarify the Scriptures and other authorities by means of deductive reasoning, often by reconciling opposing viewpoints.[10] Pedantic disputation was king, sometimes producing bizarre, hierarchically constructed yet consistent nonsense, such as the notion that there exist seven levels of heaven.

Intrinsicism in the Middle Ages formalized not only rationalism but also the doctrine of dogmatism. A doctrine is dogmatic when its conclusions are established by an authoritative body, such as the church, and held to be true without question. Everyone who subscribes to the dogma must follow its dictates absolutely. Leaders of the dogma are intolerant of other opinions, often speaking in a deprecating, imperious, and arrogant manner about rival doctrines. Those who do not accept the dogma without question or who do not subscribe to it at all are subject to censure, or worse. In the Middle Ages, heretics and pagans often got the worst.

Intrinsicism, rationalism, and dogmatism must be carefully differentiated so as not to confuse one with the others and also so their modern forms may be understood. Intrinsicism is a means of acquiring concepts. Rationalism is a method of reasoning, after the concepts have been acquired. Dogmatism is a means of acquiring conclusions (not just concepts); it is a way of holding the conclusions in one's mind and a behavior in relation to the dogma's leaders. The modern form of these three doctrines can be differentiated as follows. An intrinsicist says, "If you can't see it, I can't explain it to you." A rationalist says, "But this theory is so elegant; who cares that it's not practical?" And a dogmatist says, with appropriate scowl and tone of disapproval, "Why on earth are you reading that?," "that" being an article or book the dogmatist disagrees with or dislikes.

It is important to note that these three doctrines do not have to occur together. Aristotle's philosophy was intrinsicist, but neither rationalistic nor dogmatic to any extent. (Later Aristotelians, including

---

reasoning, often minimizing or ignoring the truth of the statements involved. If anyone doubts the unreality of rationalistic thought, see in economics the literature on the theory of pure and perfect competition, a false doctrine—so admitted by its proponents—used for over a hundred years in the American antitrust laws to punish businesses. Economists are particularly rationalistic. See my discussion of the perfect competition doctrine in Jerry Kirkpatrick, *In Defense of Advertising: Arguments from Reason, Ethical Egoism, and Laissez-Faire Capitalism* (1994; repr., Claremont, CA: TLJ Books, 2007), 122–59.

[10] Morris Bishop, *The Middle Ages* (1968; repr., Boston: Houghton Mifflin, 1987), 250.

St. Thomas Aquinas, tended to be both to a greater degree.) Intrinsicism, rationalism, and dogmatism are technically independent of one another. In the Middle Ages, however, and even today, the three often are held by the same person. This includes intellectuals, as well as laypersons.

The three together make a powerful combination. Intrinsicism—the mirror-of-nature theory of the mind—is more fundamental, thereby making possible the more onerous expressions of the other two doctrines. As intrinsicism can be viewed as an aberration of objectivism, rationalism can be viewed as an aberration of the proper use of reason. Similarly, dogmatism, inasmuch as it is an implementation of the former two doctrines, can be viewed as an aberration of both.[11]

Expunging the Thing-In-Itself

One of the most destructive consequences of the doctrine of intrinsicism was its search for "true reality," often described in terms of the search for "substance" or "things-in-themselves." This pursuit eventually became what Dewey called the search for the "philosopher's stone" because, like the investigations of medieval alchemists to find a substance with which to turn iron into gold, intrinsic essences were never found. "Tableness" most assuredly does not exist intrinsically in tables, nor "humanness" in humans. John Locke referred to substance as the "something I know not what" and Kant labeled the realm of true reality "things-in-themselves"; in the end Kant concluded that we can never know true reality because we are only aware of things as they appear to us, rather than as they really are.[12]

Over the last century, the consequence of this failed quest for things-in-themselves has been a raging skepticism, subjectivism, and relativism. These three doctrines hold that if there are no intrinsic essences or values, we cannot know true reality or what is objectively right or wrong conduct. The source of the problem is the fact, discovered in fits and starts over much of history, that consciousness is not an identity-less

---

[11] For other aberrations of reason and science that are the results of these three doctrines, see F. A. Hayek, *The Counter-Revolution of Science: Studies on the Abuse of Reason* (Glencoe, IL: The Free Press, 1952).

[12] John Locke, *An Essay Concerning Human Understanding* (1689; repr., Oxford: Oxford University Press, 1975), 95. Immanuel Kant, *Prolegomena to Any Future Metaphysics*, trans. Lewis White Beck (1783; repr., Indianapolis, IN: Bobbs-Merrill, 1950), 28–41.

mirror of reality but is an entity like any other that possesses its own unique attributes and therefore has an identity. This means that consciousness is active, not passive, in the perception and conceptualization of the world in which we live. The problem for philosophers was, and still is, "How can this active consciousness that has its own nature accurately perceive reality without distorting what we perceive?" Kant said consciousness cannot perceive reality and most philosophers since his time have agreed. Thus, the pendulum in intellectual circles today has swung from the doctrine of intrinsicism to subjectivism. In education, the pendulum has swung from coercion and obedience in the traditional mold to anything goes in the worst of the progressive molds.

This pendulum swing, however, typifies the proverbial tossing of the baby with the bath. It does not follow that because consciousness has a nature we cannot perceive reality. As Ayn Rand so aptly put it, Kant's conclusion amounts to saying: "Man is blind, because he has eyes—deaf, because he has ears—deluded, because he has a mind—and the things he perceives do not exist, *because* he perceives them."[13] John Dewey put it this way: "The problem of how a mind can know an external world or even know that there is such a thing is like the problem of how an animal eats things external to itself."[14] To state the so-called problem of the external world, says Dewey, is to assume the world's existence and a knowledge of it; the whole line of reasoning, therefore, is self-contradictory.[15] And contemporary philosopher John Searle states that once the existence of an independent reality is granted, realism of independently existing objects, words in a language that can refer to these objects, and organization of the language into objective truth naturally follow.[16]

---

[13] Ayn Rand, *For the New Intellectual* (New York: Signet Book, New American Library, 1961), 32. Emphasis in original.

[14] Dewey, *Experience and Nature*, 227.

[15] John Dewey, *Essays in Experimental Logic* (New York: Dover Publications, 1916), 281. See Raymond D. Boisvert, *Dewey's Metaphysics* (New York: Fordham University Press, 1988) for an argument that Dewey indeed has a metaphysics and that it is naturalistic and Aristotelian. Boisvert points out that such scholars as Richard Rorty and Sidney Hook have unjustly denied the significance of Dewey's metaphysics and others have caricatured it. Ibid., 3–6. For Dewey's theory of truth as correspondence, see John Dewey, "The Control of Ideas by Facts," in *Essays in Experimental Logic*, 230–49, and Dewey, "Propositions, Warranted Assertibility, and Truth," *Journal of Philosophy* 38, no. 7 (March 27, 1941): 169–86.

[16] John R. Searle, "Reality Principles: An Interview with John R. Searle," interview by Edward Feser and Steven Postrel, *Reason*, February 2000, 42–50. Searle, *Mind,*

The fundamental error of intrinsicism, because of its need to contrast the subject with the reality that it knows, lay in the separation of consciousness from its objects, the Platonic or Aristotelian forms or essences. This separation then lent strong support to the supernaturalism of the Middle Ages, along with the development of rationalism and dogmatism, and the subsequent problems of finding "true reality" in the modern period. What underlies the theory of concentrated attention, on the other hand, is a robust naturalism in which consciousness is just another entity in the reality in which we live. As one writer describes naturalism:

> Man is a piece of the earth—not an exception, nor one with something added from outside. Man is an actor in nature, not a spectator of nature. And in reverse man and his behavior are as illustrative of nature as is an atom or a solar system. There are not two worlds. Man, however, is not abased by being a piece of nature. Rather Nature becomes, among other things, that which includes man with all his ways and byways.... In brief—Nature is the kind of realm in which thinking goes on. Thinking is not a derivative from the eating of a tree of knowledge.[17]

Subject and object, consciousness and what is known by consciousness, are both a part of the same world. And that world is called nature, reality, the universe.

Today, substance, things-in-themselves, and intrinsic essences are seldom sought because they are seen as remnants of mistaken older philosophies rooted in intrinsicism and mysticism, but the expunging of things-in-themselves, as recent philosophy has been attempting to do, does not call for skepticism or subjectivism. It just means an epistemology incorporating an active consciousness is required to maintain objectivity in the awareness of external reality—and internal

---

Language, and Society: Philosophy in the Real World (New York: Basic Books, 1998), 31–33. This view, known as realism, the doctrine that a world exists external to our minds and that we can know it, presupposes a realist theory of perception, the doctrine that our senses validly perceive reality without distortion. On this, see James J. Gibson, *Reasons for Realism: Selected Essays of James J. Gibson* (Hillsdale, NJ: Lawrence Erlbaum Associates, 1982) and David Kelley, *The Evidence of the Senses: A Realist Theory of Perception* (Baton Rouge, LA: Louisiana State University Press, 1986). Realism in its broadest sense and objectivism are essentially the same doctrine, differing only in emphasis.

[17] Walter B. Veazie, "John Dewey and the Revival of Greek Philosophy," in *University of Colorado Studies, Series in Philosophy*, No. 2, 1961, 4–5. Emphasis in original. See Dewey, *Experience and Nature*, 59–60.

reality, in the case of awareness of consciousness itself. It means that a definite method, specifically a theory of concepts—for the formation of concepts is the way in which we acquire knowledge of external and internal reality—must be identified. This, we will look at a little later.

Challenging the Mechanistic Premise

The grip of intrinsicism in the modern period so influenced the development of science that the notions of free will, or volition, and introspection, the attendant method of knowing the contents of consciousness—as well as the notion of consciousness itself—have all been laughed out of the laboratories as mystical; the ideas that rule today in science are mechanistic materialism, determinism, and various forms of behaviorism. If the mind is a passive mirror of nature on which reality writes, wherein lies the will and how can the will possibly be free? Science has answered that it is not free; indeed, it says, the will is a fiction and consciousness at best is an epiphenomenon, or residue that has no causal power. Hence, materialism, the doctrine that consciousness is an illusion and that matter is the only true substance of nature, is the ruling theory in science. Consciousness and its consequent notion of free will are held to be violations of the spirit of naturalism and, therefore, must be remnants of mysticism. Introspection is just an error-filled method of inquiry used on a nonexistent entity.

All of these ideas undermine sound educational theory, for enlightened learning principles, those of the theory of concentrated attention in particular, presuppose a mind that can acquire the knowledge, values, and skills offered by teachers, an internal choice that can be performed by the student to acquire the material, and an objective method of observing the operations and contents of consciousness. The theory of concentrated attention rejects materialism, determinism, and all denials of introspection as a valid method of acquiring knowledge.

Let us take materialism first. That consciousness is a function of the brain is not disputed. It does not follow, however, that consciousness is less real, any more than the color red is less real than the light waves that produce it. Consciousness, as Searle puts it, is a higher-level feature of the brain, just as liquidity is "a higher-level feature of the system of molecules that constitute our blood." What underlies materialism is the mechanistic "push-pull" conception of causality, the notion that one thing pushes or pulls another either through direct contact or attraction, such as magnetism or gravity. The field of human action, however, says Searle, requires a broader conception, namely that causality "is a matter of something being responsible for something else happening," as in the cause of war, of economic depression, or of learning. "Push" and "pull" are not appropriate concepts in this context. Consciousness, therefore, cannot be reduced to the firing of neurons nor can psychology be reduced to physics.[18]

Some materialists say that consciousness is unnatural or nonexistent because it cannot be perceived through extrospection, but this charge can easily be reversed and used on the materialists to say, as do the idealists, that matter is unnatural or nonexistent because it cannot be perceived through introspection. Materialists dismiss introspection as a method of observation because it has produced more error than extrospection and, as a result, the sciences based on introspection, the human sciences, especially, psychology, are far less advanced than the ones based on extrospection, the physical sciences. The materialists conclude that the methods of the physical sciences, specifically those of physics, should be adopted and introspection should be eliminated. This, however, does not follow. The proper conclusion is that more work needs to be done in improving the method of introspection and, more generally, a sound epistemology that includes both introspection and extrospection needs to be developed.[19]

A consequence of materialism is the doctrine that denies free will, determinism, but this doctrine is a self-contradiction; it commits the fallacy of self-exception.[20] All events, actions, and ideas for the deter-

---

[18] Searle, *Mind, Language, and Society*, 52, 59. What Searle seems to be getting at, although he may not agree, is the revival of Aristotle's formal cause: the identity of an entity determines or causes its actions. Thus, the nature of the brain is such that it produces the actions we call consciousness. Seventeenth century scientists reduced causation to efficient causes because formal and final causes throughout the Middle Ages had been intertwined with Aristotelian teleology. This is another instance of throwing the baby out with the bath. Cf. John Searle, *Minds, Brains, and Science* (Cambridge, MA: Harvard University Press, 1984), 13–27.

[19] "We require a single method of approach which avoids the partly verbal problem of the relations of 'matter' and 'mind,' and deals with the changing structure of experienced and observed relationships." Lancelote Law Whyte, *The Unconscious Before Freud* (New York: Basic Books, 1960), 19. Whyte, a physicist by training, goes on to state that a "future theory of mental processes will constitute a special application of a more general theory of organism, and this in turn of a still more general theory of the transformations of partly ordered complex systems." Ibid., 19–20.

[20] Maurice Mandelbaum, "Some Instances of the Self-Excepting Fallacy," *Psychologishe Beiträge* 6 (1962): 383–86.

minist are determined in the sense that they could not have occurred otherwise. This statement, however, includes the determinist who must therefore be determined to believe in determinism. If this is the case, knowledge is impossible, because no idea can claim greater credence over any other, including the notion of determinism. The possibility of error—the fallibility of human consciousness—makes volition a necessary property of the mind. Knowledge is established by testing the contents of one's consciousness against the facts of reality. Identifying an object as a table when in fact it is a chair means that my conclusion, "This object is a table," could have (and should have) occurred otherwise but I failed to apply logic correctly to test my belief.[21]

Herein lies an indication of the exact nature of volition in human beings. According to Ayn Rand, volition is the ability to regulate and control conscious awareness. It means the ability to raise or lower our level of focus on any given task, to choose to concentrate or let random thoughts and emotions distract us. It also means we can actively avoid focusing on whatever we are doing through evasion. In short, a volitional consciousness is one that faces the choice to think or not to think—that is, to constantly and consistently use reason and logic to test one's conclusions against reality or to avoid such effort. Self-regulation of cognitive processes does not mean that we can control every aspect of our minds or behavior, but in large areas of our lives it does mean that we are our own self-programmers. Many of our beliefs, values, and actions derive from how we have chosen, over the years of our lives, to use our minds.[22] This idea holds great import for the philosophy of education in general and the theory of concentrated attention in particular.

---

[21] Nathaniel Branden, "The Contradiction of Determinism," *The Objectivist Newsletter*, May 1963, 17, 19.

[22] Ayn Rand, "The Objectivist Ethics," in *The Virtue of Selfishness: A New Concept of Egoism* (New York: New American Library, 1964), 11–15. Nathaniel Branden, "Intellectual Ammunition Department: What is the Difference Between the Objectivist Concept of Free Will and the Traditional Concepts?," *The Objectivist Newsletter*, January 1964, 3. The metaphor of self-programming is just that, an aid to enhance understanding; Rand has no connection to cognitive science or artificial intelligence. See Searle, *Minds, Brains, and Science*, 44, for a discussion of how, in history, the latest technology has always seemed to be used as a model of the brain; for example, some ancient Greeks thought the brain functioned like a catapult, Leibniz thought it was a mill, and pre-computer scientists in the twentieth century thought the brain was a telephone switchboard! On attention as a fundamental component of volition, see William James, *The Principles of Psychology* (1890; repr., Cambridge, MA: Harvard University Press, 1983), 1166–73.

It is ironic that science should have taken such a negative attitude toward consciousness when much of the program of thought in modern philosophy has been to acknowledge the active nature of consciousness. It is also ironic that modern philosophy should have concluded subjectivism when scientists have been producing one objective finding after another using, presumably, that active consciousness. Far from being a mirror that only reflects reality, or an epiphenomenon that is reduced to neurons, or a distorter of reality, consciousness constructs specific products, such as concepts and emotions, to enable us to interact with our environment and live effectively throughout our lives.

HOW WE THINK

If consciousness is real, active, possesses an identity, and is volitional, the question now becomes: how does this non-mechanistic entity operate to produce the beliefs, values, and actions that guide our lives? Our beliefs consist of concepts, in various combinations, our desires and action tendencies consist of emotions that stem from value judgments of objects and events we deem either "for us" or "against us," and our actions proceed from choice based on previously formed beliefs and values. The store of concepts and values that we take away from family and school as we reach adulthood greatly influences not only which career we pursue, and how we pursue it, but the character and personality we exhibit for the rest of our lives. Such is the influence of education, as John Locke asserted.[23] In this section, then, the cognitive components of learning will be discussed; in the next section the normative and behavioral components.

Implicit Measurement

One of the complaints of the materialists is that consciousness as we know it cannot be measured by the methods of the physical sciences, specifically physics. This is true, but consciousness, particularly concepts of consciousness, such as thinking and feeling, can be measured approximately. Indeed, measurement is the essential process in concept formation.

In philosophy, the theory of concepts is a major issue, known as the problem of universals, which states: how do we get universal concepts in our minds from the concrete particulars that exist in the external

---

[23] See chap. 2, p. 47.

world? Only individual humans exist, but our concept "human" applies to all human beings past, present, and future. How does this come to be? The intrinsicist view, known as realism, holds that universals exist intrinsically in reality as metaphysical forms or essences, and traditional education coercively demands that children grasp these essences.[24] Critics, however, bring up the "I can't find it" argument, pointing out that there exists no essence of humanness anywhere in human beings. The subjectivist view, known as nominalism, holds that universals are subjective products of our minds, mere names arbitrarily assigned and based on vague and shifting resemblances. Today, the theory of universals is little discussed, yet the validity of all knowledge—and therefore, education—rests on the solution to this problem.

Ayn Rand offers a solution by observing that concept formation is a mathematical process. She states that abstraction, the process by which we create universal concepts in our minds, is a process of measurement omission.[25] The concept, however, is not subjective or arbitrary because its content corresponds and adheres to the objects on which it was based. The process can be illustrated in the following steps.

First, we perceptually isolate or differentiate two or more concrete things from a wider background or category. We differentiate, for example, kitchen, dining, and living room tables as a group from the broader category of furniture that consists of tables, chairs, and beds. We differentiate the tables from their background category according to their measurable similarity, namely shape. That is to say, all furniture possesses the commensurable characteristic of shape, but we focus on tables because their shapes are more similar to one another than to the shapes of chairs and beds. This similarity is grasped perceptually.

Next, we integrate, or blend together, our perceptions of the various concretes (tables) into a new mental unit called a concept—by observing, then omitting the measurable differences among them. Thus,

---

[24] The realist theory of universals is related to the realist theory of perception, but the two are not identical.

[25] Rand, *Objectivist Epistemology*, 5–87. It is unfortunate that Ayn Rand's ideas have not been taken seriously by many professional philosophers. I would like to suggest that readers view Rand's potential contributions to philosophy as analogous to those of the German writers Goethe and Schiller. Neither of the latter was a professional philosopher—both were poets and playwrights—yet they did write philosophical essays that have been taken seriously by philosophers. Similarly, Ayn Rand was a novelist who wrote philosophical essays that *should* be taken seriously by philosophers.

abstraction is a process of measurement omission (or implicit measurement), which means that measurements exist, and must exist, but are not specified. The differences are one of degree, not kind, and are measured implicitly and approximately, in the sense of shorter versus taller and wider versus narrower. It is not necessary in concept formation to know how to make precise, numerical measurements; humankind formed the concepts of color long before precise measurement of light was discovered. Conceptualization, therefore, is a process of implicit measurement.

Third, we assign a visual and auditory symbol, called a word, to the concept to give it a label that will be easily retained, stored, and recalled when needed. The cognitive function of the word is to convert concepts into the mental equivalent of concretes. In addition to enabling us to store and recall concepts—no small aid in learning—the word-and-concept-as-concrete enables us to form higher-level concepts, called abstractions from abstractions, by identifying similarities among various lower-level concepts.

Fourth, and finally, the concept is identified by defining it. A definition is a statement that identifies the nature of a concept's referents. This is achieved by naming the background category from which the concretes were differentiated—the genus—and the concept's essence or fundamental distinguishing characteristic(s) by which the concretes were differentiated from the background category—the differentia. Thus, "furniture" is the genus or background category of the concept "table" and "flat, smooth surface with supports designed to hold other, smaller objects" is the differentia or essence that describes the shape and function of tables that distinguishes them from other types of furniture. (When children first learn the concept of table, they do not formulate anything resembling this explicit definition, because tables are easily recognized perceptual objects. However, when abstract concepts are formed, such as freedom or epistemology, rigorous definitions are necessary to maintain order in our minds.)

The concept so formed is now universal because it is open-ended, that is, it stands for and identifies all concretes of this type past, present, and future. It is valid because it is rooted in reality, referring to real similarities existing in the external world, as differentiated from a particular background. The problem of universals is thus solved because abstraction as measurement omission yields universals in our minds that are based on and derived from the facts of reality. The universal is not in the concrete, the intrinsic realist position, nor is it an arbitrary name, the subjective nominalist position. Rather, it is objective because it is a product of our distinctive mode of cognition created through a strict adherence to the object of cognition, the factual concretes. The object has set the terms; therefore, the concept is objective.

Rand's theory of concepts further holds that essences, as mental products of the measurement omission process, are determined contextually and can change as our knowledge grows. To use Rand's metaphor, the concept is a file folder, the word is a label on the folder, and the definition is written on the cover to identify the folder's content; the word and definition both serve to differentiate the concept (folder) from all others in our minds (our file cabinet), as well as to connect it to all others. The content of the folder is everything to date that we have learned about the object named by the concept. Thus, a child's folder of the concept "human" would probably be smaller than that of an adult, and the average adult's folder would be smaller than that of a medical doctor or psychologist. And the child's definition of human, based on his or her context of knowledge, might be "two-legged animal," until that knowledge has grown enough to justify the more delimited definition, "the being that possesses the capacity to reason."

Concepts (and their definitions), therefore, are short-hand devices for retaining and storing the data of reality that we perceive. They are condensations of vast amounts of knowledge—the contents of the file folders—and thus produce an economy in cognitive functioning exactly as do numbers. For example, the number "5" substitutes one symbol for any five objects or events that exist in reality, as does the number "5000." We probably can perceive and retain five objects, but not five thousand. Numbers reduce enormous quantities of data to a single symbol, thereby making the essential information that the symbol stands for immediately available to us; concepts perform the same function.

For this reason, Rand states that conceptualization and measurement are two forms of the same process. (Numbers, after all, are concepts.) One, concept formation, uses measurement implicitly; the other, numerical measurement, uses it explicitly. Indeed, the essence of a concept—its distinguishing characteristic(s)—is a range of measurements within the continuum of commensurable characteristics from which the concept was differentiated. (The shape of tables is a range within the continuum of shapes of all furniture.) The range is specified in the differentia of the definition, but no particular measurement is included.

Such is the process by which our beliefs—the concepts that we hold as true—are formed. Whether the concepts so formed are true, however, depends on how we use our minds in the formation process.

Conscious Differentiation, Subconscious Integration

Concept formation and definition, therefore, play a crucial role in learning, as educators for millennia have taught. The method required, however, is not the rote memorization of ancient, medieval, and modern rationalists, but a careful observation and classification of the data of reality that one experiences. Differentiation, as Rand's theory of concepts implies, is the essential skill needed, the ability, as it were, to separate figure from ground. The active consciousness, or more specifically, the subconscious part of consciousness, performs the necessary and automatic integrations, putting together in a new form what we have previously isolated. The driver of the differentiations is our volition, for this is what cognitive self-regulation means—the choice to focus attentively on a particular fact or not. Thus, the conscious mind differentiates; the subconscious integrates, but how exactly does subconscious integration operate and why is differentiation the key to learning?

Freud was the first to identify that humans possess a dynamic, integrating subconscious, the activities of which he called primary process; he called the activities of the conscious mind secondary process.[26] The subconscious is the portion of the mind that we are not aware of, so when asleep all activity of the mind is subconscious; when awake whatever we are not currently focusing on is subconscious. "Dynamic" means continuously active in the sense that our minds are constantly making connections whether we are awake or asleep; if awake, the connections are being made whether we are aware of what is going on in our minds or not. In short, the subconscious can be thought of as a "connection-making machine" (with no concessions to mechanistic materialism intended).

The prototype of connections made by the subconscious, according to Freud, is that product of primary process known as our dreams. However, dreams are often quite illogical, not unlike the thought pattern of schizophrenics. Indeed, the thought pattern of schizophrenics is believed by some to be a reversion to raw primary process with the

---

[26] Sigmund Freud, *The Interpretation of Dreams*, trans. James Strachey (1900; repr., New York: Avon Books, 1965), 636–48. Cf. Whyte, *Unconscious Before Freud*, 23–25.

control of secondary process entirely absent; it is also said to exhibit the error in formal logic called the fallacy of undistributed middle.[27] This last provides a clue to the nature of subconscious functioning. The fallacy of undistributed middle takes the form: all dogs are four-legged animals; all cows are four-legged animals; therefore, all dogs are cows. In a schizophrenic, the mental process might be: I am a virgin; the Virgin Mary is a virgin; therefore, I am the Virgin Mary. Such is said to be the logical mechanism of schizophrenic "thinking." By extension it would seem to be the mechanism of primary process and the subconscious mind.

If undistributed middle is the pattern of subconscious connection-making, then the following comments can be made. The error in the fallacy occurs by assuming that because the predicates in the premises of the syllogism are identical, the subjects must also be identical.[28] This is overgeneralization, because, as in the examples above, if two things hold one attribute in common, it is assumed that the two things hold all or most attributes in common. This pattern, then, if the hypothesis of undistributed middle as the model of primary process is true, would explain the unusual connections made in our dreams, as well as the errors that normal children and adults alike—not just schizophrenics—often make. Schizophrenics and sleepers have no control over their subconscious minds, so primary process operates unchecked, merrily making connections according to the fallacy of undistributed middle. Children are immature and must learn how to avoid committing this error by observing more closely that even though dogs and cows are both four-legged animals, they still possess other attributes that make them substantively different beings; that is, they must differentiate. Normal adults who commit this error have just failed in

---

[27] E. von Domarus, "The Specific Laws of Thought in Schizophrenia," in J. S. Kasanin, ed., *Language and Thought in Schizophrenia* (Berkeley and Los Angeles: University California Press, 1944), 104–14. Arieti calls the thought of schizophrenics paleologic, because it is an older or earlier version of thought in terms of evolution and the historical development of humans; later or modern thought is called Aristotelian because secondary process exhibits, at its best, the ability to follow the Aristotelian laws of logic. Silvano Arieti, *Interpretation of Schizophrenia*, 2nd ed. (New York: Basic Books, 1974), 229.

[28] The fallacy is called "undistributed middle" because the middle term in the syllogism, "four-legged animals," does not refer to all four-legged animals. There may well be, and are, more four-legged animals besides dogs and cows; that is, the range of such animals is much broader than just dogs and cows. Thus, the middle term is *un*distributed.

their cognitive self-regulation to attend to and differentiate the subjects in the premises.[29] Thus, the key to learning and, more generally, to the correct identification of the facts of reality, would seem to be differentiation.

The fallacy of undistributed middle is not the only error of overgeneralization that one can commit; the following further indicates that differentiation is important in learning. Scientists, after making a discovery, frequently overgeneralize the application of their newly discovered principle. This error—the fallacy of hasty generalization—is so common that the biologist Otto Koehler was led to say, "The truth of today is the special case of tomorrow."[30] Aristotle, for example, observed goal-directed behavior in humans, animals, and plants, then applied the principle of teleology to non-living nature; Newton applied his theory of gravity to the entire universe; and Pavlov thought the conditioned response in laboratory animals was the model of human behavior. In all of these examples, further advances were not made until the previous truths were differentiated from the contexts in which they did not apply. Delimitation, as Koehler seems to be saying, is what sometimes leads to progress in science.[31]

Learning, therefore, can be described as a process of greater and greater differentiation, an act controlled by the conscious mind, whereas integration, the blending together of data into new concepts, is performed by the subconscious.[32] Because the subconscious, when left to its own devices, will overgeneralize, the crucial role of the conscious mind is to direct and control the subconscious. Or, to put it in terms

---

[29] One logic textbook illustrates the fallacy of undistributed middle with the following, erroneous syllogism held by many educated adults: all conservatives believe in private property; all people who defend capitalism believe in private property; therefore, all people who defend capitalism are conservatives. David Kelley, *The Art of Reasoning* (New York: W. W. Norton, 1988), 199. Clearly, conservatives and advocates of capitalism are not necessarily the same people.

[30] Quoted in the Preface by Konrad Lorenz to Charles Darwin's *The Expression of the Emotions in Man and Animals* (Chicago: University of Chicago Press, 1965), ix.

[31] Delimitation, not contradiction. Einstein did not contradict Newton; he delimited the application of Newton's theory. The same with Bacon and Galileo in relation to Aristotle's teleology.

[32] Even higher-level concepts—abstractions from abstractions, which are higher-level integrations—are formed with the beginning process of differentiation, by identifying similarities among lower-level concepts. Once the correct differentiation is made, the correct integration will follow. See Rand, *Objectivist Epistemology*, 19–28.

of Rand's metaphor, our file folders (concepts) will be formed and organized in our filing cabinets (the subconscious mind) exactly the way we volitionally choose to form and organize them. If the contents of our folders do not correspond to the facts, or if our definitions do not accurately reflect the contents, and if the filing system itself is carelessly organized, our knowledge will be sorely wanting and our ability to recall and use what knowledge we do possess will be hampered. Volitional control through the awareness of differences determines how well we acquire and retrieve knowledge; the environment—especially, parental involvement and formal schooling—can help or hamper this process.

In today's intellectual climate that places little value on integration, the emphasis on differentiation is not intended to diminish the significance of putting things together in the learning process or of making integration a conscious goal of learning or education. Concepts by definition are integrations—the blending of similarities into a new unit. By extension, principles—which are combinations of concepts that state fundamental truths on which others depend—are broad integrations. The more one learns, the more one's accumulated concepts and principles must be precisely organized and integrated, lest they become a contradictory and irretrievable jumble in one's subconscious. The point here is that integration is the automatic end result of differentiation; the latter is the means and cause. Conscious differentiation puts the question: How are the two things I have differentiated connected to each other? The subconscious provides an answer.

Ranges of Measurement

A skill required for competent adulthood, but not achieved by many today, is thinking in ranges of measurement. One form of this is called "thinking in principles," the method of actively looking for and identifying common denominators among concretes that can be abstracted and formulated as principles to unite and explain all of the observed concretes.[33] A descriptive principle is a fundamental

---

[33] When Ayn Rand was twelve or thirteen years old, she adopted a method that she called "thinking in principles." At that age, she meant the process of systematically and explicitly identifying the reasons behind each idea she held and the relation of each idea to all the rest. The purpose of the former was to know why she believed what she believed, the latter—integration—to insure consistency. Later, in her novels and nonfiction lectures and essays, the meaning of thinking in principles came to focus on the "why," by looking for the abstraction that united

abstraction, stated as a proposition, that names a cause and effect relationship between the referents of two or more concepts, such as "price changes produce an inverse reaction in quantity demanded" or "force equals mass times acceleration."[34] As such, the identification of principles is a continuation of the concept formation process, but at a higher level of abstraction. The goal of identifying principles is to locate and define the essential distinguishing characteristic of the complex phenomena (the concretes) being observed, naming specifically the relationship among the referents of the concepts involved.

For example, we observe a child being spanked for not taking out the trash, another being denied dinner for not doing homework, and a third ridiculed for (what the parent considers) watching too much television; each of these children, we further observe, are resistant to the parental requests, perhaps complacent and lethargic, but definitely cheerless. The common denominator among these three concretes is, on the one side, coercion (as opposed to communication) by the parent to influence the child's behavior and obedience as the expected response; on the other side, the common denominator is unhappiness in the children. We next observe a student being given a lower grade for handing an assigned paper in late, another being made to stand for the entire class period for tipping a chair back, and a third threatened with the confiscation of pencils for repeatedly tapping them on the desk. Once again, the common theme, on the one side, seems to be coercion and obedience and, on the other, unhappiness.

If we combine the parenting and teaching examples, we can generalize, stating that authoritarianism—the notion that individuals must sacrifice their needs and wants to the will of an authority—causes unhappiness, among other personality traits, including rebelliousness, resignation, and dependence. This proposition becomes the abstraction that unites and explains all six concretes. If we continued examining concretes in the workplace, we would probably find additional confirmation of the principle.[35]

---

and explained two or more concretes. Barbara Branden, *The Passion of Ayn Rand* (New York: Doubleday, 1986), 22.

[34] A prescriptive principle, which is a guide to human action, is stated as an imperative; it names the cause and effect relationship between you, the actor, and your required action to achieve a goal. For example, "For sales success, vary your prices by product and segment" or "To achieve integrity, remain loyal to your values regardless of what others say."

[35] See Alphie Kohn, *Punished by Rewards: The Trouble with Gold Stars, Incentive Plans, A's, Praise, and Other Bribes* (Boston: Houghton Mifflin, 1993), who reviewed the motivation literature and concluded that any kind of extrinsic motivation

The criterion for knowing whether a correct principle has been identified is the rule of fundamentality in the theory of definitions. The essential distinguishing characteristic in the differentia of a definition is the fundamental one, that is, the one that causes or explains most or all of the other distinguishing characteristics.[36] "Capacity to reason," for example, is the fundamental distinguishing characteristic of the concept "human," because that characteristic causes and explains our many other distinguishing characteristics, such as the ability to speak English and to build skyscrapers. Thus, a principle is correctly identified when the cause and effect relationship names the fundamental distinguishing characteristic of the relationships united by the principle.

In the previous paragraphs, then, coercion and obedience, on the causal side of the proposition (the bowing of the will to an authority), are the fundamental characteristics of the examples given that distinguish these particular parent-child and teacher-student relationships from all others that can cause unhappiness. Thus, identifying essential distinguishing (fundamental) characteristics can be called "thinking in causes" or "thinking in essentials" and that in turn becomes an effective means to thinking in principles. Because a principle names a cause and effect relationship, thinking in principles can be thought of as "thinking in causes and effects." Sometimes the emphasis, as in this example, is on seeking to differentiate the possible causes, given an effect. Sometimes, as in the thesis of this book—the consequences of unfettered interest, attention, and independence on education—the emphasis is on seeking to differentiate the possible effects, given a cause.

The value of thinking in principles is that it prevents us from falling into one of two errors, best expressed by the familiar metaphor of the trees and the forest. On the one hand, we may become concrete-bound by focusing only on the trees and fail to see the forest. That is, we may recognize the specific examples of parenting or teaching listed

---

(rewards or punishments) is doomed to failure, whether in parenting, teaching, or managing. The reason for failure is the premise of authoritarianism, because it leads to dependent and either rebellious or resigned subjects. Intrinsic motivation, the notion that one should perform a task because one enjoys it primarily for its own sake, not for external inducements, is what stands behind the theory of concentrated attention, as well as the ideas of the more enlightened education theorists writing since the Renaissance.

[36] Rand, *Objectivist Epistemology*, 45. The difference between "cause" and "explain" is that the cause is metaphysical and the explanation is epistemological.

above without concluding that coercion and obedience run through all of them; indeed, some people would assert that spanking is coercive but withholding dinner or ridiculing a child is not, and that all of the examples of teaching are just a part of sound education. On the other hand, we may hold abstractions that are un- or ill-connected to their concretes by focusing only on the forest and thereby fail to see all of the trees (especially those closest to us) or inappropriately ascribe trees from a different forest to the one we are presently examining. This can occur when teachers recognize the above parenting and teaching examples as authoritarian, but then ignore their own coercive techniques in the classroom. For example, such a teacher might require (that is, force) students to make presentations in class summarizing the textbook that the teacher refuses to discuss; at the same time, this teacher condemns the lecture method as coercive because it allegedly forces students to accept what the lecturer says. The teacher's understanding of the principle of authoritarianism is not anchored in reality, so it "floats" (away from shore, as it were, to use a different metaphor) and becomes applied arbitrarily.

This last error—"floating abstractions" applied arbitrarily (and usually dogmatically)—is one of the consequences of rationalistic deduction for the sake of deduction, the bane of traditional education and one of the motives that led to the utter indifference of teachers to the child's educational needs and wants. If an educated adult needs to know the essence of culture, so the error goes, then children must begin, and continue throughout their schooling, to absorb the literature, science, history, etc., that the educated adult already knows. In broad outline that much is true, but the statement ignores the nature of children and the way in which they learn. And it most certainly ignores individual differences among children. The error of rationalism is that it does not maintain a connection between the concepts and principles that have been formed and the concretes from which the concept or principle was abstracted. This is where the method of thinking in ranges of measurement proves helpful as an antidote to rationalism.

Thinking in ranges of measurement is more fundamental than thinking in principles. It means focusing on and mentally retaining, firmly in conscious awareness, the range of measurements that constitutes the distinguishing characteristics of a concept. In the formation of the concept "table" discussed above, this means retaining the range of measurements of the shapes of observed tables; practically speaking, this means retaining a wide range of the variety of concretes that constitutes the meaning of the concept. A rationalist fails in just this task, tending to fixate on one narrow characteristic, and then has difficulty using concepts to identify new concretes as they arise. For example, a person who fixates on tables as flat pieces of wood with four legs will be unable to identify a flat piece of glass with three steel legs as a table, and, perhaps, will force the glass table—through deduction—into a related concept, say "coffee trays." This is how the rationalist's model of thinking becomes deduction for the sake of deduction—at the expense of or contrary to the facts of reality.[37]

Rationalism is the thinking method of relating concepts to one another while dropping most or all of the concretes that constitute the meaning of the concepts. Remembering that concepts summarize a continuum of concretes—that the concept "automobile" stands for all of the various automobiles in existence, whether subcompact, standard, or luxury, etc., and that the concept "friend" stands for all of the various types of friendship possible, including business, personal, and family—should enable one to resist latching onto one particularly narrow characteristic and then suffering the consequences of rationalism. Automobiles and friendship are not just one type of automobile or friendship; they exist in degrees. Remembering that the world is quantitative and that one's thought is quantitative—albeit not always as precisely so as in physics—will go a long way toward alleviating tendencies toward rationalism.

Thinking in ranges of measurement is more fundamental than thinking in principles because identifying ranges of measurement is where conceptual thought begins. The range of measurements is observed and retained, but moved to the background in the formation of concept or principle. The problem is that the rationalist fails to bring the measurements back to the forefront when looking at new concretes or moving on to new abstractions.[38]

---

[37] A particularly crude form of rationalism, heard by me from one of my brighter students, was the following: if the concept "life" means "action proceeding toward some end," then a rock rolling down a hill (to get to the bottom) is alive. Other rationalists, acknowledging that living organisms face the alternative of existence or non-existence, have seriously asked what the difference is between a living person and a statue—since a statue can go out of existence by being demolished. Another argued vociferously that criminals cannot be intelligent because criminals are immoral; immorality was defined as irrationality and an irrational person, therefore, could not possibly be intelligent.

[38] The rationalist's understanding of concept formation stems from the intrinsic theory of concepts, which acknowledges no measurements in the process of

Jean Piaget, the Swiss psychologist, has pointed out that deductive reasoning is a distinctive trait of adolescence. Younger children, whose thinking method is strictly concrete, are unable to move beyond the immediately perceivable. As they grow into adolescence, they become infatuated with abstractions from abstractions and the syllogism. Although they can think inductively, adolescents become consumed by deduction. Indeed, they are so consumed by deductive reasoning, says Piaget, that the idealism for which they are well-known often involves elaborately constructed and unrealistic deductions stating why they think they can save the world or write the next great novel. Piaget goes on, citing a lack of differentiation as possible cause of this rationalism:

> The indefinite extension of powers of thought made possible by the new instruments of propositional logic at first is conducive to a failure to distinguish between the ego's new and unpredicted capacities and the social or cosmic universe to which they are applied. In other words, the adolescent goes through a phase in which he attributes an unlimited power to his own thoughts so that the dream of a glorious future or of transforming the world through Ideas (even if this idealism takes a materialistic form) seems to be not only fantasy but also an effective action which in itself modifies the empirical world. This is obviously a form of cognitive egocentrism.[39]

"Egocentricity" is Piaget's term for the inability of children and adolescents to handle a variety of perspectives, tending as consequence to center on their own egos. They "decenter" (or learn to distinguish or differentiate the world, including other people, from themselves) as they move from the egocentricity of one developmental stage to the greater objectivity of the next.

Noting that the ancient Greeks were also infatuated with deductive reasoning, Piaget suggests that the attachment to deduction—of both adolescents and Greeks—is developmental; he also notes that adolescents begin to decenter when they enter the work force or begin serious professional training. The adolescent then "is transformed from an idealistic reformer into an achiever. In other words, the job leads

---

grasping essences. "Humanness" just exists in the concretes and consciousness mirrors it. This is a crucial connection between the theories of intrinsicism and rationalism.

[39] Jean Piaget, *The Growth of Logical Thinking: From Childhood to Adolescence*, trans. Anne Parsons and Stanley Milgram (New York: Basic Books, 1958), 345–46.

thinking away from the dangers of formalism back into reality."[40] Perhaps the preponderance of rationalism today and accompanying egocentricity among educated adults, especially intellectuals, is a state of arrested development. Deduction for the sake of deduction certainly is not the valid model of thought.

Application and Its Relation to Action

The correct use of deduction is to be found in the method of cognition called application. Generalization, or induction, gives us the concepts and principles from which theory is formed; application uses the concepts and principles to identify new concretes as they are met. "The process of observing the facts of reality," says Rand, "and of integrating them into concepts is, in essence, a process of induction. The process of subsuming new instances under a known concept is, in essence, a process of deduction."[41] After exposure to a number of round things, for example, a toddler forms the concept "ball," then proceeds to predict whether the next round thing encountered will also roll. In essence (and microcosm), this is the process by which we acquire knowledge and then use it to solve concrete problems. Application is the mental process prerequisite to taking action.

Generalization and application are crucial to learning and, ultimately, to living one's life. In fact, they are the processes that underlie the Herbartians' five steps of lesson planning and Dewey's five steps of a complete act of thought.[42] Both models move from inductive to deductive reasoning, or from generalization to application, which is the correct direction. Rationalism, in contrast, begins with deduction, the generalizations miraculously having arrived in the mind by mirroring intrinsic essences, and seldom, if at all, moves to induction. To use Rand's file folder metaphor, once again, generalization is the process of creating the folder, application is the process of placing a new instance in the already formed folder. Deduction, far from being the intellectual plaything of medieval Scholastics and contemporary professors, is our indispensable tool of practical living.

---

[40] Ibid., 346. "Formalism" is Piaget's term for rationalism.

[41] Rand, *Objectivist Epistemology*, 28.

[42] See chap. 2, pp. 59–60. Dewey's five steps presuppose a theory of concepts but Dewey never elaborated such a theory. Rand's theory of concepts, as well as her definition of "thought" as a "purposefully directed process of cognition," are consistent with Dewey's five steps. Rand, *Objectivist Epistemology*, 32.

Deduction is what the detective Sherlock Holmes uses to conclude that robbery was not the motive for murder, because nothing was taken from the scene of the crime; the unstated major premise is that robbery is a motive only when items are removed from the scene of the crime. Holmes would not be able to draw this conclusion if he had not previously formed the concept "robbery." Similarly, a medical doctor diagnoses a disease by subsuming observed symptoms, such as high fever and respiratory inflammation, under the previously formed concept "flu." Indeed, truck drivers deduce how to shift gears and steer trucks they have never been in before because of the knowledge they have acquired earlier through training and experience.

Deduction is what we all perform when we encounter specific items or ideas that are new to us. (Familiar items that we have seen many times before are recognized through the automated routine of habit.) Previously acquired knowledge, in the form of concepts and principles, is applied through deductive reasoning to identify these concretes. When we apply the general term to a specific item, we say, in effect, "Aha! This belongs in that folder," and the toddler concludes, "This new round thing is a ball."[43] If we do not have the folders stored in our subconscious, we will not be able to make the identifications; new generalizations through induction will be required. If the folders are not well organized and related to one another (integrated), we will have difficulty making the identifications; considerable volitional effort to reorganize will be required. Children who lack knowledge, and ignorant adults, exemplify the former situation, adults who carelessly tend to their subconscious minds exemplify the latter.

It must be stressed at this point that both generalization and application are equally important cognitive processes, hence their use in the Herbartian and Deweyan models. A proper education must teach children both methods and, especially, how to maintain a correct balance between the two. Sometimes one method is emphasized more than the other, but both are always present, often used in a continual back

---

[43] In the process of forming abstractions from abstractions, ideas, or previously formed abstractions, are held in our minds as concretes; similarities among these "concrete abstractions" are then identified and united to form a higher-level abstraction. This is how, for example, we arrive at the concept "human-made object," by identifying similarities among such concretes as "furniture," "automobiles," and "computers." Thus, any idea, or abstraction, encountered in our daily life, say, in the newspaper or just in conversation, becomes a concrete that must be categorized—that is, put into its proper file folder.

and forth manner. For example, applied sciences are largely deductive, drawing the broad principles that comprise their foundations from the fundamental sciences on which they rest. From these broad principles, and in conjunction with inductions from the facts that constitute the context of the applied science, narrower, more concrete principles are identified.[44]

Application, moreover, is more than a tool for recognizing new concretes; it is a necessary requirement for action in a new situation. All action takes place in a concrete, particular context. A doctor whose patient exhibits the symptoms of fever and respiratory inflammation must not only deduce the cause of the symptoms presented, but also must deduce the proper treatment based on stored knowledge concerning these kinds of symptoms. An engineer who seeks to build a bridge must not only deduce that a particular location on a river meets the requirements of bridge-building principles, but also must deduce the proper materials to be used and specifically how to put them together to construct the bridge. All action in new situations, as opposed to habitual action in situations that are exact copies of what one has done before, requires deductive thinking, the skill of application.

As can be seen in the above examples, application to act in a new situation carries with it a responsibility to discover all of the relevant facts before acting. The doctor who does not uncover all of the relevant concrete symptoms can easily misfile them in the wrong "folder," thereby prescribing an incorrect treatment. Similarly, the engineer who fails to collect sufficient data on the site can apply the wrong principles and, as a result, build a weak and possibly dangerous bridge. And reacting to the apparently hurtful behavior of a friend requires the same diligent fact-finding. Digging to uncover facts is essential in any kind of practical endeavor, yet this is precisely what rationalism tends to discourage.

One of the telltale signs of rationalism in everyday life is the penchant some people have for "figuring things out" in their heads, stubbornly refusing to consult facts that could provide a quick solution to their problem. Examples include refusing, while reading, to look up a word in the dictionary, preferring to deduce its meaning from one's present context of knowledge, or refusing, after getting lost while driving to an unfamiliar location, to look at a roadmap or to ask for directions. These "dangers of formalism," as Piaget refers to them, are the

---

[44] Cf. Kirkpatrick, *In Defense of Advertising*, 31–32.

equivalent of a weather reporter announcing that it is raining outside, because the data say so, but, at the same time, refusing to look out the window to see the brightly shining sun.

Application, therefore, is the cognitive tool we use to recognize new concretes and to provide plans of action in new situations. It is primarily the tool of using our previously acquired knowledge whereas generalization is the tool of acquiring that knowledge. Both skills, which describe the essentials of the thinking process, are necessary in any type of education. What remains to be discussed is how behavior results from our cognitive processing and the implications of these processes for relating to others on a personal and social basis.

HOW WE ACT

Actions are determined by our beliefs and values, and beliefs and values, in turn, are acquired from our parents and teachers or on our own through reading, study, or experience. The previous section concentrated on the formation of beliefs, the cognitive or factual knowledge, consisting of concepts and principles, that we hold to be true. The present section focuses on the normative aspects of life, the formation of values and emotions that determine the goals we pursue. Since the aim of education is independence, both physical and, more importantly, psychological, this section also touches on the means, especially through education, to achieving mental health free of defense mechanisms that lead to psychological dependence.

Value Formation, Emotions, and Behavior

It is important to emphasize at the outset that the cognitive and normative processes of consciousness are not separate faculties or activities. Consciousness is an unending stream of activity the processes of which are separated only by abstraction. Thus, concept formation and value formation are aspects of the same mental process. That is, a toddler forms the concept "ball" and, at the same time, evaluates the round thing as being either "for" or "against" him or her, that is, as potentially benevolent or harmful. The automatic result of the evaluation is an emotion, which would be some kind of pleasure or pain, depending on the specific conclusions drawn about the ball. The toddler's evaluation will then determine how he or she reacts the next time a ball is encountered, either to approach or to avoid it. In microcosm, again, this example of the ball illustrates the process of motivation and behavior. A few points need elaboration.

Evaluation is the mental process of relating objects and events to ourselves in terms of the beneficial or harmful effects the object or event might have on us. Objects and events judged to be beneficial become values; those judged harmful become disvalues. The natural inclination, or desire, is to approach or acquire values and to avoid or destroy disvalues. Initially, we may not know which things are potential values and which are not, so we experiment. A curious toddler, for example, pulls a cat's tail only to be hissed at and possibly scratched. The result of this incident may be a negative evaluation of the cat—or it may not, if the child realizes that pulling a tail is as unpleasant for a cat as having an arm yanked by parents. Volition is cognitive self-regulation and this means that two people can end up with quite different evaluations of the same concrete event, depending what they choose to focus on.

Emotions are automatic, psychosomatic pleasure-pain responses to evaluations.[45] Pleasureful emotions result from positive evaluations, painful ones from negative evaluations, but there are many different kinds of positive and negative emotions, and some are quite complex. Each emotion expresses a definite thought, based on the evaluation, that can be put into words. For example, "joy" expresses the thought, "Something I value highly has been achieved." "Fear" says, "Something is threatening me (or mine)." And "sadness" says, "I have lost something (or someone) I value."[46] Emotions can be thought of as a kind of automatized knowledge together with the pleasure-pain response that is instantly evoked when the object of that knowledge is encountered.

Emotions are automatic in the sense that, given an evaluation along with perception of the object of evaluation, the emotion follows immediately. We are not able directly to control or prevent the occurrence of our emotions, given our evaluations, but we can change the thought that stands behind the emotions. Our emotions contain knowledge that expresses the evaluation of the object or event, as well as knowledge of the nature of the object or event being evaluated. The "something" in fear, for example, that is threatening us may in fact be real, imagined, or mistaken. A child's fear of the dark is certainly based on an

---

[45] Linda Reardan, "Emotions as Pleasure/Pain Responses to Evaluative Judgments: A Modern, Aristotelian View" (Ph.D. diss., Claremont Graduate University, 1999), 18–29.

[46] Edith Packer, "The Art of Introspection," *The Objectivist Forum*, December 1985, 4–5.

imagined or mistaken something. When shown, perhaps over several nights in succession, that there is no something in the dark that can cause hurt, the child's evaluation will change and so will the emotional reaction to the dark.

Values and disvalues are the keys to understanding motivation and behavior. When we value something as benevolent, and then that something comes within our perceptual range, our emotional action tendency to approach the something follows, and more often than not, we act. When we do not act, other values and disvalues are operating, sometimes subconsciously, to deflect our behavior in different directions. The so-called will power of not acting on a desire is a different value and desire (or disvalue) that is influencing us to act otherwise. My aversion, for example, to upset stomachs might deflect my behavior away from consuming the pepperoni pizza, which I value highly, that has come within my reach. Volition operates in the process of forming our values, much formation of which occurred in the early years of our lives, and in the process of changing our values, which can occur at any time in the present, including the moment of confronting a particular desire. "Acting from reason," instead of emotion or inclination, properly understood means, before acting, assessing our values and desires according to an objective standard, which includes the full context of all of our values; it does not mean acting without emotion or against desire, because all action is motivated by emotion.

A crucial function of education, whether through parenting or schooling, is to teach which values are the objectively correct ones to pursue. Contrary to what many public school educators have advocated for over a hundred and fifty years, it is impossible not to teach values in a formal setting. For most of the history of the American public school movement, the values of white Anglo-Saxon Protestants have dominated. Today, the pendulum has swung to the other extreme of demoting and denigrating anything European or western, including and especially the social system known as capitalism. The point is that values are inherent in the teaching process. However, nearly all of our most deeply held values come from our parents or, if our parents default on their responsibility, from the peers of our youth; these values are the ones that continue to influence us throughout much of our lives. So, why do people act the way they do? Why do some behave poorly, even viciously, and why do others behave in a civilized manner? Answer: look at their values.

Self-Esteem and Independence

Judging another person's overt behavior is not easy, because as outsiders we are not privy to the other values and disvalues that influence that person. Being aware of our own motivation can also be a challenge, because so much of what causes our actions is subconscious. Sometimes the values that motivate us are not just subconscious but almost inaccessibly subconscious because they are repressed. Repression is a defense mechanism that attempts to protect us from anxiety by preventing certain subconscious content from becoming conscious; in the end, however, this only causes frustration and unhappiness and leads to dependence. The path to independence requires drawing the correct conclusions about ourselves—that is, having the right thoughts—when confronted with obstacles to the achievement of our goals. This process begins quite early.

Young children, especially infants and toddlers, are natural explorers and achievers. They are inherently curious and, if given the chance, will spend long periods of time and great effort examining an insect or building a boat. Unfortunately, they are not often given the chance because their parents interrupt them to make them do what the parents want them to do, and their teachers make them put down what they are interested in and move on to the next task that is not so interesting. Of course, far worse happens to many children, including serious verbal and physical abuse. The phenomenon of interruption, however, can be taken, as Montessori did, as the prototype of how a child's self-esteem and independence are prevented from developing. The process works as follows.

When children are prevented from pursuing their own interests, they feel an assortment of emotions, ranging from disappointment to hurt to anger. Further, they likely internalize the message that what they value is not important and, after many such repeated experiences, conclude as a core evaluation that they are not important.[47] What counts is what their parents and teachers want. This is a prescription for low self-esteem and dependence, because the values they form are ones of pleasing

---

[47] The qualifier "likely" is necessary in this sentence because volition, again, means that children can—and some rare ones do—conclude that this ill-treatment does not reflect on their self-worth. Core evaluations are fundamental subconscious conclusions (evaluations), formed in childhood, about oneself, reality, and other people, that are held as self-evident truths and operate automatically to influence one's future development and present actions. See Edith Packer, "Understanding the Subconscious," *The Objectivist Forum*, February and April, 1985.

others (or avoiding their disapproval). Their reality becomes, not the world that is waiting to be known and conquered, but what other people think of them. Thus, a mental habit, or psycho-epistemology, is established of always looking over their shoulders, so to speak, to see how other people are reacting every time they pursue one of their other values.[48] This soon breeds anxiety, that seemingly objectless fear we feel when there is no apparent cause present. To combat anxiety, the child may develop defensive maneuvers, the most common being the defense mechanism of repression followed by some type of defense value.

Repression typically attempts to prevent us from being aware of or experiencing certain emotions, usually painful ones, when we encounter their cause. Thus, when a child is concentrating on a project and is yanked away from it by a parent, the child may decide, after a number of these painful experiences, not to feel hurt anymore. The child's subconscious will thereafter automatically prevent the hurt from surfacing when the parent interrupts. Repression does not work because the hurt is still there, in the subconscious, and the mechanism of forbidding awareness of painful feelings can spread to other areas of life. To further combat the anxiety experienced when being interrupted, the child may adopt a defense value, which is any value held in the mind as a defense against anxiety because that value makes one momentarily feel good about oneself. The defense value is not genuine to the child, although it may be a legitimate, rational value if held in a different way by someone else; a defense value is held as a prop against pain, making the holder feel special in his or her own eyes and in the eyes of others. Thus, this child who is constantly interrupted by a parent may adopt the defense value "I'm good because interruptions don't bother me—I can handle working in short bursts" or "I'm good because I always do what my mother or father wants me to." Either way, the child's independent self has ceased to grow and compensatory "searches for glory" have become the norm.[49]

---

[48] Psycho-epistemology is the unique method by which each individual uses his or her mind. Rand, *For the New Intellectual*, 21. Nathaniel Branden, *The Psychology of Self-Esteem* (New York: Bantam Books, 1971, 98–100. Cf. Harry Bear, "The Theoretical Ethics of the Brentano School: A Psycho-Epistemological Approach" (Ph.D. diss., Columbia University, 1954) and Joseph R. Royce, *The Encapsulated Man: An Interdisciplinary Essay on the Search for Meaning* (Princeton, NJ: D. Van Nostrand, 1964), 5, 71, 107.

[49] Karen Horney refers to the pursuit of defense values as the search for glory through self-idealization. Karen Horney, *Neurosis and Human Growth: The Struggle toward Self-Realization* (New York: W. W. Norton, 1950), 17–39.

Independence is a personality trait, as well as the conscious and subconscious conviction, that we alone, as individuals, are responsible for our lives, that each of us alone—because no one else can get inside our heads to do it for us—must develop and possess the mental efficacy to identify our goals in life, then generate action for, and direct it to, the achievement of those goals. Independence presupposes self-esteem, the conviction of self-worth and mental competence.[50] Self-esteem and independence are developed from the earliest years by enabling and teaching children to do as much as they can on their own. This includes not just being able to put a shirt on by oneself or to tie one's shoelaces but also to make decisions for oneself and, most importantly, to identify the nature and causes of the emotions one is feeling. This last, a skill that many adults do not possess, will give children the confidence to pursue their own values. When confronted with an obstacle to the achievement of one of their goals, such as friends or adults harshly criticizing their plans, such children will have the ability to assert their self-esteem and to pursue the plans anyway. This is independence.

Creativity and Imagination

For many decades progressive educators have promoted creativity and imagination as antidotes to the authoritarianism of traditional education, which last, the progressives correctly point out, stifles individual interests and choices. Children must be encouraged, so the argument goes, to use their imaginations by engaging in creative activities, often working as members of groups. Froebel's emphasis on imaginative play

---

[50] Edith Packer, *The Role of Philosophy in Psychotherapy*, pamphlet (Laguna Hills, CA: The Jefferson School of Philosophy, Economics, and Psychology, 1987), 9. In today's public school context of awarding prizes in an attempt to improve a child's self-esteem, it is necessary to emphasize that such programs are virtual defense-value factories (as is the whole comparative grading system). Indeed, the concept of self-esteem that is being used by these programs is the essence of defense values, the purpose of which is to make children feel special—and superior to their classmates. The result is a pseudo self-esteem. Bumper stickers on cars, for example, that say, "My child was first at such-and-such school!" encourage children to think of themselves as special in the eyes of others, not competent in their own eyes, which would result, say, from successfully solving problems on their own. Boasting and bragging, whether by the child, the child's parents, or the child's teachers is always a sign that defense values are operating. People who are genuinely smart do not go around bragging that they are smart. Many geniuses have been humble about their intelligence.

was a major source of this idea.[51] However, it is important to understand the exact nature of these concepts before they can be applied to the educative process.

Imagination is the ability to retain in one's mind something that is not now present before the senses. Creativity is the ability to rearrange existing objects or ideas and put them in a form that has not been done before; to create something means to come up with something new. Creativity obviously requires imagination, because the new object or idea, which does not yet exist, must be projected and held—that is, imagined—in the mind of the creator. Every healthy human being is at once imaginative and creative, because the nature of abstract thought presupposes imagination and the formation of concepts is by its very nature creative. As the child forms the concept "ball," imagination is being used to create the concept. Thus, all learning is creative to the person who is learning. This type of creativity is called "ordinary creativity," the type that everyone experiences. "Great creativity" is the type that the rare innovators perform when they come up with something that is new, not just to themselves, but to all of humankind.[52]

The kind of creativity and imagination that the progressive educators are talking about, however, is the fantasy play that originated with Froebel. Montessori summarizes Froebel's approach this way:

> A wooden brick is given to a child with the words: "This is a horse." Bricks are then rearranged in a certain order, and he is told: "This is the stable; now let us put the horse into the stable." Then the bricks are differently arranged: "This is a tower, this is the village church, etc."[53]

The undefined nature of a wooden brick or block is essential to Froebel's fantasy play. Giving a child the distinct figure of a horse or an accurately designed miniature stable would, according to Froebel, prevent the stimulation of the child's imagination.

Montessori disagrees with this whole approach to child rearing and education. She points out that a child who straddles a stick and

---

[51] There were other, later influences in the United States, such as the expressionist art movement that led some to view the child as a creative artist. Lawrence Cremin, *The Transformation of the School* (New York: Vintage Books, 1961), 203–07.

[52] The distinction between ordinary and great creativity is from Silvano Arieti, *Creativity: The Magic Synthesis* (New York: Basic Books, 1976), 10–11.

[53] Maria Montessori, *Spontaneous Activity in Education*, trans. Florence Simmonds (1917; repr., Cambridge, MA: Robert Bentley, 1971), 258.

whips it as if riding a horse, or pretends that several wooden blocks arranged in a particular order are a horse and stable, may be exercising imagination but, more significantly, is expressing an unsatisfied desire. Such a child would much rather have a horse than a stick or wooden block. In contrast, states Montessori, the more affluent child who has a horse possesses no need to engage in such fantasy play. To give another example, my grandmother, as a child on a western Kansas farm, played a game called "Stonies" or "Stone People," by using pebbles to represent adults and children in a village or household; one could say that she was exercising her imagination but she was more correctly expressing her desire to be grown up, to be engaging in adult activity. Lack of money and access to stores prevented her from having figurines, which she would have much preferred.

Indeed, Montessori argues, Froebel's approach to education breeds credulity, not imagination, for it is the adult who imagines that a wooden block is in fact a horse or, a little later, a tower or church; the child is then expected to believe these conjurings of the adult as if they were reality. "The building of towers and churches with horses," continues Montessori, that is, with blocks that earlier represented horses and now are supposed to represent towers and churches, only generates mental confusion in the child. "There are, indeed, men who really take a tree for a throne and issue royal commands," but they are insane. Such credulity as is expected of the child in Froebel's approach to education is a mark of the uncivilized (or mentally ill), not a trait that should be cultivated in the "naturally ignorant and immature." Montessori concludes, "Education, therefore, should not be directed to credulity but to intelligence. He who bases education on credulity builds upon sand."[54] Effective use of the creative imagination presupposes a firm foundation in reality.

And "reality, exactitude, work," not "imagination, make-belief, play" are what children need most, says Montessori.[55] The reason Montessori objected so vociferously to fairy tales and Froebelian fantasies, as her grandson explains, is that people in the early twentieth century believed "children were too small, too stupid or too immature to understand reality. They thought children lived in a world of make-believe and adults should use that means to communicate with them. It was not just telling them stories, whether realistic or imaginary, but

---

[54] Ibid., 258–60.

[55] Quoted in E. M. Standing, *Maria Montessori: Her Life and Work* (1957; repr., New York: Plume/Penguin, 1984), 343.

cheating them by making them believe what was not true. That is what she was fighting against."[56] Even today, it is astounding how little reality young children are offered in books, movies, and television shows. Is it any wonder that nightmares about supernatural monsters occur with regularity in young children and that some even try to fly like Peter Pan by jumping out of an upper-story window?

The deliberate intent of the authors of many fairy tales—and of many of today's books, movies, and television shows—is apparently to scare the living daylights out of children. In the Middle Ages the motive, no doubt, was to scare the original sin out of them, but instilling fear in preschool children, consistent with the traditional approach to education, can have only one consequence: to cow them and therefore make the children easier to control and command. The ultimate in cowing comes from religious stories that threaten the prospect of going to hell. What is needed today is greater creativity, not by the children, but by the authors of these stories—creativity that dramatizes reality and at the same time does so without undue scariness.[57] And to say that "reality will not sell" is either ignorance or evasion of Montessori's success.

From the time they are born, children desperately need to learn what is real and what is not. G. K. Chesterton put the issue concisely: "When we are very young, we do not need fairy tales. Mere life is interesting enough. A child of seven is excited by being told that Tommy opened the door and saw a dragon. But a child of three is excited by being told that Tommy opened a door."[58] The mythical dragon frightens and confuses the young child. The blurring of lines between reality and fantasy in adult-contrived stories delays and harms development. The adult and the products of adults, at least in the early years, should represent firm reality.

This is not to say that Montessori never told fairy tales or other imaginative stories to children. She was critical of both in print to emphasize the need for reality but, as her grandson relates, "She liked a good story of whatever kind, and we hung on her lips as

---

[56] Mario M. Montessori, Jr., *Education for Human Development: Understanding Montessori* (1976; repr., Oxford: Clio Books, 1992), 109.

[57] Cartoons simplify reality and that is probably their appeal to young children. However, many more realistic stories portraying realistic problems and challenges are what are needed.

[58] Quoted in Standing, *Montessori: Life and Work*, 336.

children. If it was fiction, she said so; if not, she told us that too."[59] And therein lies the crucial teaching point, namely that parents and teachers must tell children when something is real and when it is not. They must say, "This story is not real; it is pretend or imaginary. It cannot really happen." Over time, children begin to comprehend the distinction between reality and fantasy. Encouraging children to fantasize only moves them further from reality.

This also is not to say that fantasy play has no place in the life of a preschool child. If left alone and not interfered with or interrupted, children do engage naturally in a variety of fantasy plays. How is this to be explained? Piaget calls it "an assimilation of reality into the self; it is individual thought in its purest form; in its content, it is the unfolding and unflowering of the self and a realization of desires."[60] That is, it is self-expression. If left alone or participated in by the parent as, say, a pretend character, such fantasy play becomes an expression of the self that either is a rehearsal for later life or an intellectual and emotional working out by the child of what is real and what is not. It is a needed phase of development. However, when adults interfere and impose fantasy on the child, say, by expecting the child to believe that a wooden block is a horse, the child's developing confidence and independent judgment are undermined.

This means that there is a place in education for "creativity" and freeplay of the kind that some progressives have advocated, but not for the reasons they have given. Such activities as finger painting, drawing, singing, playing musical instruments, acting, dancing, etc., as well as ordinary play, are not, at a fundamental level, engaging the child's creative imagination, as the progressives claim; they are giving the child an emotional outlet and an opportunity for unrestricted self-expression. Child psychologist Haim Ginott identifies the essential value of music lessons:

> The main purpose of music education in childhood is to provide an effective outlet for feelings. A child's life is so full of restrictions, regulations, and frustrations that media of release become essential. Music is one of the best avenues of release: it gives sound to fury, shape to joy, and relief to tension.[61]

---

[59] Mario Montessori, *Human Development*, 109.

[60] Jean Piaget, *Science of Education and the Psychology of the Child*, trans. Derek Coltman (New York: Orion Press, 1970), 156. Cf. Mario Montessori, *Human Development*, 28–32, 110–11.

[61] Haim G. Ginott, *Between Parent & Child* (New York, Avon Books, 1965), 95.

As long as the music lessons are not turned into a duty or chore with "restrictions, regulations," and the inevitable "frustrations" that follow such adult-imposed edicts, or into a vehicle by which the parents can show off to other adults, the child will be able to experience his or her self and emotions fully and refuel for subsequent work. So it is with the other activities mentioned above.

Finally, it is the height of pretentiousness to assume that a child of four or five is creative when drawing a house or acting in a play. Creativity in the arts does not occur until one has acquired a high degree of basic skill, which the many lessons over the years are intended to develop. The child enjoys the activity for its own sake and therefore views it as play—as defined by Froebel and Dewey—where means and end are simultaneous. Thus, the child performs the activity for the immediate emotional effect it brings, not for some subsequent end of having brought into existence a new product to be enjoyed by others, or, as in the case of cognitive learning, for the end of preparing the child for independent adulthood. Adults, it is true, often gush over these alleged creative activities of children and in the process they do indeed produce in children a subsequent end: the desire to please. This, however, breeds dependence, a trait opposite the goals of sound parenting and education.

VOLITION AND LEARNING

The presence of volition in human beings means that knowledge and skill cannot be forced on the child. This is the reason for calls in modern education to free the child from the coercion of teachers and the school system. If children are not free to choose what they want to learn, they will close their minds to all learning, or learn just enough to get by—namely, to pass a test and obtain a degree. Coercion destroys self-motivation, directing attention to an external end. In today's educational system, the goal of students is to acquire credentials, not to learn. The presence of volition also means that even the best teachers will not necessarily get through to all students, since each student is his or her own self-programmer and can choose not to learn anything. Because cognitive self-regulation is itself a skill, the operations of the volitional consciousness must be taught to children from the earliest ages. This skill includes the ability to identify the nature and causes of one's own emotions, preferably as they are being experienced, which means the ability to introspect the nature of one's mental processes and to correct them if need be. It means, of course, also the ability to apply the principles of logic in all aspects of one's life, everyday, in one's relation not just to reality but also to oneself and to other people. Cognitive self-regulation means the ability to use reason and emotion together in harmony in one's life to achieve independence and happiness. Teaching the child how to achieve this independence and happiness is a tall order.

VOLITION AND POLITICAL FREEDOM

The presence of human volition further means that freedom is a fundamental requirement of social existence. As Ayn Rand argued often, laissez-faire capitalism is the only moral social system because it recognizes the conditions of human survival by protecting individual rights and banning the initiation of physical force, especially such force as may be originated by the government. Government-run education, which initiates physical force by extorting money from a country's citizens to provide education for some of the citizens' children, is clearly a violation of this premise. The only moral educational system that recognizes the volitional nature of human beings is a free-market educational system of competing, for-profit learning services.

4

The Theory

I hold that the aim of life is to find happiness, which means to find interest. Education should be a preparation for life.

—A. S. Neill[1]

To INSTILL IN THE YOUNG a purpose in life is the fundamental aim of education.

Purpose in life is defined by one's chosen values, especially career. By giving us pleasure in the pursuit of material and psychological values and in the enhanced standard of living that results from the pursuit, productive work uses—or should use—our conceptual consciousness to its fullest. When choice of career is established, the pursuit of family and leisure values (which include friends) can then further give meaning to our lives. Career is primary because it forms the core of who we are and unifies with it all of our other values into an integrated whole; it bolsters our developing self-esteem. "Purpose," as the dictionary tells us, "suggests a more settled determination" than intention or intent;[2] thus, at the end of formal schooling, the young adult should be fully equipped with the knowledge, values, skills—and confident determination—required to pursue a produc-

---

[1] *Summerhill: A Radical Approach to Child Rearing* (New York, Hart Publishing, 1960), 24.

[2] *Webster's Ninth New Collegiate Dictionary* (Springfield, MA: Merriam-Webster, Inc., Publishers, 1985), 629. Nothing mystical is assumed by this discussion of purpose in life. "Goal" is a less preferable synonym of purpose.

tive career in a free society. The purpose of education is to instill a purpose in life.

The theory of concentrated attention provides the means of achieving this "settled determination" by nurturing self-esteem and independence. Rejecting coercion and rationalism, the theory frees the young and encourages them to be actively curious and practically self-assured. Recognizing that consciousness is our means of knowledge and guide to action, and that values and emotions form an integral part of both, it advocates training the young not just in the skills of generalization and application, but also in the arts of evaluation, introspection, and execution. Rejecting the progressive view that skill can be taught without content and that repetition is "drill and kill," it advocates a subject matter appropriate to the child's age and interests and practice to acquire all knowledge and skills. The theory of concentrated attention, then, in essence, is a theory of nurture, rather than one of coercion or neglect.

We turn now to the main tenets of this theory, beginning with the purpose of education.

PURPOSE

Three concepts—interest, attention, and independence—form the core of the theory and constitute the criteria of educational accomplishment. If successful, the education will have enabled the young to choose values that will give their lives meaning and significance.

Interest, Attention, Independence

Concentrated attention is heightened awareness of one object out of the many that exist in our field of awareness. "Focus" and "concentration" are synonyms of "attention" but, as used here, "concentrated attention" means an extreme or high degree of awareness of the object, as opposed to a low level of awareness of, or inattention to, background noise, such as a ticking clock or a lawn mower humming a few houses away. This means that "attention" is essentially a continuously quantitative concept and that "concentrated" is the modifier. Thus, at any point in time we can experience a heightened level of awareness of one object, say a book that I am reading, while still perceiving at a low level another object, the ticking clock. We know that we are aware of such objects in the background as ticking clocks because, when the clock stops ticking, we feel that something is wrong. An attention that is concentrated is one that is both intensive and sustained, rather than shallow or fleeting.

A person who does not exhibit concentrated attention is one who is easily distracted from the object under consideration—by, say, the ticking clock or humming lawn mower. Thus, what is initially low in one's awareness is allowed to rise to a level that hampers perception of the object at hand. Over time, the mind wanders from object to object and we say that such a person cannot sustain attention. The ability to prolong attention on one object is the sustained component of concentrated attention. However, because paces of learning vary from person to person and length of time spent concentrating on a topic does not automatically determine amount of learning, intensive attention can produce results more quickly. Geniuses grasp more in one learning session than the average person and no amount of time spent by average persons can approach what the genius can accomplish.[3]

Thus, concentrated attention, if sustained, will not necessarily lead to genius, but it can lead to greater learning. As William James puts it:

> Whether the attention come by grace of genius or by dint of will, the longer one does attend to a topic the more mastery of it one has. And the faculty of voluntarily bringing back a wandering attention, over and over again, is the very root of judgment, character, and will.... An education which should improve this faculty would be *the* education *par excellence.*[4]

Montessori's example of the three-year-old girl working with wooden cylinders for a prolonged period of time illustrates how the Montessori method encourages the development of the sustained component of concentrated attention.[5] In young children, it is the ability to sustain attention over time that initially needs to be developed. In later years, the skill of increasing the amount of content grasped at one time can be taught. When the two skills are combined—intensive and sustained attention—economy of learning results and acquisition of knowledge escalates.

---

[3] William James, citing a number of writers approvingly that there exists a strong correlation between sustained attention and genius, concludes that genius causes sustained attention, not the other way around. William James, *The Principles of Psychology* (1890; repr., Cambridge, MA: Harvard University Press, 1983), 400.

[4] Ibid., 401. Emphasis in original.

[5] See chap. 1, pp. 26–27.

What drives concentrated attention is interest and concentrated attention, in turn, drives independence. Interest is an emotion, a desire that directs attention to a particular object; this means that in the present, or at an earlier time, the object is (or was) evaluated positively and accepted as a value. We are interested in, and therefore attend to, what we value. As Dewey put it, interest is the identification of the self with the object, that is, we take possession psychologically, or take psychological ownership, of the object and declare it to be ours. By declaring the object to be a value, we are saying that it is something that will benefit or enhance our lives; thus we want to possess it in some form to experience the pleasure of having it. To be interested in something is to want it as a value, and to have it requires that our attention be directed toward it. As an emotion, interest says, "I like that object and want to know more about it."

Attention drives independence by directing effort to the achievement of a goal. One of the worst errors parents and teachers make when working with children is to interfere with the child's efforts to accomplish certain results. These interruptions occur from birth to well into adulthood.[6] A newborn infant, for example, if left alone, will exert enormous effort and exhibit a biologically programmed concentrated attention by crawling up its mother's stomach to reach a breast. A toddler will emphatically protest with the words "self, self" when the parent is trying to do something for the child, such as unscrew a bottle cap. Teenagers will angrily tell their parents to "get a life" (or something stronger) when the parents constantly badger them about certain careers that the parents think will be more lucrative, enjoyable, respectable, etc., than the ones the teenagers are planning to pursue. In all of these examples, the infant, toddler, and teenager are seeking independence by directing their attention to specific goals; the adult has the power to prevent the accomplishment of that independence through constant interruptions. And every interruption that does occur deflects attention away from the task at hand to the adult who does it for the child. This breeds the opposite of independence.

As all cognitive processes are a continuous stream, interest and attention are not separate faculties of consciousness; we identify and separate them only by abstraction. Nevertheless, there is a temporal relationship between the two. As discussed above, interest is

---

[6] Coercion and physical punishments are far worse interruptions. The discussion here assumes kind, well-intending adults.

present before attention becomes focused on a particular object, and it is interest that focuses the attention. However, attention can precede interest, as may occur, say, on a mountain hike when coming upon a flower that one has not seen before.

Awareness of the flower is unavoidable because it is in the middle of the path. Our attention has been caught, but now we have several options. If we do not like flowers, we might step on this one or cut it down! If we are indifferent to flowers, or preoccupied with our goal of reaching the end of the trail, we might ignore this one and quickly step around it. Or, curiosity might lead us to smell its fragrance and wonder what its name is, or, if we have a pre-existing interest in flowers, we might stop to examine this one and speculate about its species. In this example, our attention was awakened by an outside influence, then a pre-existing interest determined our attention and behavior in relation to the flower. In the last case, curiosity directed our attention to look more closely at the plant. Interest here still drives attention even though the initial attraction of attention was not caused by interest.[7]

This last is the pattern by which naturally curious babies and children acquire interests in the first place. Curiosity is a milder, less specific form of interest, but it is still a desire to know. Thus, when objects come into the field of awareness of babies, they immediately want to know what the objects are and what can be done with them. The objects may be put into their mouths, dropped on the floor, or thrown across the room, or all three; the babies are exploring the nature of the objects and deciding whether they like them or not. As toddlers becomes verbal, they will begin to state explicitly about an object, "I like it" or "I don't like it." In this manner, values and disvalues are acquired and curiosity and interests are determined. These will later guide the older child's explorations both in and outside of school.

The store of interests—the kinds and quantity of values—that we acquire in childhood and youth determines the level of curiosity we exhibit later in life and thus what we will attend to. Giving children the freedom to discover as many interests as possible encourages the development of an active curiosity. Allowing children to pursue spe-

---

[7] Similarly, attention certainly would be caught if a bear had been in the middle of the path instead of a flower. The fight/flight response is interest-driven attention where the attention is usually triggered first. How we respond in such situations depends on our previously acquired knowledge of what is the correct thing to do. Park rangers, for example, say that if a bear charges us, we should freeze—because the bear is *probably* bluffing!

cific interests without interruption for long periods of time stimulates growth, maturity, and independence. Non-intrusive parenting and teaching culminates in practical self-assurance and ambition, thereby enabling children to make their way in the world and to succeed. Not giving children this freedom is as harmful psychologically as not feeding them is physically.

A Theory of Nurture

Interest, attention, and independence are, respectively, an emotion, a cognitive skill, and a personality trait. As such, they are not something that one deliberately sets out to teach, although each can be enhanced with good parenting and teaching. If parents and teachers leave children alone sufficiently to develop on their own, interest, attention, and independence will develop naturally. Teaching—and parenting, which in large part is teaching—therefore, is essentially a task of nurturing the naturally curious child.

The theory of concentrated attention is one of nurture because to nurture means to feed and protect while otherwise not interrupting the natural development of, say, a plant, animal, or child. For human beings, the extended meaning of "to feed" denotes providing knowledge, values, and skills necessary for mature adulthood. "To protect" means simply to guard against harm. If otherwise left alone, the child's interests will naturally direct attention toward independence. Herein, however, lies difficulty in applying the concept of nurture to parenting and education. Many parents and educational theorists interpret feeding and protecting as meaning stuffing and controlling, the most extreme form of this to be found in Plato's totalitarian state in the *Republic*.

Since the Renaissance the direction of educational theory has shifted from coercion to nurture. This shift has included in its intellectual arsenal the organic metaphor, which states that the bud should be allowed to grow and blossom naturally on its own. Over-watering, over-feeding, and over-pruning suffocate the plant and prevent the bud from blossoming and the blossom from bearing fruit. Thus, parents who obsess over their toddlers' lack of eating and hand-insert food into their mouths, who prevent children from going into the garage to explore, and who practice the maxim "children do not tell adults what to do—adults tell children what to do" are suffocating their children and preventing them from developing naturally. Today, much of this "over-parenting" stems from ignorance, for example, of what constitutes good eating habits in toddlers (and of the fact that babies do not starve themselves) and inconvenience, say, of refusing to follow children into the garage to make sure they do not poke themselves with a rake or drink antifreeze; over-parenting also stems from explicit authoritarian premises, as in the third example above.

Similarly, educators who impose without choice rigid methods and curriculum on students are smothering the students' interests and preventing them from developing their own values and, consequently, a sense of themselves. The solution, say the modern theorists, is freedom to develop on their own. Progressives in the twentieth century, however, took the organic metaphor to the extreme of doing virtually nothing for the child, offering only minimal guidance. "Freedom" and "laissez-faire" in education came to mean "do nothing." What perhaps the organic metaphor needs is an additional image to support and clarify it: guardrails that guide children into certain areas, on the path to independence, and, at the same time, prevent them from going off the path and over the side, thereby harming themselves.

The image of the guardrail does not mean to imply a rigid "straight and narrow" path within the rails—some freeways today, after all, have ten or more lanes per direction—nor does it imply a complete lack of guidance, which is impossible, because every family and school has a culture that children absorb whether it is taught to them or not. Parents do in fact guide their children in the sense that they daily expose them to specific careers and family and leisure values. From birth, children soak up the knowledge, values, and skills of their parental environment. Parents differ according to the specific options they expose their children to and the extent to which they expose them to other options. The guardrail image means that within the rails children are, or should be, given an extensive variety of options from which to choose.

Telling (coercing) children that they must become, for example, truck drivers (or doctors or lawyers) is the narrowest of the straight and narrow paths within the rails. Buying them books and introducing them to people in all walks of life, on the other hand, enables them eventually to choose a career that interests them and will give meaning to their lives. Thus, the guardrail metaphor is intended to imply, within the rails, a wide latitude of choice from among a rich and abundant collection of knowledge, values, and skills provided by parents and teachers.

The rail image as a bar to behavior applies only to very young children, to protect them from physical harm, such as recklessly running out into the street or playing unsupervised with plastic bags, or to prevent them from harming others or destroying others' property. As children mature, frequent communication, that is, teaching, not rules, about how to protect themselves, pursue values, and respect the rights of others become the guides to behavior.

Rules are commands to act or not act a certain way. Obedience may be rewarded; disobedience is certainly punished. Because attention becomes fixed on the reward or punishment, not on learning how to behave, rules have no place in a theory of nurture. The principle of modern child rearing and teaching, which Montessori endorsed, is "control the environment, not the child," which means child-proofing the environment by putting plastic bags out of sight or reach and locking the door to the garage. Control of environment becomes the guardrail or bar to harmful behavior. If children still want to play with plastic bags or go into the garage, then the adult's obligation is to carefully supervise such activities—with appropriate teaching about the handling of plastic bags or rakes, and the dangers of antifreeze. It is not to respond with a menacing "Don't you play with that" or a threatening "Don't you dare go in there." Indeed, when a stray plastic bag or unlocked garage door is found by a child, the fault lies with the adult, not the child.

By adolescence, an understanding of how to resolve conflicts with others through mutual need recognition and discussion to reach agreement should make unnecessary the coercive and arbitrary rules that teenagers today detest and readily disobey. Assertiveness—the pursuit of values—without harming oneself or others, not obedience to authority, is the hallmark of independence. And the art of negotiation is the means of relating to others on a mature, adult basis. Thomas Gordon points out that adults do not say to other adults with whom they disagree, "You're grounded! Go to your room!" Why should such coercive techniques be used on children and students? Negotiation is the rational solution to adult conflict, so it also should be with children and students.[8]

Interest, attention, and independence are the criteria of educational success because the goal of education is to enable children's interests

---

[8] Thomas Gordon, *Parent Effectiveness Training*, rev. ed. (New York: Three Rivers Press, 2000), 218–21. Gordon, *Teacher Effectiveness Training* (New York: Peter H. Wyden, Inc., 1974), 217–21. Some adults—especially legislators and heads of state—do use coercion against other adults, violating their rights (often in the name of democracy). This would seem to imply that the root of dictatorship is the parent/child relationship: if it is okay to coerce children, why should it not also be okay to coerce adults?

to focus their attention on areas of study that they enjoy and that eventually will lead them to independence and happiness in a career, family, and leisure life they love. To the extent that specific educational methods and content contribute to the development of interest, attention, and independence, to that extent those methods and content should be adopted. To the extent that they prevent children from pursuing their interests and focusing attention on what will make them independent and happy, to that extent those methods and content should be avoided.

Other Forms of Attention

At this point concentrated attention needs to be differentiated from several related concepts. Meditation is one. In education concentrated attention is used to fuse thought and emotion together to efficiently and effectively acquire the knowledge, values, and skills required for a child's mature adulthood. Meditation of the religious type empties the mind of all thought and emotion except a mantra; in education this type of attention to a single object would be a distraction. Secular meditation, however, is intensive attention to one object and its purpose is contemplation. When used in this manner, problem solving can be enhanced through subconscious integrations that occur during the heightened state of awareness. Enhancing the skill of concentrated attention enhances the skill of meditation, which makes the latter a special case of the former.

Daydreams are another concept that need to be distinguished from concentrated attention. In traditional schools, as Dewey pointed out, daydreams divide interest and distract attention. As a defense against boredom daydreams split attention between two objects of awareness: the subject of study and the more pleasant images of what students wish they could be doing. As a defense against anxiety daydreams attempt to provide a pleasant escape from what is causing fear and insecurity; daydreams cannot succeed in providing escape because the anxiety does not go away unless addressed directly through introspection, to reprogram one's subconscious premises, and action to go against the paralyzing fears. Focusing on one pleasant mental image, however, when attention is not required somewhere else can be relaxing and when combined with contemplative meditation can allow subconscious integrations to be made to solve problems. Daydreams can also be the fuel that fires ambition, by projecting goals and visualizing oneself achieving them.

Defensive attention requires additional comment, because it can be confused with the healthy version of concentrated attention. The workaholic is probably the best example in adults. In the child, defensive attention may manifest itself as prolonged time spent searching the Internet, practicing a musical instrument, or reading books—normally worthwhile pursuits. If done, however, in the midst of or to escape the shouting of parental fights, for example, defensive motivation is likely operating. What seems like concentrated attention in fact is a compulsive behavior to fight off anxiety. A driven or frantic quality accompanies the unhealthy behavior, whereas spontaneity and a natural desire to pursue the activity motivates healthy actions. Defensive attention is split between anxiety—the feelings of fear and helplessness—and the need to maintain the illusion of power and control. The anxiety is usually repressed and the need for power and control is biologically programmed, so what such a person is left to feel is a seemingly uncontainable drive to do something. Thus, long hours spent in the office, at the computer, practicing, or reading temporarily relieve the anxiety.

The difference between the two types of attention can be explained simply as the difference between motivation by love and motivation by fear. Persons exhibiting concentrated attention love their activities and experience genuine pleasure in their accomplishment; persons exhibiting defensive attention feel dread or burdened in the pursuit of their activities and enjoy little more than relief from anxiety in their accomplishment. Recognizing and differentiating these two types of attention in a family or school setting is not easy, but the ability of parents and teachers to identify and minister to the unhealthy form is crucial to the successful development of independence. What further complicates matters is that most of these people are motivated in part by a genuine love for the activity and at the same time in part by a need for relief from anxiety. The science of psychology has much work to do in the twenty-first century to help parents and teachers cope with all forms of defensive behavior.[9]

A concept closely related to concentrated attention that has been much researched in the last couple of decades is the "flow experience." Flow is defined as "the state in which people are so involved in an activity that nothing else seems to matter; the experience itself is so

[9] The foregoing relies heavily on Edith Packer, *The Obsessive-Compulsive Syndrome*, pamphlet (Laguna Hills, CA: The Jefferson School of Philosophy, Economics, and Psychology, 1988).

enjoyable that people will do it even at great cost, for the sheer sake of doing it."[10] The greatest cost of a flow experience was supposedly paid by Archimedes, who is said to have lost his life to a Roman sword because he was so absorbed in his mathematical work that he did not notice the presence of soldiers.[11] In the past this state was described pejoratively as absent-mindedness. Today, flow is considered an instance of optimal experience.

Flow in fact can be described as the optimal state of concentrated attention, for it reflects total concentration on an activity such that all outside influences are not noticed, including time and the need for food. The experience is exhilarating and accomplishment seems effortless, because everything comes together in the performance of an activity and nothing seems to go wrong. Athletes speak of being in the "zone." Attention is both intensive and sustained; confidence is heightened and energy flows smoothly. Indeed, this last is the reason why the experience is called "flow": performance flows smoothly and effortlessly. It is as if one is caught up in the flow of things, flow being metaphor for the pleasure-filled, perceived effortlessness of the undertaking.

Experienced teachers know that stretching—presenting material just slightly beyond the context and capabilities of the student—is one of the best ways to encourage learning. So also it seems that the state of flow is entered when one is challenged just slightly beyond one's capabilities. If the challenge is too great, anxiety results; if too little, boredom.[12] The window of opportunity for a flow experience is the same narrow range as that sought in successful teaching. Thus, flow and concentrated attention have much in common, but the goal of education is not to achieve flow experiences; flow is just a pleasant consequence sometimes achieved as the result of concentrated attention.

From the discussion of interest, attention, and independence, we now turn to the questions, "How are knowledge, values, and skills to be made available to the child?" and "Which particular knowledge, values, and skills should be taught?" The answers to these questions refer to method and content of education. First, to method.

---

[10] Mihaly Csikszentmihalyi, *Flow: The Psychology of Optimal Experience* (New York: Harper & Row, 1990), 4.

[11] A good story, but apocryphal. *Encyclopædia Britannica Online*, s.v. "Archimedes," http://0-search.eb.com.opac.library.csupomona.edu:80/eb/article-9109383 (accessed April 23, 2007).

[12] Csikszentmihalyi, *Flow*, 74.

METHOD

While interest, attention, and independence are not directly taught to the child, they must be encouraged and allowed to develop through a skillful method of education. Two of the three main components of method of education—the teaching and learning process and teacher-student contact—will now be explored. The third component of method, the organizational structure of education, which for the theory of concentrated attention is a free market of educational entrepreneurs, will be discussed in the next chapter.

The Teaching and Learning Process

To teach is to transfer knowledge, values, and skills from one person to another, either by formal instruction or by example. By extension we can say that the teacher may be a book, movie, audio recording, or Montessori's didactic materials, the transfer of knowledge coming from the products of another person. To learn means to acquire knowledge, values, and skills, either from a teacher or by experience alone. Learning is a process of conceptualization, not memorization, and the result of conceptualization is understanding of the nature of something or of how to do something. To recite memorized bits of information is not evidence of learning; it reflects only the ability to retain and retrieve certain words or motions, like a parrot, but not be able to use the words or motions, except in a limited way. Actors, for example, must not just memorize their lines but learn them; they must understand and demonstrate in action the motivations of the characters that speak the lines.

To learn by experience alone, when deliberate teaching is not taking place, means to observe the behavior (or example) of others and to adopt as one's own, sometimes imitatively, sometimes in improved fashion, some or all of the others' knowledge, values, and skills. Similarly, learning by experience also means to observe the events of nature and to draw conclusions about what is observed, thereby increasing one's knowledge. This is the essence of scientific research, but observing events and drawing conclusions also applies on a more commonplace level. The experience of hiking in the mountains, for example, when a falling rock almost causes injury can lead a hiker to conclude that better observance and greater anticipation will be needed on the next hike. The phrase "experience teaches" is idiomatic for self-teaching, or rather, learning without a teacher.[13]

The formal teaching and learning process involves four steps, two performed by the teacher and two by the learner. In simple terms, the process can be described as follows: (1) present, (2) learn, (3) do (make mistakes), (4) correct (or self-correct). The teacher presents new material and the students receive it. Next, the students do something with the new material, which usually includes making mistakes. Finally, the teacher corrects the mistakes. Sometimes, as in Montessori schools, teaching materials are designed to be self-correcting; sometimes students can catch their own mistakes and correct them without help from the teacher. Indeed, all self-teaching that takes place beyond formal schooling requires this skill of correcting one's own errors.

Music lessons provide a good model of the teaching and learning process. The teacher assigns a new passage to work on, explaining tempo, dynamics, and mechanics of performance. The student listens and perhaps sight reads the passage. Some corrections may come from the teacher at this point, but essentially the next step is for the student to go home and practice the passage, correcting as many mistakes as can be done on one's own. At the next lesson the student plays the passage for the teacher who then offers suggestions for improvement, that is, makes more corrections. The music lesson model is a one-on-one tutorial, but it is the model that can achieve in-depth learning and, at the same time, accommodate individual differences.

The music lesson model demonstrates that learning requires considerable effort on the part of students, especially practice, and that learning and doing are distinct steps that in fact do not occur simultaneously. Practice, or repetition, as an expression of concentrated attention is essential to learning, not just because such skills as finger-brain coordination when playing a musical instrument are not automatic, but because our mind is not a mirror that reflects the material presented to it. A conceptual consciousness must volitionally process

---

[13] After giving one student a specimen to examine, nineteenth century naturalist Louis Agassiz stressed the importance of observation (or experience) as teacher. He said, "Take this fish and look at it." Hours later, when the student wanted to know what to do next, Agassiz said, "Look at your fish." And still later, "Look, look, look." For three days the student looked at the fish, then on the fourth, Agassiz presented him with a new specimen. Lane Cooper, ed., *Louis Agassiz as a Teacher: Illustrative Extracts on His Method of Instruction* (Ithaca, NY: Comstock Publishing, 1917), 40–48.

new material in order to fully understand it. And "processing" means relating new concepts or principles to the other knowledge we have stored in our subconscious and observing new instances of the concepts or principles in our daily experience. To use Ayn Rand's metaphor, new file folders must not only be opened, labeled, and filed; they must have content added to them. Practice at the conceptual level means thinking about recently acquired ideas, relating them to one another and to one's store of previously acquired ideas, and, especially, actively looking for concretes that exemplify the ideas. The result of this process is understanding, rather than rote memory.[14]

Rote memorization occurs when understanding is either not present or is ignored while the person practices; it is completely appropriate in many kinds of learning. A musician, for example, who must play a thirteen-note run in one beat of time cannot possibly think about each note or finger position; thus, memorization, even though the music itself may be in front of the musician, is the key to an excellent performance. Similarly, shoppers who see a sign that says "3 for a $1.00" instantly know—or should instantly know—the price of one item, because many years earlier they learned by rote memory the multiplication tables. "Drill" becomes "kill," even in the development of musicianship, when fear and anxiety are the motivators, rather than interest.[15] The solution is to eliminate the fear and anxiety and their (usually) coercive causes, not the necessary drill.[16] And the drill does not have to

---

[14] "The Comprachicos," in Ayn Rand, *The New Left: The Anti-Industrial Revolution* (New York: Signet Book, New American Library, 1971), 207–08. This excellent essay on how the worst versions of progressive education deform the minds of children misses the point that traditional, authoritarian education does the same, as does, and probably in a worse way, authoritarian and insensitive parenting. It also takes a quotation from John Dewey (on page 207) out of context. Rand is correct that Dewey did not advocate individualism or egoism in her senses of the terms, but in the pages of the work cited (*The School and Society*) he is talking about the bad effects of bureaucratic competition in traditional education. See chap. 5, pp. 163–66, for my discussion of bureaucratic competition.

[15] For centuries mathematics in western culture has been taught rationalistically— that is, abstractions first, then the concretes (maybe). This approach—"here are the symbols and rules, now memorize them"—does not aid understanding. Further, group teaching ignores differences in pace of learning, which probably more than anything else causes the fear and anxiety that students feel when learning their multiplication tables. Finally, compulsory education laws and the bureaucratic system that we have today tend to destroy any natural interest students may have in learning things quantitative.

[16] Eliminating drill because it may cause fear or anxiety in some students is another example of the progressives' throwing the baby out with the bath. Traditionalists

be Jesuitical contests at the chalkboard, but some form of repetitious exercise is required to program the memory.[17] Teachers acknowledge that they learn far more about a subject than their students, primarily because of the additional study required to digest a subject into an essentialized oral presentation, but also because of the repetitions, that is, the practice, they are able to perform from term to term.

Learning and doing are separate steps because learning is the step of acquiring knowledge, whereas doing is the step of applying it; in traditional education doing means writing papers and taking exams. "Learning by doing" is a misleading concept because in all cases of supposed learning by doing, the learning still comes before the doing. For example, on-the-job learning, as opposed to what takes place in the classroom, results from teaching by another employee and trial-and-error self-teaching; in the former case, learning clearly occurs before doing, in the latter, awareness of the error and what to do to prevent its future occurrence come before the next step is taken. The same is true of all so-called learn-by-doing classroom projects and even of learning to ride a bicycle "by doing it," which, in this case, either the parents have explained to their children the importance, with every step, of shifting their weight to the opposite direction of the bike frame or the children painfully learn themselves through trial and error. The advantage of formal learning *before* doing is to prevent some of the more egregious and possibly harmful errors from happening in the first place. After the formal learning, "doing it" means fine tuning the skill through additional trial and error learning.[18]

---

equally miss the mark when they complain that calculators prevent children from learning their decimals. Knowing the rules of decimals, however, is prerequisite to the effective use of calculators.

[17] Montessori teaches arithmetic inductively, where the children work—individually or in small groups—with specially designed bead sets, counting frames, and multiplication boards, to enable them to understand why the arithmetical operations are performed the way they are. By working with these materials, children develop their own sets of tables, then move on to more complicated operations, including squares and cubes. Each additional step reinforces what was grasped in the earlier steps. Thus, graded exercises using concrete materials provide the needed repetition for both automatization and understanding. Geometry is taught in similar fashion—to six- and seven-year-olds. Maria Montessori, *The Montessori Elementary Material* (1917; repr., Cambridge, MA: Robert Bentley, Inc., 1971), 205–97.

[18] And trial-and-error learning is what results from repetition. Considering how pervasive repetition is in our modern society, it is astonishing how hostile progressives feel toward drill. Not all repetitive learning is rote memorization but every walk of life has its tasks that are highly routinized. Football players must

There is a deeper significance to repetition than polishing the skill, which is usually thought to be its purpose. Repetition is an affirmation of self, a way of experiencing our values over and over again. Repetition gives us a firmer sense of who we are. Adults may immediately play newly purchased CDs a dozen or more times, not just to learn the music, but also for the enlivening sense that "this is me." Joggers run daily not just for the physical exercise but for the "high" they feel during and after the run. Children do the same. As Montessori puts it:

> To have learned something is for the child only a point of departure. When he has learned the meaning of an exercise, then he begins to enjoy repeating it, and he does repeat it an infinite number of times, with the most evident satisfaction. He enjoys executing that act because by means of it he is developing his psychic activities.... The exercise which develops life consists *in the repetition, not in the mere grasp of the idea.*[19]

This phenomenon also probably explains, at least in part, the incessant question asking of young children, including the repetition of the same question that was just answered—for the second, third, or fourth time.

Teaching is the process of taking knowledge that the teacher possesses and seeing to it that that knowledge is grasped and understood by the learner. Presentation and correction, in other words, are the functions that teachers perform. This does not mean, however, that presentation must be a formal lecture and that correction must require an examination or letter grade. Again, music lessons provide the model. Sermonizing a music student about his or her performance while ignoring skill level and desire, say, not to become a performer in public does not convey the teacher's skill at all. And handing out gold stars and letter grades turns the learner's attention immediately away from what must be done to learn to play a musical instrument to what must be done to earn an extrinsic reward (or to avoid a punishment).[20] When interest

---

memorize their plays, actors must memorize their lines, and bus drivers their routes. Memorizing the multiplication tables is just the beginning.

[19] Maria Montessori, *The Montessori Method*, trans. Anne E. George (1912; repr., New York: Schocken Books, 1964), 357–58. Emphasis in original.

[20] "Do this and you get that (or avoid that)" is how Alfie Kohn describes the reward and punishment system of motivation. The problem is that attention becomes focused on the "that" at the expense of the "this." Alphie Kohn, *Punished by Rewards: The Trouble with Gold Stars, Incentive Plans, A's, Praise, and Other Bribes* (Boston: Houghton Mifflin, 1993).

and attention are placed at the center of education, teaching means first and foremost being aware of the student's needs and wants, then adapting the teacher's knowledge to those needs and wants.[21] This is why patience and empathy are said to be requirements of good teachers.

Having said the above, the much-maligned lecture method nevertheless holds a well-deserved place in education—because it is efficient. The knowledge contained in a well-crafted oral presentation is easier to grasp than that in a book or series of books. Given that the rate of speaking is slower than the rate of silent reading, the well-organized lecture (when not presenting newly unpublished material) by its nature essentializes the content of the written word. This enables the listener to acquire ready-made, organized file folders within which to file subsequent details. Books provide the details. Thus, hearing a lecture and, either before or after the lecture, reading a book on the identical subject is a powerful combination for learning. That today's students often do not listen to the lecture (or read the book or, at the university level, even buy the book) is an indictment of the coercive educational system that destroys interest and erects barriers between the teacher and student; it is not a condemnation of the lecture.[22]

Indeed, the lecture and tutorial are the only genuine methods of formal instruction.[23] The tutorial is a one on one session—one teacher, one student—as in the case of music lessons, and the feedback and correction are immediate. When two or more students are present, a lecture is taking place—mass as opposed to personal communication—and the feedback takes longer and the corrections become more involved. The 25–40 student classes that we have today and are euphemistically labeled "lecture-discussions" are a perversion of the two methods. The purpose of the lecture is mass communication; the purpose of the tutorial is individual attention. The two do not mix well in one session of more than a handful of students.[24] The solution,

---

[21] Needs are objective conditions of the task at hand, the requirements of learning; wants are optional tastes and preferences.

[22] Cf. Jerry Kirkpatrick, "In Defense of Lecturing, or: It's Time to Cut Down on TV in the Classroom," in Jeffrey T. Doutt and Gary F. McKinnon, eds. *Marketing Education: Exploring New Directions* (Proceedings of the Western Marketing Educators' Association Conference, April 1990), 80–85.

[23] Cf. Gilbert Highet, *The Art of Teaching* (New York: Vintage Books, 1950), chap. 3.

[24] In Montessori schools, the lesson on how to use a particular didactic material is given by the teacher to no more than a few students at a time, sometimes to only one. Thus, the teaching method is tutorial or very small lecture.

at least at the secondary and university levels, would seem to be to have a few mass lectures (or even recordings of a few excellent lecturers) to communicate large amounts of knowledge and many tutors to provide the needed individual attention and correction of error.[25] More on this idea in the next chapter.

Relating to the Student

Eliminating coercion from the teaching and learning process is not an easy task. Many parents and teachers today repudiate corporal punishment, yet resort to other techniques that either produce obedience or, at minimum, intended or not, communicate distrust and disrespect. These techniques, or "roadblocks to communication," as Thomas Gordon calls them, utilize a language of unacceptance and can be classified roughly into four categories: (1) commands, threats, and insults; (2) moralizations, criticism, hard-sell lectures, and praise; (3) distraction and denial; and (4) interrogations, analysis, and advice.[26] The classification is proposed to represent a continuum of techniques ranging from worst (category one) to bad (category four). What the techniques all have in common is not seeing the child or student as a person with self-initiated thought processes and real values, emotions, and conflicts, but as an object to be manipulated. They communicate dislike and are patently unkind.[27]

Commands, such as "go to your room," and threats, such as "if you don't stop talking, you're going to the principal's office" are just as much physical punishments as hitting or spanking a child, because behavior is unwillingly changed or about to be changed. Even insults, like "If you had any more brains, you'd be a half-wit," usually succeed in silencing an uncooperative child, which is what the parent or teacher wants

---

[25] "Only individual attention to each student can keep the whole class abreast and truly teach. A lecture is a sizing of the canvas in broad strokes. The fine brush and palette knife must be used close up to finish the work of art." Jacques Barzun, *Teacher in America* (Garden City, NY: Doubleday Anchor Books, 1954), 39.

[26] The list, with some liberties taken, is from Gordon, *Parent Effectiveness Training*, 47–53; it is not intended to be exhaustive and there is some overlap. See also Thomas Gordon, *Discipline That Works* (New York: Penguin Putnam, 1991), 175–79. The discussion that follows rests on the work of Gordon, including *Teacher Effectiveness Training*, plus Haim G. Ginott, *Between Parent & Child* (New York: Avon Books, 1965) and Ginott, *Teacher & Child* (New York: Collier Books, 1972).

[27] In the tradition of Gordon and Ginott, see Alfie Kohn, *Unconditional Parenting: Moving from Rewards and Punishments to Love and Reason* (New York: Atria Books, 2005) for excellent parenting advice.

to accomplish. Moralizing, criticizing, hard-sell lecturing, and prais-
ing all aim at influencing behavior but in a less coercive manner than
the techniques in category one; manipulation would not be an
inaccurate description of these techniques. "You shouldn't act like
that" (moralization), "you obviously didn't spend much time on this
paper" (criticism), "you need to burn the midnight oil every night like I
did when I was a student" (hard sell), and "you're brilliant" (praise) are
statements that seek compliance with the adult's desires.

For example, the descriptive statement "you made a connection
between those ideas that neither I nor many adults could have made"
allows children to draw their own conclusions about how good or
smart they are; evaluative praise and criticism are nothing more than
external rewards and punishments, which breed dependence by preventing children from making their own judgments.[29] Instead of the
above criticism on a student paper ("you didn't spend much time on
this"), it would be far more helpful to say, "Additional time, perhaps,
researching and thinking about this topic would enable you to elaborate and explain exactly what you want to get across to the reader.
Check the following sources...." Correction, as Ginott says, means
direction, "pointing out how to do what has to be done."[30]

---

[28] Ginott, *Parent & Child*, 43–59.

[29] "Direct praise of personality," says Ginott, "like direct sunlight, is uncomfortable and blinding. It is embarrassing for a person to be told that he is wonderful,
angelic, generous, and humble. He feels called upon to deny at least part of the
praise.... [And he] may have some second thoughts about those who have praised
him: 'If they find me so great, they cannot be so smart.'" Ibid., 47.

[30] Ibid., 51. Ginott, *Teacher & Child*, 103–05. Cf. Montessori's enigmatic phrase that
teachers must "teach, teaching, not correcting." Quoted in E. M. Standing, *Maria
Montessori: Her Life and Work* (1957; repr., New York: Plume/Penguin, 1984), 219,
italics omitted. Correcting a young child at the time an error is committed, says
Montessori, creates defensive withdrawal. The task of the teacher is to note the
error, then, at a later time and without comment about the previous error, teach
the correct way of doing things.

Categories three and four in the above list both avoid attempting to understand the child's emotions, category three explicitly so, category four under the pretense of helping the child solve a problem. "Let's talk about something more pleasant" (distraction) and "You don't really feel that" (denial) effectively ignore any problem the child may have and either ends discussion or prompts vehement protests. Category four is a trio of techniques that most would consider helpful in their relationships with children and students. However, "where did you get such an unpopular idea?" (interrogation), "you feel that way because you're not doing well in class" (analysis), and "just make a schedule of the homework you have to do and stick to it" (advice) make the child feel unseen and unaccepted. More often than not the child feels, "Here is another adult lording it over me; who I am does not count for anything."

Repeated use of these techniques over time produces, by the end of secondary school (and sooner), a young person who looks—and is—beaten. It is not surprising, then, that these kids develop a wide variety of coping mechanisms, ranging from withdrawal to aggression. Yet there do exist, in addition to Ginott's principle for praise and criticism, better techniques for relating to children and students that treat them with respect and trust. These techniques begin by having adults practice active listening to help the children identify their emotions. In the course of a discussion the adults may communicate their own emotions and, in the case of conflict, the two sides, led by the adults, may utilize negotiation techniques to recognize mutual needs and alternative solutions to the disagreements.[31]

Active listening, according to Gordon, is the process of attending to a child's words and behavior, uncovering the hidden emotional message, then feeding it back with empathy to the child for verification. For example, when a young girl says to her mother "I hate you!," the mother should not hit her daughter or resort to one of the communication roadblocks discussed above.[32] Rather, to listen actively, she must decode the feeling behind her daughter's words and reply with

---

[31] These techniques of effective communication should also be used in adult relationships, but more often than not the roadblocks interfere.

[32] Or call "time out," which usually is a another form of "go to your room," because the child must go somewhere—to a penalty box, as it were—to serve the time that is out. The concept of time out, however, is mixed. When emotions run high, taking time to cool off can be helpful, but the way many parents and teachers use it today it is just another strong-arm tactic. Kohn calls the time out a "version of love withdrawal." Kohn, *Unconditional Parenting*, 25.

something like, "You're really angry at me!" The daughter may then respond, "I sure am!," because her feeling has now been affirmed. Further, she feels that her mother understands her because her mother has shown that she accepts her daughter's anger. The mother has said, in effect, "It's okay to be angry at me." Hitting and the roadblocks deny the acceptance.[33]

And it must be okay to feel this anger or any other emotion. As Ginott puts it, every child has "a constitutional right to have all kinds of feelings and wishes.... We set limits on acts; we do not limit wishes."[34] Empathy is crucial in the feedback because the ability of the mother to imagine what her daughter is feeling and to some extent to feel the same emotion is what convincingly communicates understanding and acceptance; empathy is non-judgmental acknowledgment of an essential expression of self, which, when received, enables a child to gain perspective on an emotion that otherwise might be overpowering, confusing, or unknown. As a result of the mother's empathetic response, the girl may feel more warmly toward her mother and open up about why she is angry. If the mother continues to listen actively, her daughter may resolve her own problem with the anger withering away.

To give a similar example, this time in the setting of school, a boy might exclaim, "I hate math!" To listen actively, the teacher must not respond with this all too common teacherly advice: "Well, if you'd study harder, you might learn to like math." Rather, the teacher must probe the emotion behind the statement by saying, for example, "You're afraid you won't be able to keep up with the rest of the kids" or "You're disappointed in the score you got on the last quiz." Again, identifying and naming the emotion indicates understanding and acceptance of the student's

---

[33] Gordon, *Parent Effectiveness Training*, 58–70. One childcare expert said the following in regard to the "I hate you" statement: "A child who says this kind of thing is usually frightened. His own powerful fury frightens him and he is still very unsure just how great his power is. He does not know that it would be virtually impossible for him really to damage you. He longs for you to keep control of him while he is out of control of himself. If you let yourself get angry because of his words and shout back at him, you add to his alarm. You have no real reason for anger. He is using great self-control in shouting rather than kicking. So try to stay calm and be the grown-up he so badly needs." Penelope Leach, *Your Baby and Child: From Birth to Age Five*, 3rd ed. (New York: Alfred A. Knopf, 1997), 506–07. The last sentence is also excellent advice for parents and teachers of much older children (and for adults in their relations with other adults); being the grown-up is what active listening is all about.

[34] Ginott, *Parent & Child*, 110–11.

plight. By saying that it is okay to feel this way, the student is now able, with, it is hoped, the help of the teacher's further active listening, to sort out his difficulties with math and to devise a plan for mastering this bane of elementary school children.

In addition to active listening, parents and teachers need a technique by which conflicts may agreeably be resolved, that is, without resort to coercion or other roadblocks to communication. The first step in this process puts emphasis on description of the facts and emotional communication, not on evaluation of the child. The second step is problem-solving negotiation to find a solution acceptable to both child and adult. In the first step the adult communicates what Gordon calls an I-Message by factually describing the child's behavior, the feeling it causes in the adult, and the factual effect the behavior has on the adult. For example, a teacher might say, "When you walk into class late, I feel distracted and annoyed; it makes me lose concentration and waste time repeating the instructions I just gave." The emphasis is on facts—the emotional and behavioral effect of the child's conduct on the teacher—rather than on attacks of the child's character or personality. Sarcasm, such as "Don't know how to read a clock?," makes the child feel threatened. The I-message might actually generate an apology.[35]

The student might have a legitimate reason for coming late to class, in which case a conflict of needs exists between the two. When adults confront a conflict peaceably, they define the nature of the problem facing them, generate alternative solutions, and discuss the pros and cons of each alternative to arrive at a mutually acceptable solution. For example, the student explains to the teacher her need to work on the school yearbook, a temporary assignment, and that deadlines are nearing. The teacher insists on the need not to be interrupted and to have to start class over. Subsequent discussion leads to the solution of having a classmate record the beginning of class so the yearbook staffer can listen quietly to the teacher's instructions after she arrives. Similar negotiation techniques can and should be used between adults and children or students in all situations of a conflict of needs; it means treating the young like the grown-ups they so eagerly want to become.[36]

---

[35] Gordon, *Teacher Effectiveness Training*, 142–45. Gordon, *Parent Effectiveness Training*, 129–37. Cf. Ginott, *Teacher & Child*, 84–99.

[36] The example is from Gordon, *Teacher Effectiveness Training*, 222–24. In the course of discussion to resolve a conflict, Gordon points out, it is important to distinguish needs from solutions. The teacher needs an orderly classroom and presentation, not every student seated at the beginning of class before instructions

Resorting to coercion or one of the communication roadblocks is a declaration of war on the child, the objective of which is to command obedience, not to encourage independence.

The significance of the I-message here is that the student can readily see a tangible, concrete effect of her behavior on that of the teacher—loss of concentration and waste of time having to start the class over. If, instead, the student arrives on time and the teacher says, "When you come to class with that pink hair (or sloppy clothes or pierced tongue, etc.)…," a conflict of values, as Gordon calls it, exists and the difference between a conflict of needs and a conflict of values is that the value situation—the pink hair—produces no tangible, concrete effect on the teacher. Conclusion for the teacher: do not try to change what the youth holds as a strong, symbolic and personal value. Or, as the youth might put it, "It's none of teach's damn business what color my hair is!"[37]

How properly to relate to the student—and more broadly, how adults, especially parents, should properly relate to children—is a large and untapped area for improvement. Writing in 1989, Thomas Gordon states, "I have found it difficult to identify more than a handful of psychologists or educators who support the position that I have espoused for over a quarter of a century—namely, that discipline [meaning to control, punish, penalize, correct, and chastise children] is an ineffective, outmoded, and harmful way to rear and educate children."[38] The problem for adults who are opposed on principle to any form of physical or mental abuse of children is that the adults themselves were most likely raised by and taught the same methods Gordon refers to as harmful. The reactions of adults toward child behavior are automated

---

are given. The latter is one of several possible solutions to the teacher's need not to have to repeat the instructions. Needs are abstract requirements, solutions are concrete options for meeting the need. Ibid., 272–74.

[37] Ibid., 285–89. Gordon, *Parent Effectiveness Training*, 295–308. Values that have no tangible, concrete effect on parents or teachers are tastes and preferences that are morally optional. In some cases they may seem bizarre, or worse, to an adult, but they harm no one except the adult's arbitrary sense of how children and teenagers should look and behave.

[38] Gordon, *Discipline That Works*, 201. The definition of discipline is on page 4 of the same book. It probably should be acknowledged at this point, as many education writers do, that the etymological root of "discipline" is "pupil" and that the verb means "to teach." Nevertheless, current usage clearly means "to command obedience." Thus, I prefer to *teach* my child and students, to encourage independence, not to discipline them.

and therefore are difficult habits to unlearn. The problem of how better to relate to the child is one of education—of the adult.

The Prepared Environment

The term "prepared environment" is Montessori's, but it can apply equally to the setting of the Dewey school. It refers to any material or aid that can attract the attention of the student, involve him or her in the process of learning, and in fact provide most of the teaching. For Montessori, the activity of the child is called work; for Dewey, it is an experience. For both, the environment should be child-friendly with child-sized chairs and tables (at the preschool and elementary levels) and be safe for the child to move around in. Thus, the prepared environment represents a guardrail venue that gently guides the child toward maturity. For both Montessori and Dewey, the teacher is the one who prepares the environment; in the classroom the teacher retreats to the role of facilitator of learning, rather than primary communicator of knowledge.

In extended meaning and especially for older children, the teacher logically becomes part of the prepared environment to further guide the child to independence, which may be achieved through lectures and tutorials. And books also become essential materials to involve the child in learning. Dewey assumed this would be the case in higher levels of education,[39] as did Montessori. According to the theory of concentrated attention, all materials and methods are to be evaluated by the criteria of interest, attention, and independence. Whatever stimulates interest, holds attention, and contributes to the development of independence is to be retained as part of the prepared environment. Whatever dampens interest, weakens attention, and inculcates dependence is to be discarded.

Montessori's materials for pre- and elementary school levels are probably better than Dewey's occupations because the former are more conceptual and focused on the development of independence than the latter. But this does not mean that Montessori's method is the only legitimate one for those age levels. Further research—and competition in a free market in education—will determine whether other methods will prevail.

---

[39] See chap. 2, p. 63.

CONTENT

Content of education comprises the knowledge, values, and skills that are required for mature adulthood in a free society. Some will be recommended for anyone who considers him- or herself to be an educated adult, most will be optional. No content will be required for everyone because, in a free market in education, there is no education czar, or board of education, dictating who will learn what. All content will be freely chosen by the education consumer in a marketplace of ideas.

The following discussion does not pretend to decree which knowledge, values, or skills should be taught at any particular level of education—primary, secondary, or higher. It merely presents an outline of the end results a sound educational system should produce in the educated adult.

The Skills of Concentrated Attention

Progressives have long touted method over content, meaning that the real aim of education is to teach students how to think, not to teach any particular subject matter. While on the surface this last may have some appeal, the skill of thinking is in fact a content—a subject matter—of education, not a method, that can and does need to be taught to children of all ages. Method of education refers to what educators do to educate; content is what the educated students acquire and demonstrate that they have learned. Further, the skill of thinking, or more broadly, the skill of the effective use of one's mind, includes much more than Deweyan problem solving.

Every educated adult should thoroughly understand and, especially, know well how to employ the following cognitive skills: generalization, evaluation, application, introspection, and execution. Although these skills cannot be taught in technical detail until adolescence and thorough understanding probably cannot be achieved until adulthood, they can be taught in rudimentary form to the youngest child, when properly adapted to age and stage of development. The first three skills were described in the last chapter; certain additional points will be emphasized here, followed by discussions of introspection and execution.

Generalization. Generalization and application begin when the child first starts to talk, probably before, and evaluation begins at birth. Flawless use of these skills is not automatic, thus the obligation of parents and teachers to teach—rather than to command, hit, and control—is paramount from the earliest ages. Generalization to form the concepts of concrete objects is readily achieved by young children without much aid from adults, provided parents and teachers eagerly use the correct words to name the objects that interest the child. Abstract concepts, however, and, particularly, abstractions from abstractions require careful (and patient) explanation (and repetition of explanation) by the adult.

One example of learning an abstract concept occurred when my daughter was quite young. From the time she was just a few months old my wife and I had often read her the Berenstain Bears book *Old Hat, New Hat.* When she was eighteen months old, we bought a new refrigerator, often referring to it as the "new refrigerator." By that age she was mimicking everything we said, so she also referred to the refrigerator as "new." A few days later, on one of the many occasions when she was pointing to the refrigerator and calling it "new," a light went on in her mind and she charged across the room to look for her book *Old Hat, New Hat.* She had just grasped the meaning of the concept "new." The teaching here resulted first from deliberately choosing a book that discriminated two concepts, such as "old" and "new," and then deliberately using those terms subsequently to describe anything that in fact was old or new. The arrival of the refrigerator was the culminating point that brought about the generalization required to understand the concept "new."

One of the most significant feats of generalization that a young child accomplishes is learning how to read, write, and do arithmetic. Reading is achieved by learning how to decode—that is, to generalize—the sounds of written signs. In an alphabetic language this means generalizing the sounds of the language's letters and letter combinations; in English, there are 44 such sounds.[40] Cursive writing is

---

[40] Jeanne S. Chall, in *Learning to Read: The Great Debate*, 3rd ed. (Ft. Worth, TX: Harcourt Brace, 1996), reviewed nearly 100 years of research on learning to read and concludes that phonics is the clear winner. Learning to read can be achieved at quite an early age. Winifred Sackville Stoner's daughter learned at sixteen months, as described in Stoner's book *Natural Education* (Indianapolis: Bobbs-Merrill, 1914). Another child, described in Lewis Terman, "An Experiment in Infant Education," *Journal of Applied Psychology* 2 (1918): 219–28, learned at twenty-six months. Parental coercion, though, was likely involved in these two cases. At Sudbury Valley School, where children are not made to learn anything at any particular time, including how to read, Daniel Greenberg reports that some early readers subsequently do not read a lot and some late readers do. Greenberg's own daughter did not express an interest in learning to read until age nine; by nine and a half

primarily a physical skill but it is driven by the generalization that there are only three strokes in the Latin alphabet. Arithmetic, the hardest of the "three R's" to learn, requires the child to generalize four meanings of ten Arabic symbols before beginning to program the memory to calculate quantity. Learning all three of these skills requires considerable practice, that is, repetition.[41]

From upper elementary school on, complex concepts should be taught in accordance with the rules of definition, and by adolescence thinking in principles and thinking in ranges of measurement can be introduced. The rules of definition, particularly genus and differentia, equivalence (not too broad or too narrow), and essentiality, insure that our concepts are tied to the facts they denote and are related to one another in a objective way. The negative rules—avoid circularity and negative, vague, obscure, or metaphorical language—further refine our understanding of the concepts being defined. Far from being a semantic game (a favorite pastime of rationalists), precise definition is the means of tying our concepts firmly to reality by maintaining a well-organized file cabinet of folders that can be retrieved instantaneously for future use. Precise definitions are the building blocks of education.[42]

Once children have learned the art of definition, they can be taught actively to look for and identify connections that exist among the phenomena of nature; this includes all three levels of nature: the physical, the biological, and the human. Thinking in principles and, especially, thinking in ranges of measurement are the superstructure of education that tie the building blocks together into an integrated whole.[43]

---

she was a "complete reader." Dyslexia, he says, is nonexistent at his school. Daniel Greenberg, *Free at Last: The Sudbury Valley School* (Framingham, MA: Sudbury Valley School Press, 1995), 31–35.

[41] For excellent discussions of the generalizations involved in learning how to read, write, and do arithmetic, see Samuel L. Blumenfeld, *How to Tutor* (Milford, MI: Mott Media, 1977), 29–39, 137–46, and 179–98. The three strokes of cursive writing are the over- and undercurve of the oval and the push-pull slant. The four meanings of Arabic numerals are position in sequence (three comes after two, which comes after one), total (three), the counting process (one, two, three), and place value (ones, tens, hundreds, etc.).

[42] See David Kelley, *The Art of Reasoning* (New York: W. W. Norton & Company, 1988), 32–43.

[43] And no one has better achieved this feat of integration in education than Montessori. The seeds are planted in pre-school, but starting at the lower elementary level, she introduces children to the world of knowledge through a series of "Great Lessons." Stories more so than lessons, they are designed to spark the imagination and interest of young children about the universe; the origins of the earth,

Thinking in principles focuses on identifying causes; thus, the ability to distinguish necessary from sufficient conditions and to use John Stuart Mill's methods of agreement and difference (including the joint method), concomitant variations, and residues should be taught and thoroughly practiced in all areas of knowledge.[44] Causal explanation is not just the foundation and content of science but also is the necessary tool by which we come to know and understand the events of our daily lives.

Thinking in ranges of measurement acknowledges that the universe is continuously quantitative and that a volitional consciousness chooses the dividing lines between concepts, based on the purpose to which the concept is put. This is why translation from one language to another is a significant challenge; inventors of the various languages have drawn the dividing lines of their respective concepts at different points along the continuum of reality. Thinking in ranges of measurement also means that essences are not embedded in the concretes of reality, dictating that a specific concrete belongs in only one category and not in another. Different contexts call up different assortments of instances of a concept or principle. The student, therefore, needs to learn the skill of visualizing, at some level of awareness, the collage of varying concretes that constitutes the referents of a particular concept or principle. Practice of this skill will go a long way toward preventing the development of rationalism.

Evaluation. Evaluation, a skill seldom if ever taught today, is the art of relating a fact to oneself and concluding that the fact is either beneficial or harmful. In the animal world, the most basic form of evaluation is the sniff-and-taste test performed by, say, the family dog or cat who comes upon some substance on the front lawn. If the substance passes the test, it is eaten; if not, it is left alone. Human beings perform a similar test to determine their food preferences. Most evaluations, however, are not as automatic as the sniff-and-taste test, though they may seem

---

life, and human beings; and the development of language, communication, and mathematics. In a broad sweep, Montessori introduces the young child to physics, chemistry, geography, biology, history, literature, and math. The imagination thus sparked, the child is then encouraged to pursue specific topics to fill in the detail. Paula Polk Lillard, *Montessori Today* (New York: Schocken Books, 1996), 54–76. Maria Montessori, *To Educate the Human Potential* (1948; repr., Oxford: Clio Press, 1989).

[44] For a discussion of, and exercises on, how to identify causes, see Kelley, *Art of Reasoning*, 273–88.

so to people who act on their emotions without stopping to identify the evaluations that stand behind the emotions. The process of evaluation presupposes a standard or criterion that often is far more sophisticated and complex than our taste buds. Thus, considerable knowledge and thought may be required to arrive at a final judgment.

Unfortunately, most values are passed on to children and students in the same way that concepts of concrete objects are: as assertions of fact. Concrete objects are identified by saying "This is a ball, this is a table, this is a rock." Values are conveyed by saying "That's not nice, you're naughty, that's a disgusting movie, the government owes you a job." Values are also passed on as commands or duties, which have the force of unquestioned fact: "Say 'please' and 'thank you,' share, don't lie." And values are acquired by imitation, by observing the behavior of admired others. Standards and the process of comparing facts to the standards are never discussed. The child memorizes, imitates, and often is not allowed to question why something is said to be a value or disvalue. Yet value formation is a skill as necessary for mature adulthood as is concept formation; it unquestionably needs to be taught explicitly from the earliest years onward.[45]

The simplest way to teach evaluation is to give reasons why something is good or bad, the reasons given being the standard of evaluation. For example, saying "please" and "thank you" is a courtesy that shows respect to another person; the absence of these words shows disrespect. Teaching the child to tell the truth because both deceiver and deceived are harmed—the deceiver is harmed by subsequently not easily being able to discern fact from fantasy—establishes the self-interested, life-enhancing basis of morality. Evaluating a movie, however, or whether or not the government owes everyone a job, requires an enormous amount

---

[45] It should be emphasized that there is no unbreachable gulf between facts and values, as many philosophers seem to think. Whatever is required, factually, to achieve a goal is what one ought, factually, to do. Objective values are a special kind of fact derived from the nature of the goal pursued; the goal constitutes the ultimate end of action and therefore forms the standard of evaluation. Thus, to sustain and enhance life, one *ought* to pursue a productive career; to successfully sell products, one *ought* to communicate features and benefits to prospective customers; and to build a toy boat, one *ought* to collect hammer, nails, saw, and wood, and possess a knowledge and skill of toy boat building. See Ayn Rand's one paragraph dismissal of the so-called is/ought problem in *The Virtue of Selfishness: A New Concept of Egoism* (New York: New American Library, 1964), 7–8. As Rand demonstrates, the ultimate goal that guides human action is life itself; all values derive from that fundamental fact.

of knowledge and thought before judgment can be made. Dogmatic assertion of fact in the former case ignores the prerequisite knowledge of esthetics and movie-making and, especially, of the principle that it is possible to dislike a good work of art and to like a bad one;[46] in the latter case, evaluation requires knowledge of economics and political philosophy and, at minimum, an awareness that there are alternative judgments about the government's proper role in society.

Application. The skill of application is demonstrated in its simplest form by pointing out that "this is an instance of that." Observing at the concrete level that a new round object is an instance of the concept "ball" is not difficult for young children. The challenge occurs when having to recognize instances of broad abstractions and when using abstractions to guide action in concrete situations. After presenting a lengthy example of some concept recently explained, teachers occasionally encounter such responses as "I don't see it," or worse, blank stares. The reason students don't see "it"—the example as an instance of the concept—may be because of poor presentation by the teacher, particularly a failure to tap into the students' contexts of knowledge, but from the students' perspectives, not seeing may result from insufficient and poorly organized knowledge. Hierarchically integrated knowledge that has been tied firmly to reality from the first learning experience is what leads to fast identifications of new concretes.

Intelligence undoubtedly plays a role here, for the quick wit is one who sees "it" before the less intelligent others do. This emphasizes the need in education for more individual attention, especially adaptation of teaching to pace of learning, as well as to interest. Illumination, the step of the creative process in which connections and identifications are made, is what occurs when the "it" is seen as an instance of "that." Whether experienced by the more intelligent or less, creative insight results from conscious differentiations that enable subconscious integrations to make the needed identifications. When taught to adolescents, and practiced, the steps of the creative process—preparation, incubation, illumination, and verification—would make an excellent adjunct to the skills of concentrated attention.[47]

---

[46] See Ayn Rand, "Art and Sense of Life," in *The Romantic Manifesto: A Philosophy of Literature* (New York: Signet Book from New American Library, 1971), 43.

[47] The specific steps of the creative process were identified by Graham Wallas, *The Art of Thought* (New York: Harcourt, Brace & Co., 1926), 79–107. They do not differ significantly from Dewey's five steps of a complete act of thought. Both series are based on methods of thought used by scientists.

Application as precondition to action requires substantial research to identify, say, the cause of a problem before action can be recommended to resolve the situation. Digging for facts and attention to detail is the only way to describe the effort exhibited by competent doctors diagnosing the cause of a disease and engineers identifying the location of a new bridge. Failure to uncover one crucial fact in the history of a medical patient, for example, can make the difference between life and death. Not all cases of application are as dramatic as the doctor-patient relationship, but commitment to facts to build a context is essential to being able to use previously acquired knowledge to solve a problem.[48] Students need to be taught that vigorous fact-finding is not a task reserved to doctors and engineers, but is the key to good judgment in all areas of life, personal and professional.

Still, there are those who have great difficulty grasping a concrete as an instance of a generalization and who seek few facts to help make decisions. The only remaining explanation of such behavior is the person's psychology. This takes us to the importance of teaching the art of introspection to all students.

Introspection. Education of the mind does not only mean an acquisition of knowledge of the external world and a skill to operate within it. It includes knowledge of the internal reality known as our conscious and subconscious minds and, especially, the skill to attend to errors of the mind's use. Introspection is the tool we use to identify the contents of consciousness.

Logic and an awareness of logical fallacies are the means of monitoring our reasoning powers, but an equally important use of them in introspection is the maintenance of psychological health and happiness, by identifying the nature and causes of our emotions. Many people today can name their emotions only in a vague, general way, such as "I feel upset," "I feel jealous," "I feel okay." Some cannot name even that much. Yet understanding exactly what one feels and what causes that feeling is crucial to resolving internal conflicts and paving the way to a happy, productive life. The technique of identifying emotions and their underlying thoughts, as well as the technique of correcting incorrect subconscious premises, needs to be taught to children at their youngest and reinforced throughout the growing years to adulthood.

---

[48] The bureaucratization of medicine today through health maintenance organizations has so reduced the amount of time that doctors can afford to spend with patients that fact-finding, the taking of a patient's history, is disappearing.

Psychologist Edith Packer describes the process of emotional introspection as a series of six steps.[49] First, the emotion one is experiencing must be named; an emotional summary, such as "being upset," must be broken down into its component emotions. Second, the universal evaluation underlying each emotion must be identified; for example, the universal evaluation underlying fear is "I am in danger" and the one underlying anger is "An injustice was done to me." The third step identifies the personal evaluation behind each emotion, that is, the concrete experiences and thoughts that the individual has generalized into the universal evaluation; thus, a young man paralyzed by fear at the prospect of asking an attractive young woman for a date might recall instances from his adolescence when he thought he was an ugly bum who would get his head bitten off if he attempted even to talk to an attractive girl.

The fourth step of emotional introspection examines the truth or falsity of the personal and universal evaluations, that is, assesses them against the facts. The young man above learns to look at himself in the mirror to see that he is not ugly and to reflect on himself as not irresponsible or worthless; he applies logic to his own subconscious premises to see that there exists no objective basis to feel danger in asking for a date. If the personal and universal evaluations are incorrect, and one continues to feel the unpleasant emotion, the fifth step identifies the reasons for holding the false evaluations, which often, though not always, stem from inappropriate core evaluations acquired in childhood. The young man may discover that the way his mother related to him made him feel fearful of people in general such that he would feel worthless at the first sign of disapproval; thus, his fear of asking for a date is his subconscious talking, telling him to expect feelings of worthlessness at a moment's notice.

The sixth and final step reinforces correct evaluations in order to reprogram the subconscious mind to establish new thinking habits, thereby providing the opportunity to experience newer, more pleasant emotions. The young man now must practice new thinking methods by catching his fear before or as it occurs when asking a young woman for a date and by reminding himself that his fearful reaction is not founded on fact but on incorrect subconscious premises

---

[49] Edith Packer, "The Art of Introspection," *The Objectivist Forum*, December 1985 and February 1986.

from the past; above all, he must act repeatedly against his fear by asking for dates and thereby retrain his subconscious.[50]

The fifth and sixth steps of emotional introspection are the most difficult and the whole process for adults may require professional help. If taught to children from the earliest years, however, the art of introspection could help prevent the development of psychological problems that would require professional help in later years or, at minimum, the lack of self-awareness that leads to aimlessness and unhappiness. It certainly would help remove obstacles to concentrated attention that are erected by the child's psychology.

It is this last—the child's psychology or, more specifically, psycho-epistemology—that often causes a failure to see, for example, that a particular concrete is an instance of a generalization or that a generalization can be drawn after observing a series of concretes. Psycho-epistemology is the unique method by which each individual uses his or her mind—unique, because we all make different decisions and draw different conclusions about a myriad of issues, all of which are stored in our subconscious minds from the time we are able to talk. "Use of the mind" refers to the programmed interactions between the volitional aspects of the conscious mind and subconscious processes.

Since automated mental processes (mental habits) are what routinely guide us in our daily lives, psycho-epistemology refers most significantly to the way in which subconscious premises influence our conscious perception of facts, that is, our perception of reality. By adolescence, a child's psychology is well established and difficult to change. For this reason alone, the art of introspection should be taught—in manner adapted to age and stage of development—from the youngest years.[51]

---

[50] The acronym NUPARC might be used to aid learning this art. **N**ame the emotion, then the **U**niversal and **P**ersonal evaluations. **A**ssess the evaluations against the facts, identify the **R**easons for the incorrect evaluations, then **C**orrect and reinforce new premises through practice.

[51] Without assuming Freud's determinism, "The power of the subconscious to influence our perception of facts" is a statement that cannot be emphasized too often. An earthquake is seen by one person as the wrath of God to punish us for our sins, by another as an unfortunate natural disaster. A husband interprets his wife's "maybe" as a "definite," party hosts ignore their guests' glaring disinterest in parlor games, and a newspaper reporter sees corruption in business as a sign of capitalism's demise, whereas another sees it as the product of government regulation. An adult yells at three adolescents; one cowers, the second becomes hostile and walks away, the third continues to work as if nothing had been said. In all of these examples, the content of each person's subconscious affects the way in which the facts are perceived, interpreted, and responded to. Volitional control of

Execution. The rationalism of traditional education, as well as the alleged empiricism of the progressives, normally precludes teaching anything resembling execution, except perhaps in a shop class or occasionally, and not too well, in an English composition class. However, putting ideas into action to get something done is essential to living a happy, productive life. The concept of defining a goal and setting priorities on the steps that must be taken to achieve the goal seems simple enough, but it is astonishing how many people do not know how properly to execute an idea. Some are good at getting things done at work, but hopelessly lost in their personal lives, or good at gardening and terrible at shopping. Interest may play a role here, and psychology, but the skill of execution, which includes practice (repetition) and, at the more advanced levels that require other people, the art of negotiation, should be taught throughout the school years.

Acquisition of Culture

One way or another, every school—ancient, medieval, or modern; eastern or western—communicates its culture to students. Curriculum debates focus on what specifically should be transferred to the young, and the emphasis varies by time period. In a free society, one in which education is provided by the marketplace, the principal culture to be transferred is the knowledge and values required to understand, sustain, and enhance the social and economic system of market liberalism, or capitalism, and the skills to live successfully in that context.

The essence of this system is the protection of individual rights, especially property rights, which leaves individuals free to pursue their own values, and to develop their own skills, as they see fit, without interference from anyone else, especially the government. The developed skills aim at producing, or contributing to the production of, life- and civilization-enhancing goods and services. To fully understand and appreciate market liberalism, and to participate in it as a productive member, the gamut of basic and applied sciences—physical, biological, and human—must be taught at all levels of education (adapted, again, for

---

the conscious mind can sometimes overrule and change the subconscious method we each exhibit, but the older we get, the more difficult the task becomes. Psychoepistemology determines the psychological component of personality.

age and stage of development).[52] This in particular includes history and political economy; it includes the values of reason, science, and technology; it includes the ethics of rational egoism, especially the principles of trade and the abolition of initiating physical force; and it includes an understanding and appreciation of art.

Specialization vs. "Well-Roundedness." The above, which might be described as a standard liberal education (with a skew toward capitalism), is not a core curriculum to be prescribed to every child who goes through the educational system. There is no education czar, or board of education, dictating what should be taught to whom and when it should be taught. In the free market, interest and pace of learning guide the teaching and learning processes.[53]

This is not to say, however, that broad interests and wide-ranging, general knowledge are not assets to productive careers. The young should be encouraged—without coercion—to acquire as much of a liberal education as their interests warrant. The debate over specialization vs. general education is a false dichotomy. Reading, writing, and doing arithmetic are the most general of general education skills and theoretical and historical knowledge provide the foundation on which specialization is built. Specialization focuses on the concretes of the problem at hand, but general knowledge provides the base that guides thinking toward alternative solutions and ultimately to the best solution to the problem. With little or no general knowledge, problem solvers are technicians, restricted to a narrow range of concretes that they have acquired in their immediate experience. Specialists, on the other hand, bring greater quantities of knowledge to bear on the problem and can therefore offer more creative solutions.

In fact, in a division-of-labor economy everyone is a specialist, some better than others. Acquiring knowledge for its own sake may be a pleasant leisure-time pursuit, but it is not a profession that the market rewards with money. In the past, acquiring knowledge for its own sake was an activity reserved for the privileged elites of aristocracy; today, it is a remnant of the rationalistic method of thinking and

---

[52] It is the rationalism of traditional education that says geometry and algebra, for example, as well as physics and chemistry, cannot be taught until tenth or eleventh grade. Montessori teaches all the sciences in elementary school.

[53] Although from about the fourteenth century to today liberal education has come to mean the education of a free person, its original meaning was general education. *Artes liberales* was the Latin translation of *enkyklios paideia*, Greek for general education.

a manifestation of intelligence defense values, both of which thrive in academic circles.[54] The purpose of acquiring knowledge is to guide choices and actions and enhance life, which last is achieved primarily through productive work in the marketplace; the aim of acquiring knowledge is not to prove to some educational authority that one is "well-rounded," whatever that expression means. Indeed, the epithet "well-roundedness," a vague term at best, like Herbart's "many-sided interest," probably is a slap at egoism, designed to insinuate that anyone who is not well-rounded is selfish—self-absorbed, crude and vulgar, narrow and short-sighted, ill-developed, inconsiderate, etc. Add your own label. The distinction should be: educated for chosen purpose in life versus ignorant.

The debate over specialization versus general education in the last one hundred or more years stems from the progressives' concern for interest, motivation, and individual differences and the traditionalists' insistence on broad, liberal education for everyone.[55] The challenge, clearly, is to combine both. What about classical and medieval literature, not to mention non-western literature and culture? These, in a western culture, are specialties studied and taught by a small segment of the educated population. The free market will pay for them, albeit probably not to the extent that the scholars would like to be paid. Proper essentialization of history should cover these areas in general terms; a child whose curiosity is piqued by one or more of the fields can then pursue them in greater depth on his or her own by learning from the specialists in those fields.[56]

---

[54] An intelligence defense value says something to the effect, "I am good (or special) because I am smart." It carries with it, as do all defense values, an air of superiority over others and, often, a compulsion to demonstrate the superiority. "An Interview with Edith Packer on Psychotherapy (Part II)," interview by Jerry Kirkpatrick, *The Intellectual Activist*, May 1994, 15–18. Cf. Karen Horney, *Neurosis and Human Growth: The Struggle toward Self-Realization* (New York: W. W. Norton, 1950), 17–39.

[55] Diane Ravitch, *The Schools We Deserve* (New York: Basic Books, 1985), 88. The progressives, though, held mixed premises. Lawrence Cremin, in *The Transformation of the School* (New York: Vintage Books, 1961), 201, credits Malcolm Crowley with suggesting that progressive educators combined "two quite different sorts of revolt: bohemianism and radicalism. The one was essentially an individual revolt against puritan restraint; the other, primarily a social revolt against the evils of capitalism." I support the former revolt, not the latter.

[56] Although I enjoyed studying both in my school years, the Latin and Greek languages certainly do not have to be learned by every child. Vocabulary exercises that emphasize Latin and Greek roots can be, and have been, developed to deepen

What about the child who wants to do nothing but play the piano or compete at gymnastics? There are such children today and their education does not suffer. Some have private tutors; others work long hours, attending school and pursuing their special interests. It must be remembered that parents do have a say in the child's education. If raised in a loving and multi-value environment—meaning that the child is not retreating into music or sports as an escape from parental turmoil or being coerced and manipulated by "stage mother" parents—the child should have a strong curiosity to learn related subjects and skills. An astute music teacher, for example, could repeatedly bring up the physics of sound, the chemistry of the materials musical instruments are made of, and the relation of music to the other arts and literature. By reading constantly, the composer Johannes Brahms gave himself an extensive general education, acquiring over his lifetime a sizeable library. (Sometimes as a young man he supposedly even read books while playing the piano for money in dance halls).[57]

Subject Matter vs. Interdisciplinary Studies. The debate between traditionalists and progressives over this topic has not justified the amount of ink it has consumed. All knowledge is interconnected, which means that disciplines or subject matters are identified and separated only by abstraction. This, however, does not mean that the disciplines are less real than the integrated whole. Indeed, there is an epistemological efficiency in breaking knowledge into disciplines for teaching purposes. Epistemologically, a specific discipline is isolated from its related fields, studied in detail as a distinct subject, then put back together with the parental and sibling fields. That subjects today are not connected to one another, but often are taught in complete isolation, and that students do not see or understand the connections, is an indictment of the teaching profession, not of the notion of subject matter or separate disciplines.

Interdisciplinary courses may have their place in education—if well taught—but the same can be said for subject matter courses. Execution, and knowing how to execute properly, is crucial for getting things done. This applies especially so to successful teaching.

---

the child's understanding of language. What I lament most in recent times is the demise of Roman numerals, particularly the use of "M," as in "5M" for 5000, which, of course, has now become "5K."

[57] Paul Holmes, *Brahms: His Life and Times* (Southborough, England: Baton Press, 1984), 12–13. Jan Swafford, *Johannes Brahms: A Biography* (New York: Random House, 1997), 29.

CONCENTRATED ATTENTION AND POLITICAL FREEDOM

Intensive and sustained attention requires the absence of interruption. In an educational context, the relationship between teacher and student (and student's parents) is one of voluntary cooperation. When third party intervention enters the picture, as happens when the government becomes involved in education, dictating purpose, method, and content, concentrated attention breaks down. Political freedom, the absence of governmental interference, is prerequisite to sound education. The theory of concentrated attention, therefore, requires private entrepreneurs to train, in a civil and respectful manner, knowledgeably productive and self-reliant citizens of a free society.

5

Bureaucracy and Education

There are two methods for the conduct of affairs within the frame of human society, i.e., peaceful cooperation among men. One is bureaucratic management, the other is profit management.

—Ludwig von Mises[1]

SPONTANEOUS ACTIVITY IN EDUCATION requires spontaneous activity in economic life, and vice versa. The one reinforces the other.

The term "spontaneous" means natural and self-generated, not subject to external constraint or cause. Thus, in education children are free to choose what they want to learn according to their own interests and at their own pace; similarly, in a free society citizens are free to choose their own goals and to pursue them according to their own values and abilities. The "unplanned," spontaneous order of capitalism needs the countless plans of independent, individual minds trained in a free market in education so as to extend the division of labor to more innovative areas of production, thereby increasing the wealth of everyone. The "unplanned" and spontaneous free market in education needs the countless plans of educational entrepreneurs, some of whom may be geniuses, to develop and execute innovative approaches to education, thereby extending the power of free-market education to further cultivate independence of thought and satisfaction in life. The trappings and mentality of bureaucracy, however, thwart both systems.

---

[1] *Bureaucracy* (1944; repr., Cedar Falls, IA: Center for Futures Education, 1983), v.

The organizational structure of education is the subject of this chapter. Because a system of free-market education, or anything resembling it, has never existed, it is easier to explain what a free market in education is not than to project what it actually might become, if allowed to develop. The chapter, therefore, begins with a discussion of bureaucratic management and its influence on education as we have come to know it. Next, a suggested description is presented—including caveats that its structure ultimately would be determined by the interaction of entrepreneurs and paying customers—of a for-profit educational service market. Finally, the chapter concludes with a discussion of privatization and how the transition to a free market in education might be accomplished.

BUREAUCRACY AND ITS TRAPPINGS

Capitalism is a radical idea, little understood today. The notion of free-market education is even more radical and less understood.

In academic circles the doctrine of pure and perfect competition masquerades as the theory of laissez-faire capitalism and late nineteenth century America poses as capitalism's history. Intellectual leaders, politicians, the press, and the general public are clueless about capitalism's true nature and value; most are social liberals and hold unacknowledged Marxist premises, along with the Enlightenment view that universal education means government-provided, compulsory education.[2] Of those who do understand the correct theory and history of capitalism, many do not fully appreciate the mechanism by which a free market in education would work. They assume that such accompaniments of our current bureaucratic system as grades, examinations, credits, degrees, and even academic freedom, tenure, and accreditation would exist—but be more objective and fair—in a free market. To understand what a free market in education would be like, we must first turn to a discussion of bureaucracy and bureaucratic management.

Bureaucratic Management[3]

Bureaucratic management is the planning, implementation, and control of actions required by governments to administer their laws and affairs.

---

[2] Most conservatives hold the same Marxist premises and Enlightenment view of education.

[3] The following discussion relies heavily on Ludwig von Mises, *Bureaucracy*; Mises, *Socialism*, trans. J. Kahane (1936; repr., Indianapolis, IN: Liberty Classics, 1981), 163–65, 190–91; Mises, *Human Action*, 3rd rev. ed. (Chicago: Henry Regnery Company, 1966), 303–11.

Rules, derived from the laws, and a budget, handed down by a higher author-ity, ultimately the executive, legislative, and judicial branches of govern-ment, are the vehicles by which the laws of the land are implemented and executed in the various governmental bureaus. Because governments hold the legal monopoly on the use of physical force, bureaucratic management can be described as the management of coercion. Under capitalism the police, military, and courts of law, as well as executive, legislative, and judi-cial branches of government, are bureaucracies; the rest of society is run by private businesses following the principles of profit or entrepreneurial management. A socialist system is totally bureaucratic—one organization in which everyone is a hired employee of the state.[4] A mixed economy exhibits bureaucratic management (beyond the minimum required for a capitalist society) to the degree that the government intervenes in the economy by regulating and taking over private businesses.

Profit or entrepreneurial management is the planning, implementation, and control of actions required by private businesses to produce need- and want-satisfying, profit-making products for the market. No rules or regu-lations, other than the laws against violating individual rights, control the decisions and actions of entrepreneurs. Making a profit is the entrepreneurs' ultimate goal and the means to that end is customer satisfaction. Form of organization, financial structure (which includes budgets for the various departments), selection of personnel, product design and development, pricing, advertising, and distribution are all determined by the compa-ny's projected success in the marketplace. The criterion of a decision's or action's success is its contribution to profit through customer satisfaction.[5] Bureaucratic management has no such standard of economic calculation; its sole measure is compliance with the rules and budget established by the higher authority.

Because its decision-making is guided by the free interaction of buyer and seller, profit management can be described as the man-agement of voluntary cooperation; coercive interference by outsiders,

---

[4] Lenin and other socialist writers likened the socialist state to a giant post office. V. I. Lenin, *State and Revolution* (1917; repr., New York: International Publishers, 1988), 43–44, 83–84.

[5] Effective executives, according to management consultant Peter Drucker, focus on contribution to results of the organizations they serve, not on compliance to policies or rules. Drucker's criteria are broad enough to be applied to bureaucratic managers, but only private businesses have the added yardstick of profit through customer satisfaction. Peter Drucker, *The Effective Executive* (New York: Harper & Row, 1966), 52.

especially the government, is forbidden by laws against the violation of individual rights. When intervention does occur, in the form of government regulation, the entrepreneur's attention is deflected from customer satisfaction and profit making to compliance with the law. A breach between the normal affairs of business management and customer satisfaction has been established. The entrepreneur becomes a bureaucrat. To the extent that private businesses are regulated by the government—by rules and laws that go beyond the protection of individual rights—to that extent they will be bureaucratic, that is, to that extent they will cease to be private businesses and will become bureaus of the state.

Bureaucratic management is "top down," backed by the coercive powers of the state. Profit management is "bottom up," backed only by success at winning and continually satisfying paying customers. When a complaint is made to a bureaucrat, the response often is (in style and content, if not also in actual words): "Rules are rules, fella; I don't make 'em, I just enforce 'em." When made to a private business, the response is, or should be: "I'm sorry. That won't happen again. I will take care of your problem." Individual bureaucrats can be helpful, even innovative, and individual entrepreneurs, or their employees, can be rude and obtuse, but bureaucrats keep their jobs by complying with rules, not by being nice, whereas in a free market rude entrepreneurs can lose customers to competitors who advertise—and deliver—pleasantness. When a business begins to sound like a bureaucracy, one must look for the government regulations that redirect attention of the workers away from customer satisfaction to conformity to a rule.

That customer satisfaction is the means to the end of making a profit has been well established by capitalist economists.[6] Marx and the socialists (and Plato) are wrong. Bureaucrats are not omniscient and therefore cannot know what every customer's needs and wants are. Regulations of business, in addition to violating the rights of buyer and seller to voluntarily negotiate an agreement, impose by law what the bureaucrats—that is, the philosopher-kings or, today, the PhD-kings— think the customers should need or want.

Today's mixed economy is exceedingly bureaucratic, because all businesses are highly regulated and many are owned outright and operated by the government. The post office, for example, is a socialized

---

[6] See, especially, economists of the Austrian school, for example, Mises, *Human Action*, passim.

business at the national level; it enjoys the pretense of economic calculation and responsiveness to the market by being able to subtract
costs from revenues and to conduct marketing research surveys. Over-
whelmingly, however, it is a rule-bound, regulation-driven bureau of
the state. Its monopoly on the delivery of first class mail only magnifies
its insensitivity to the criterion of customer satisfaction. Such "private"
businesses as utilities, insurance companies, and banks are de facto
bureaus of the government, run ostensibly as private businesses, but
sanctioned and regulated as monopolies and cartels of the city, state,
or federal governments. At the other end of the spectrum, sole proprietors in small towns become bureaucratic when they must obtain
city and county licenses, purchase permits, and comply with zoning
regulations. As small businesses grow, in numbers of employees and
sales revenues, increasing quantities of regulations become applicable
to them and must be met.

Compliance to rules and regulations usually requires a form to be
filled out, hence the well-known paperwork of bureaucracies. If the
rules and regulations are not complied with or the forms are not filled
out correctly, hands may be slapped, or fines or imprisonment may
be imposed. As small businesses grow, so does their paperwork—and
the threats of hand slapping, fine imposition, and imprisonment. Some
paperwork naturally exists in private, free-market businesses, but not
much. Job applications are one example, but note the difference in attitude between private businesses and government agencies. In the fine
print at the bottom of job applications for private businesses, a comment usually reads something like: "If any statement in this application
is false or misleading, the new hire may be dismissed." For the government agency, the fine print adds: "or fined or imprisoned."[7]

The reason private businesses do not generate volumes of paper is
that paperwork tends to ossify decisions into command and control
rules. The market, however, is constantly changing. Businesses are not
run by rules, but by general guidelines, typically called policies, that
to a great extent help define the nature of the business based on the
products it sells and the customers it serves. Whenever either one of
these two variables changes, product or customer, so must the policies
change in order to keep the company moving toward greater profits

---

[7] This is the difference between economic and political power. The government
agency brandishes a gun, backed by the police power of the state. The private business only benefits from the power of persuasion. See chap. 1, p. 34.

and customer satisfaction. Bureaucratic rules and regulations often fly in the face of what needs to be done to increase profits and customer satisfaction. A strong incentive therefore exists to ignore or to find loopholes in the rules and regulations.

Bureaucratic intrusions into the marketplace are a major cause of so-called business corruption. Mixed economies often are correctly described as "government by lobby," because groups of businesses, labor unions, and other organizations—lobbies or special interests, in other words—are constantly vying with one another for government handouts and privileges. Temptation to manipulate government officials and to offer monetary incentives is strong. The temptation, naturally, works the other way, and probably more strongly, with bureaucrats harassing and threatening entrepreneurs, lest the latter produce certain payments and other perks for the bureaucrats. The solution here is to remove government from all business affairs.[8]

It must be emphasized at this point that private nonprofit organizations are bureaucracies as much as the post office or public schools and government-run universities. Like the post office, nonprofits can subtract expenses from revenues or donations and put on a pretense of profit management. (Most, however, abhor such a thought.) At root they are creatures of the state. Nonprofit organizations exist by virtue of the tax laws.[9] Management attention, thus, must often be focused on the tax consequences of action, and on other regulations governing nonprofits, not always on the interests of the nonprofits' constituencies.[10] The significance of this is that today's private schools, nearly all of which are operated as nonprofit organizations, do not remotely constitute a model of what a free market in education might be like.

---

[8] Gary S. Becker, "If You Want to Cut Corruption, Cut Government," *Business Week*, December 11, 1995, 26. Bribes and grease payments are more common in countries that are heavily bureaucratic. Black markets are free markets trying to operate under the burden of regulation; because of their illegality and the threat of imprisonment or worse, black markets tend to attract the less savory elements of society. Getting the government out of business and vice versa, not stiffer penalties, is the way to eliminate black market trade and corruption.

[9] "Nonprofit" means that any excess of revenues or donations over expenses cannot be distributed to members or donors, as can be accomplished in for-profit organizations. Some nonprofits are indeed highly profitable!

[10] Under capitalism, philanthropies would be operated as profit-making institutions. This includes charitable foundations set up for the sole purpose of giving away money; the fund of money to be given away is invested to earn income, while the management of the organization incurs expenses that are deducted from the income.

The small percentage of for-profit private schools that do exist must still comply with the many regulations that govern education at the national, state, and local levels. Add the socialized nature of the education market in which they must compete, as well as the mimicking of their socialized competitors, and private schools today, it must be concluded, are highly bureaucratic.

Contrary to the conventional wisdom of social liberals, which includes management writers and professors, private corporations today are not bureaucratic because they are large, hierarchically structured organizations with several layers of management. They are bureaucratic because they must comply with so many government regulations that they have become virtual bureaus of the state. The conventional view of bureaucracy makes no distinction between government-run and private, profit-making organizations. Size, structure, and chain of command in this view make an organization bureaucratic. These characteristics, however, are not fundamental. The essential distinguishing characteristic of profit management, when contrasted with its bureaucratic version, is the ability to make decisions and to take actions based on market prices, that is, to make economic calculations of profit and loss. Bureaucrats have no such market-based yardstick. They only have the laws to tell them what to do.[11]

Bureaucratic Education

Like the post office, public elementary and secondary schools and state-run universities are socialized businesses; unlike the post office, they are not national institutions, although regulation of education in recent decades has become more and more nationalized. Elementary and secondary schools are controlled at the local level but must comply with state regulations, as well as federal laws that apply. State-run universities are state institutions, but they also must comply with federal laws. And private schools and universities are subject to state regulations and federal laws. Bureaucratic education is so rule-bound and regulation-driven that it is best described as a monopoly or medieval guild—there is little difference. First, the monopoly.

---

[11] Mises, *Bureaucracy*, 22–31. The conventional view of bureaucracy, as understood by social liberals and management professors, comes in large part from the German sociologist Max Weber. See "Bureaucracy," trans. H. H. Gerth and C. Wright Mills, in S. N. Eisenstadt, ed., *Max Weber on Charisma and Institution Building* (Chicago: University of Chicago Press, 1968), 66–77. Cf. William P. Anderson, "Mises versus Weber on Bureaucracy and Sociological Method," *Journal of Libertarian Studies* 18, no. 1 (Winter 2004): 1–29.

The Education Monopoly. Any intrusion into the marketplace by government is monopoly in the political sense. Monopoly is a government-granted privilege that favors one group of entrepreneurs, workers, or consumers at the expense of others who would otherwise compete with the favored. The privilege is maintained by initiating physical force against those others, through various laws and regulations, thereby hindering or preventing the others from entering the market. Government ownership of a business, as in the case of the post office and schools, is the most obvious form of such monopoly, but occupational licensure, protective tariffs, minimum-wage and pro-union legislation, antitrust laws, and government franchises granted to utilities also constitute monopolistic favoring of some at the expense of others. In this political sense of monopoly the socialist state is not only totally bureaucratic; it is also the one giant monopoly that Marxists for decades have accused capitalism of moving toward.[12]

The alleged motive for such monopolistic legislation is to protect smaller businesses, workers, or consumers from untrammeled business practices. The actual effect, and often the real motive, is to restrict the market to the control of the monopolists. Sometimes, because of a restricted supply, the favored few enjoy high prices, wages, and profits, as in the case of the medical and legal professions and labor unions. Primarily, the goal is to dictate who will produce what, in which quantities, and who will distribute what, to whom, in which quantities. Prices, wages, and profits may or may not be directly controlled by the government. In government-run education, though, everything is controlled. Teachers and professors may not make as much money as trial lawyers and surgeons, but their market is just as monopolized, if not more so.

The education monopoly in the United States is not as restrictive as that of the post office, or as education monopolies in other countries, because private schools are allowed to compete (to some extent) and regulation is not totally nationalized. Nevertheless, distortions in the

---

[12] George Reisman, *Capitalism: A Treatise on Economics* (Ottawa, IL: Jameson Books, 1996), 376–87. The economic concept of monopoly as a single seller in a defined market, Reisman goes on to point out, is an invalid concept, because when examined carefully either everyone is a monopolist or no one is. Ibid., 389–92. Cf. Yale Brozen, *Is Government the Source of Monopoly? And Other Essays* (San Francisco: Cato Institute, 1980) and Murray Rothbard, *Man, Economy, and State: A Treatise on Economic Principles* (1962; repr., Los Angeles: Nash Publishing, 1970), 2 vols. in one, vol. 2, 585–93.

educational marketplace that otherwise would not exist in a free market are noticeable, most particularly the discrepancy between tuitions charged by public, government-run schools and their private counterparts. This discrepancy stems from the same source as the disparity that exists in rents between controlled and uncontrolled rental apartments in such cities as New York. Both distortions are caused by price controls designed to favor one group of consumers at the expense of others. Those others must then subsidize the controlled apartments and schools and the full costs of their own operations with abnormally high prices; decontrol of both markets would produce prices somewhere in between the highs and lows of the private and controlled sectors.[13] The most significant distortions in the educational marketplace, however, stem from the guild-like paraphernalia of bureaucratic management, all of which affect the quality of service provided.

The Education Guild. Government control of education is said to be necessary in order to protect parents and students from the alleged ruthlessness and inferior quality of free-market profit-seeking. The result of control, however, is to create a closed brotherhood not unlike that of medieval guilds. Indeed, modern educational institutions, particularly universities, originated in the Middle Ages as guilds.[14] Today, their character is essentially unchanged,[15] and their aim, as in guilds, is to control production and distribution.

---

[13] Reisman, *Capitalism*, 240–41, 248–54. Under capitalism, real prices decline. The highs and lows of the above examples exist in our current mixed economy. In a free market, there is no reason to doubt that the real costs of education (or rental apartments) would fall below the current nominal rates.

[14] James Bowen, *A History of Western Education*, vol. 2, *Civilization of Europe* (New York: St. Martin's Press, 1975), 42–44.

[15] "What about the academic regalia—all those Medieval robes, caps and hoods?" asks Thomas L. Johnson in *The Real Academic Community and the Rational Alternative* (Fredericksburg, VA: Lee Editions, 1980), 136. Would one find such attire in a free market of education businesses? "It is true," says Johnson, "that certain businesses do have their employees dressed in similar outfits, or many businesses have a particular character, like a clown, dressed in a certain way and acting as a representative or symbol of the business. But one does not find, as one does in the academic community, a group of academic 'clowns'—the professors, administrators, and board members—dressed in Medieval clerical garb forming and marching in academic processions that look almost identical to religious processions.... Titles and robes are always found wherever one group of people is trying to lord it over another group of people. Kings and dictators get themselves up in fancy costumes and demand that they be called by an array of titles. Military and academic personnel do the same. But not businessmen."

One distinctive characteristic of medieval guilds was the special project or "masterpiece," a kind of final examination that journeymen had to complete in order to become masters. The purpose of the "masterpiece" was to determine who should be allowed to become a full member of the guild. In the universities, which had organized themselves during the Middle Ages on the model of craft and merchant guilds, students who completed final examinations were granted a certificate, the *licentia docendi*, or license to teach. Thus, the modern degree came into existence as an occupational license, granted by the church, the governing body of the time. In later centuries, the state took over as dispenser of degrees. Examinations were required in order to determine who deserved the license.[16]

The use of a qualifying examination is not unique to education or to medieval guilds; it is an essential characteristic of bureaucracy. Without a market-based yardstick to help make personnel decisions, bureaucracy usually falls back on patronage. To avoid the arbitrariness inherent in patronage systems, and thereby to set up an alleged objective measure of talent, bureaucratic management employs the examination as a means of screening applicants.[17] The model of modern bureaucracy is nineteenth century Prussia, brought to the United States as the Pendleton Civil Service Act of 1883.[18] The

---

[16] Bowen, *Civilization of Europe*, 119. Charles Homer Haskins, *The Rise of Universities* (1923; repr., Ithaca, NY: Cornell University Press, 1957), 11. Gabriel Compayré, *Abelard and the Origin and Early History of Universities* (1893; repr., New York: Greenwood Press, 1969) 139–64.

[17] The church, which controlled medieval schooling, was, and continues to be, a bureaucracy. It was modeled originally on the bureaucracy of the Roman Empire. The first civil service examinations came into existence during the early Han dynasty in China (206 BC - AD 220). William A. Smith, *Ancient Education* (New York: Philosophical Library, 1955), 83–86. The Chinese examination system was admired by Europeans and brought to Europe in earnest during the eighteenth and nineteenth centuries. Teng Ssu-Yu, "China's Examination System and the West," in Harley Farnsworth MacNair, ed., *China* (Berkeley and Los Angeles: University of California Press, 1951), 441–51. The Roman Empire sparingly used competitive examinations and then only to select certain teachers, especially rhetors and grammarians; examinations seem not to have been used for any other governmental service. H. I. Marrou, *A History of Education in Antiquity*, trans. George Lamb (1956; repr., New York: Mentor Books, 1964), 409–11. Examinations of any kind were rare in Greek and Roman schools. Evaluative grades (or marks) and degrees were nonexistent.

[18] Murray N. Rothbard, "Bureaucracy and the Civil Service in the United States," *Journal of Libertarian Studies* 11, no. 2 (Summer 1995): 3–75. The solution recommended by the Founding Fathers of the United States to an entrenched

problem with examinations is that the choice and wording of questions can be just as arbitrary and subjective as a patron's judgment. The examination system in bureaucracy—and in education—is a pretense at objectivity.[19]

The Paraphernalia of Bureaucratic Management.[20] Examinations, grades, credits, degrees, accreditation, as well as academic freedom and tenure, are all trappings of bureaucratic intrusions into the educational marketplace. They are extensions of the rules and regulations required, as in any monopoly or guild, to control the production and distribution of education. They are the certifications that give rise to the epithet: "Today, we live in a credentialed society." They are in fact the rewards and punishments that accompany the modern forms of status and privilege granted by the government. They are the trappings of authoritarianism.

Compulsory education laws are explicitly authoritarian, but what drives bureaucratic education is the degree. The degree is a standardized piece of paper that can only be granted to students who have completed a series of examinations and earned certain grades and numbers of credits, all in an accredited school. The degree does not indicate amount of knowledge learned or qualification for a particular job in the free market. And it is standardized only in the sense that the pieces of paper from various schools say the same thing, namely "High School Diploma" or "Bachelor of Arts." The programs of study in the various

---

bureaucracy was "compulsory rotation in office." Patronage was endorsed, provided the patron's term in office was short.

[19] Testing is a contrived situation that seldom corresponds to the reality it is supposed to represent. Supermarket shoppers in one study performed arithmetic calculations far more accurately in the store than on a formal test. Jean Lave, Michael Murtaugh, and Olivia de la Rocha, "The Dialectic of Arithmetic in Grocery Shopping," in Barbara Rogoff and Jean Lave, eds., *Everyday Cognition: Its Development in Social Context* (Cambridge, MA: Harvard University Press, 1984), 67–94. And one boy, considered the dumbest in his class, was discovered by his teacher to be a paid scorekeeper in a bowling alley, simultaneously tracking the progress of two teams of four players each. The teacher promptly created word problems, requiring students to calculate scores for games of bowling. The boy could not do the problems. James Herndon, *How to Survive in Your Native Land* (New York: Bantam Books, 1972), 92–97. Test-taking is a skill that can be learned, but "why learn it?" is a question that has not been well answered, other than to please some authority who will then issue a certificate of passage. (Scorekeeping at bowling is something that I, a PhD holder, have not yet mastered!)

[20] Much of the following is indebted to the difficult-to-find and unjustly neglected book by Thomas L. Johnson, *The Real Academic Community and the Rational Alternative*, cited above in footnote 15.

schools are anything but standardized. As such, the degree is a sham. (In some countries, such as Japan, where the curriculum is dictated and controlled at the national level, a high degree of standardization may be achieved, but at the price of considerable regimentation.)

At best—and worst—the degree is a credential, or union card, that allows one to join the club of the educated and to enter the bureaucratized workplace. The higher the status of the school, the higher the station in the workplace the student enters. In the United States, where the economy remains adequately free and upward mobility is relatively uninhibited, high school and college dropouts can sometimes still outshine holders of PhD degrees. In less free countries, however, students may be shunted into vocational school and a blue collar life based on examination scores in the sixth or eighth grade, with little or no hope of subsequent improvement. Bureaucratic education is designed to direct students into areas that the "expert" bureaucrats think the students should go.[21]

It is true that in the last one hundred years educational bureaucrats worldwide, more or less, have promoted education as the means of advancement, and generally this has been successful. More people today acquire some knowledge, to help them advance, than their counterparts of a hundred years ago; what they learn today, however, is probably less intensive or in-depth than what the few learned in the past.[22] Nevertheless, status and privilege are inherent in the system. Status, because position in society depends on which school or university the student attends. Privilege, because the government controls the spoils—the special titles of "diplomate," "bachelor," "master," or "doctor"—by selectively dispensing the degrees. Status and privilege are unearned advantages that the free market erases; failure to achieve status and privilege is an unearned disadvantage that the free market corrects. Freedom of opportunity is the norm under capitalism.[23]

---

[21] Rule by experts, along with the restriction of supply, is the essence and motive of licensing. See S. David Young, *The Rule of Experts: Occupational Licensing in America* (Washington, D.C.: Cato Institute, 1987).

[22] Extensiveness, rather than intensiveness, has been the primary goal of progressive education. Extensiveness versus intensiveness is the core of much debate between the progressives and traditionalists.

[23] It is also true that bureaucratic education, both in the United States and elsewhere, is based to some extent on merit, meaning that students who are graduated have probably learned something. This is because bureaucratic management of private businesses still retains some legitimacy of the business. The post office

The question that must be answered is: Why would these trappings of bureaucratic management not exist in a free market? The answer: For the same reason that there are no certifications granted to shoe buyers and classical music concert attendees. In a free market customers are not examined, graded, and anointed with a credential that says "good shoe buying behavior" or "weak appreciation of classical music," with an added scolding that reads "you didn't do your homework before attending this concert, did you?" In a free market the customers examine and grade the sellers of goods and services, not the other way around. Seller reputation then determines, among the competing entrepreneurs, who succeeds or not.

Educational entrepreneurs in a free market hang out shingles that say something to the effect: "Ideas For Sale" or "Knowledge For Sale." Parents and students then buy educational services based on their needs and wants (interests) and their judgments of which entrepreneurs are most likely to meet the needs and wants. Entrepreneurs teach by catering to the students' individual differences as much as possible. If some students are slower than others, entrepreneurs cannot flunk them and boast of their schools' high rejection rates because that would result in losses of revenue; rather, the entrepreneurs must innovate and discover methods of reaching the slower students or go out of business.[24] Employers hire students based on the reputations of the teachers the students studied with; in the more technical fields some employers might choose to administer, as part of the interviewing process, a brief qualifying examination to applicants, to be assured that the new hires possess the required knowledge for the job.

In this scenario of a free market in education, reputation, not degrees (or licenses or rules and regulations), guide choices and actions. Reputation is the collection of value judgments market participants hold about how well a particular entrepreneur has met the customers'

---

still delivers mail, albeit not as efficiently, inexpensively, or often as it might if it were privatized and freed of regulations. Similarly, bureaucratic education, one does have to admit, still attempts to educate students. Those who pass and pass with honors have indeed earned recognition for their accomplishments. From the perspective of free-market analysis, however, it is a question of exactly what did these students learn, what might they have learned in a truly free market, and, more importantly, what about the losers in the system?

[24] See Robert Love, *How to Start Your Own School* (Ottawa, IL: Green Hill Publishers, 1973), 76–83, for a discussion of how this point was impressed on the teachers of a traditionally run private school. Viewing the students (and their parents) as customers meant that expulsion was not an option, unless the teacher had an alternative plan for replacing the lost revenue.

needs and wants. Entrepreneurs with poor reputations do not last long in the market, unless they are propped up by bureaucratic interventions. Compliance to the rules and regulations governing degrees, which in practice means compliance to accreditation requirements, says little about meeting the actual needs and wants of educational customers. Thus, despite voluminous complaints of educational customers today about bureaucratic indifference, many flagrantly incompetent schools remain in "business" because they have complied with the rules.

Accrediting commissions in the United States boast that they are voluntary, non-governmental institutions, yet they also note that they came into existence in the early twentieth century to fend off outright government takeover of standard setting in education.[25] This defensive maneuver to establish self-regulating accrediting commissions immediately makes the commissions creatures of the state and makes accreditation a governmental function.[26] Today, accrediting commissions owe their existence to the U. S. Department of Education. While accreditation is technically voluntary and means little to students, it means a great deal to school administrations. Government favors, especially money, come only with strings attached, meaning that the school must be accredited.

In the absence of accreditation, or direct government regulation of education, degrees probably would not exist in a free market. The entrepreneur's name or the school's name would represent the quality of education received. When reputation is allowed to perform its role in a free market, pieces of paper called degrees, licenses, and seals of approval become superfluous. In addition, there is no need in the free market for such broad scale standardization as the degree allegedly represents. As markets mature, products do tend to become standardized, but not completely so, because needs and wants still vary from individual to

---

[25] *WASC Accreditation Handbook* (Alameda, CA, 2001) 8. Also available online at http://www.wascsenior.org/wasc/Doc_Lib/2001%20Handbook.pdf. The telephone companies at about the same time were spared nationalization by being granted "natural monopoly" status, which means they remained technically private but were regulated by the government. Accrediting commissions are "natural monopolies" in education certification.

[26] "Self-regulation" of any kind is antithetical to the free market and represents a defense against governmental regulation or takeover. Some students of the free market, in exasperation and ignoring the power and significance of reputation, still protest, "There has to be some form of accreditation or certification!" But the proper response to this protest is: Who will accredit the accreditors? Who will certify the certifiers?

individual and innovation shakes up the standardized models. There is no reason to think this variation and innovation would not also occur in a free market in education. This means that there likely would be no core or standardized curriculum in free-market schools.

If degrees are absent, credits, grades, and examinations are also not likely to exist in a free market in education. Credits are merely a counting system for the modern cafeteria style of curriculum: accumulate so many credits and the degree is granted. In earlier years, when every student took the same courses, credits were not necessary. Examinations (broadly construed to include term papers and other types of assignments) are needed to qualify for the degree. Grades are rankings of students on the examinations; a cutoff point determines who passes, and therefore progresses toward the degree, and who does not. Grades do not necessarily indicate what students have learned. Grades are rewards and punishments handed out by the agents of bureaucracy, the teachers. The red ink pen is the teacher's gun.

That the red ink pen is a gun can be seen from the cringe students exhibit when teachers pull out their pens. Students are servile, even the so-called good ones, and cower in fear of what the powerful teachers might do to them. Teachers possess political power by virtue of the authoritarianism imbued in the bureaucratic system. The rules and regulations of education compel teachers to treat students as numbers on a roster that must be summed, averaged, and ranked in order to determine who advances and who does not. The monopolistic nature of the system prevents students from taking their business elsewhere, because there is no elsewhere to go; all schools must comply with the same regulations. In a free market the entrepreneur is the one who cringes at the fear of losing customers to the competition. Irate customers can demand changes in the product or the return of their money. Students today do not dare show anger at their teachers, lest their grades suffer.[27]

In the absence of government involvement in education, the issue of academic freedom and tenure becomes moot. Protection of individual rights under capitalism guarantees the freedom to speak, teach, and write whatever one wants, provided the listeners, learners, and readers are listening, learning, and reading voluntarily, that is, through mutual agreement. Similarly, the protection of individual rights also

---

[27] On the servility of students, see Craig Haney and Phillip Zimbardo, "It's Tough to Tell a High School from a Prison," *Psychology Today*, June 1975.

guarantees the right of entrepreneurs and employees to voluntarily agree upon terms of employment, lifetime or otherwise. Academic freedom arose in a bureaucratic system in which the church, then the state, sought to control what was taught and written; today, it is the means by which the establishment of tenured faculty dictates politically safe doctrine.[28] In a free market tenure would be a joke. It is a major source of poor quality education.

Bureaucratic Competition. Bureaucratic intrusions into the marketplace create the credentialed society we now live in by deflecting attention away from the genuine interests of consumers to the rules, regulations, and certifications required by the government. The credentialed society produces an unhealthy form of competition that is the opposite of its free-market counterpart. Economic competition is a rivalry among entrepreneurs for the same, finite source of revenue.[29] The means of winning this rivalry is to please consumers, by producing better products, in greater quantities at lower prices, than the competition. In economic competition consumers exert their power of the purse to influence entrepreneurs and the course of production and distribution. Bureaucratic competition, on the other hand, because of distortions created in the marketplace, such as an artificially restricted supply, is a rivalry among consumers for the limited goods and services available. It is akin to competition in the animal kingdom in which the food available is strictly limited by nature.[30] In education bureaucratic competition is a rivalry among students for the limited grades and degrees that are doled out by the authorities.[31]

The scramble for a limited supply of credentials in education, that is, for grades and degrees, is sometimes acknowledged by critics as a cause

---

[28] Or, as in Europe, it means that the faculty agree with the government's viewpoint. Mises, *Bureaucracy*, 81–83.

[29] An expanding quantity of money, caused by credit expansion or the printing press, is a bureaucratic intrusion that distorts the operation of economic competition, by favoring those who get the newly created money first.

[30] Reisman, *Capitalism*, 343–45. Cf. Mises, *Human Action*, 273–79. Workers in a free market compete with one another for a finite amount of money available for wage payments, but consumers rarely compete with each other for products. Strong demand signals entrepreneurs to produce greater quantities of products.

[31] Grade and degree inflation are just another symptom of bureaucratic subjectivity. The existence of grade inflation, though, is disputed in Alfie Kohn, "The Dangerous Myth of Grade Inflation," *The Chronicle of Higher Education*, November 8, 2002. Available online with update and references at http://www.alfiekohn.org/teaching/gi.htm.

of the noticeable decrease in curiosity and enthusiasm for learning in the classroom that students exhibit by the age of ten (fifth grade). "Children come to school *curious*," says John Holt; "within a few years most of that curiosity is dead, or at least silent. Open a first or third grade to questions, and you will be deluged; fifth-graders say nothing. They either have no questions or will not ask them. They think, 'What's this leading up to? What's the catch?'...Curiosity, questions, speculation—these are for outside school, not inside."[32] Holt's solution, near the end of his short life, was to abandon the state-run system and promote home schooling, which itself is subject to a host of bureaucratic regulations.

Some critics mistakenly equate bureaucratic and economic competition. The phrase, "it's being turned into a business," has been used to describe both the medical profession and education. Both, however, are being turned more and more, as the decades go by, into bureaus of the state, rather than businesses. The medical profession, because it is now dominated by health maintenance organizations, which are creatures of the state, and education, because it is increasingly becoming nationalized by federal regulations. References to "bottom line" management in both fields are attempts by the bureaucrats to imitate profit management, but there is no unfettered market to make true economic calculation possible. Both professions were bureaucratic long before the advent of recent developments; it is just that bureaucratic management, and the bureaucratic form of competition, has increased its grip in recent decades.[33]

Education and social critic Alfie Kohn, failing to distinguish the two forms of competition and, in particular, to understand the economic variety, states, "The more closely I have examined the topic, the more firmly I have become convinced that competition is an inherently undesirable arrangement, that the phrase *healthy*

---

[32] John Holt, *How Children Fail*, rev. ed. (Reading, MA: Perseus Books, 1982), 263. Emphasis in original.

[33] In a similar vein, performance evaluations in private businesses have become bureaucratized by regulations, requiring employees to produce reams of paper in order to compete with one another for limited favorable ratings from their bosses, lest they not get a raise, or perhaps even be fired. "I hate it," referring to the process, is the refrain of those who go through it. The process is uncannily similar to the gauntlet that professors go through to get tenure.

competition is actually a contradiction in terms."[34] Bureaucratic competition in education *is* unhealthy, as Kohn demonstrates, and Kohn does identify an unhealthy side effect, namely that it encourages a "fight to the death" desperation that one sees in the animal kingdom.[35] Not physical desperation, but psychological. The comparative nature of the bureaucratic raffle and ultimate ranking of students generates in many winners an intelligence defense value; in the losers it produces a deep sense of inferiority. The projected worth of both types of student is misleading and unearned.

What gives bureaucratic competition its coercive sting is that everything the bureaucrat says and does is backed by the police power of the state. In economic competition entrepreneurs have no power to dispense government-granted privileges (licenses) to customers or incentive to give them gold stars or chastisement. In a free market in education modest examining or questioning may occur in the "do" (third) and "correct" (fourth) steps of the teaching and learning process discussed in chapter 4.[36] Such action will be undertaken only with the permission of the student (or parent) and certainly will not have the power or significance it has today. Ranking is less likely to occur because, by catering to individual differences, there will be no need for comparison or sorting and no readily available standard to do so. Games are usually a source of pleasure and can be a stimulus to improvement, so learning competitions may occur, but, again, without the importance they have today. In the broader context, economic competition among schools for customers and for placement of students in higher schools and in the workplace will occur.

Here is another instance that demonstrates the difference between bureaucratic and economic competition. It is sometimes said jokingly that what schools today produce and sell are students. The product of education is a student possessing certain credentials and the customers of a particular school are higher schools and the workplace. This is said jokingly but it also is true that the bureaucracy views the

---

[34] Alfie Kohn, *No Contest: The Case Against Competition*, rev. ed. (New York: Houghton Mifflin, 1992), 9. Emphasis in original. Kohn is a social liberal, which explains his antagonism to economic competition.

[35] Kohn does not make the allusion to the animal kingdom.

[36] See p. 122.

education marketplace in this manner. In a free market in education, however, the product of education is knowledge and the customers are the students. The higher schools are not buyers of students, but sellers of knowledge to the students who have purchased the services of the lower schools. The workplace, that is, businesses, are buyers of labor, and what entrepreneurs hire are employees possessing certain knowledge, values, and skills, not credentials. If students today feel like they are just numbers on a roster—or products on a shelf—that is exactly how the bureaucracy views them.

One further, unattractive point about bureaucratic competition needs to be made: the winners it produces sometimes are the less savory elements of society. Bureaucratic management means compliance to rules, not the creation of value. Focusing on rules, rather than on production, means adhering to and enforcing the coercive power of the government, rather than developing and executing need- and want-satisfying products. In varying degrees, greater or lesser, bureaucrats enjoy power. The more bureaucratic the society, the more power becomes a motivator.[37] In education this means that administrators, in varying degrees, value adhering to and enforcing the rules of the system; they also enjoy generating new rules to enforce. It means that faculty who spend much of their time fighting administrative battles, rather than teaching, enjoy the power struggle (or, at least, the perception of doing something important in the bureaucracy).

Students who succeed in the system, as they will gladly verify, are "good at the game." This means that they are good at bureaucratic education, which means they are good at taking examinations and writing term papers, or they are good at finding out what teachers want and feeding it back to them, or at grubbing for grades and grade changes, or at cheating. The students who are good at taking exams and writing term papers, it should be mentioned, do seem to learn something, although it is uncertain exactly what. In a credentialed society, though, where the credentials are backed by the state, cheating is encouraged. When extrinsic motivation prevails, rewards and the avoidance of punishment are what counts; the credential, not the

---

[37] In bureaucratic dictatorships, it is the worst who get to the top, as Friedrich A. Hayek demonstrated in *The Road to Serfdom* (Chicago: University of Chicago Press, 1944), 134–52, and Ayn Rand dramatized in her novels *We the Living* and *Atlas Shrugged*.

knowledge learned to acquire the credential, is the prize. Some students, perhaps many, will do whatever it takes to get the credential.

Bureaucracy and the *Theory of Concentrated Attention*. The intent of the theory of concentrated attention is to train knowledgeably productive and self-reliant citizens of a free (capitalist) society. The means to that goal is to allow private entrepreneurs to prepare a civil and respectful environment in which students are free to pursue their interests, develop intensive and sustained attention, and achieve independence of thought while acquiring the essential knowledge, values, and skills necessary to flourish under capitalism. The ultimate end is to nurture a purpose in life.

Bureaucracy and its trappings, it should be obvious by now, are inimical to this theory. Interruption, deflection, and command and control are the tools of bureaucratic intrusion into the marketplace. They are unethical and violate individual rights when used on private businesses and citizens; they are particularly harmful when used on teachers and students, because force and fear are the enemies of learning. Force, the unchosen rules and regulations of the bureaucrats, and fear, of punishment for noncompliance with the unchosen rules, shut down the mind or, at least, drive it underground. Force and fear prevent the emergence of individual selves, impede the growth of mental powers, and encourage the development, at once, of submissive and manipulative personalities. The ultimate end of bureaucratic education is obedience to authority.

We turn now to a suggested description of a for-profit educational service business, operating in a free market.

THE EDUCATIONAL SERVICE BUSINESS

The absence of grades and degrees, rules and regulations, and education czars in a free market in education raises the questions: What will the schools be like? And who will determine the purpose, method, and content of education?

The Free Market in Education

In answer to the second question: the market will decide. That is, education consumers and entrepreneurs, not government "experts," will have the power cooperatively to shape the market, by determining what, how, and to whom knowledge is to be provided. Entrepreneurs will provide the philosophy and infrastructure of education, perhaps following the theory of concentrated attention, perhaps not. No one will have the power to coerce them to follow any specific purpose, method, or content. Parents and their children will be the consumers and will provide the fees with which to purchase the entrepreneurs' services. Buying and abstaining from buying by consumers will ultimately determine which are the better schools and philosophy of education. If the premises of the theory of concentrated attention are based on fact, there should be a convergence of schools toward the theory's acceptance. Execution of the theory's tenets would still vary.

The first question, on the description of free-market schools, requires lengthier discussion. Any attempt to describe what does not exist is always risky, and I have no crystal ball to gaze into to see what might happen if a move to deregulate and privatize education were to occur. Nevertheless, certain projections can be made, based on the history of education and the nature of free-market services. The present distinctions between primary, secondary, and higher education derive from Hellenistic Greece and the notion of preschool education stems from post-Renaissance Europe. Because these divisions are based on psychological stages of development, there is no reason to think that they would change in a free market. Rigid groupings by age, however, would not occur; Montessori and others have demonstrated the value of multiple ages in the same class. Study by course and semester or quarter may or may not be prevalent, depending on how the content and calendar of a particular school is structured, which in turn depends on the needs and desires of the customers.[38]

The free market in education would be more differentiated than it is now, in types of schools available and subjects offered, because of the widely varied interests of students that are not now satisfied. Interests are not satisfied today because they seldom are the criteria by which educational offerings are made;

---

[38] "Bankers' hours," it should be noted, are a phenomenon of monopolistic privilege. With modest deregulation banks today are open a little longer than their former 10 AM to 3 PM and some are even open on Saturdays. Doctors, lawyers, and professors, however, still do not usually work weekends. A free-market service firm must be open and available when the customers need them. Educational services in a free market, therefore, may take on a totally different schedule and calendar than exists today. The computer industry's "24/7" indicates the ultimate in service. The free market gives privilege to no one.

bureaucratic edict dictates and a monotonous sameness results.[39] As stated before, when free markets mature, they do tend to become standardized, but they are not monolithic; the shoe and food markets today are mature, but differentiation is still the key to maintaining a competitive edge. Standardization from degrees will not exist, because there will be no degrees. Primary schools will be local, and there will be more of them, catering to the specific needs of each area. They may be owned by one company, but each branch will determine its own objectives and strategies in the face of competition with the other local primary schools. Secondary schools will be less local, but not too much so; the centralized, 1000-plus student high schools of today will become a relic of bureaucratic folly.[40] Universities probably will be smaller and more specialized.[41]

In the absence of grades and degrees it has already been stated that entrepreneurs will have to offer greater value—that is, value without the threat of punishment or failure—than educational administrators now offer. The objective of all teachers in the free market will be to ensure that they succeed in getting through to all of their paying customers, including the slower ones, lest they lose money and face the threat of going out business. The teachers will be graded and examined, not the students, and they, not the students, will face competition. They will be challenged to discover more efficient and effective ways of teaching a wide variety of personalities and interests.

Teachers are salespersons of the knowledge, values, and skills promoted by the entrepreneurs of their schools. If the customers do not like what the sales representative offers, they do not buy, or if they are in the process of buying and are dissatisfied, they stop

---

[39] The worst of the sameness is statewide adoption of textbooks and curriculum. Some countries decree nation-wide adoption.

[40] The move to large, comprehensive high schools was encouraged by former Harvard University president James B. Conant in *The American High School Today* (New York: McGraw-Hill, 1959). "By 1996," says Diane Ravitch, "nearly half of all American high school students attended a high school with an enrollment of more than 1,500 students, and 70 percent attended a high school larger than 1,000 students." Diane Ravitch, *Left Back: A Century of Failed School Reforms* (New York: Simon & Schuster, 2000), 362.

[41] In Hellenistic and Roman times, primary education focused on the fundamentals of learning (reading, writing, speaking, and a modicum of arithmetic), secondary (grammar) schools taught a general education (grammar and literature), and universities provided professional specialization.

and, at times angrily, demand their money back.[42] Teachers in a free market are peddlers of ideas; as such, they will have to own up to the responsibility and difficulty of retaining satisfied, paying customers. That today's teachers would be enraged at such a characterization of the profession reveals, in addition to their hostility to capitalism, the comfort of privileged elitism they enjoy from the education monopoly. In a free market teachers will not be able to say to students, with disdain during posted office hours, "I can't talk now. I have a meeting," because competing teachers who are kinder will make more money by talking to the students (and there will be few, if any, meetings in free-market schools, because there will be few administrators).[43]

For the most part, education is a retail service.[44] Its product, like all services, in contrast to goods, has distinctive characteristics that make its productivity a challenge to improve. The educational service is intangible in the sense that its features and benefits cannot be as easily perceived as that of a good; thus, it is difficult for customers to know ahead of time what exactly they are buying. The educational service also is inseparable from the person of the seller, that is, production and consumption of formal education are simultaneous, whereas a good can be separated from its producer and put on a shelf; a service cannot easily be distributed. The quality of the educational service is variable, because the labor element that produces the service can have good days and bad days, whereas a good is machined to within narrow tolerances every time it comes out of the factory; the customer, therefore, some days buys a good service, some days a bad one. And

---

[42] It is sometimes said in private businesses that everyone in the company, not just the sales reps, should once in a awhile be required to talk to and attempt to pacify an irate customer. Such an encounter would enable all those not in sales to better appreciate why the company is in business.

[43] The "appalling lack of civility" is how Charles Silberman described the behavior of teachers and principals toward students in public schools. Charles Silberman, *Crisis in the Classroom* (New York: Random House, 1970), 10. On meetings, one wag said that the best meeting in private business is no meeting at all, because work does not get done when a meeting is being held. The second best meeting is a stand-up discussion in the hall. The third best is in a room with no furniture, so no one can become comfortable and, as a result, talk too much. The fourth best meeting, if it has to be held, is in a room with uncomfortable furniture. Meetings are the bureaucrat's favorite time waster. The priority of the teacher who cannot spend time talking to the student is clear: a meeting with *other faculty* is more important than the needs and wants of students.

[44] The training of teachers is a wholesale service.

the educational service is perishable because, unlike a good facing low demand, it cannot be saved for another day; the service must be purchased at a time the provider is available.

Essentially, services are labor performed for others, supported sometimes by tangible goods and equipment, such as an automated car wash, sometimes not, such as a business consultant. Educational services are closer to the latter. Service productivity is improved by reducing the labor element. Ultimate improvement results from the elimination of labor altogether, replacing the service with a good. The refrigerator, for example, eliminated the need for ice delivery services. The automobile reduced the need for many mass transportation services, and the television has replaced or reduced the need for numerous forms of out-of-home entertainment. The most profound innovation in educational history was the printing press that made it possible for every student to acquire his or her own book. Inexpensive paperbacks, audio-visual equipment, and, of course, computers have advanced learning to levels unheard of just a lifetime ago.

The introduction of these tangible goods into education, however, does not mean that teachers in a free market will be replaced. Printed books have not replaced teachers in six hundred years; the computer and Internet will not do so in the next one hundred. Teachers will not be replaced for the same reason that parents cannot be replaced by computers or other machines. The personal, especially emotional, touch, by a parent or teacher is primary in the nurturing process. Even older students, including those in college, need warmth and encouragement from their teachers, something they seldom acquire in the bureaucratic setting.[45] Teachers will not be replaced because some services meet a fundamental need that cannot be eliminated by a good.[46] Books provide detailed knowledge, but a good lecturer can summarize the essentials and motivate the listener to read more. Videos can demonstrate scientific experiments, but performing an experiment under

---

[45] I have noticed that students at my university crave attention, which they do not seem to get either at home or school. Being a number on a vast bureaucratic roster prevents one from acquiring much attention.

[46] Transportation, for example, has been radically improved since the invention of the wheel but airlines today are still services. The introduction of jet aircraft has simply made the service more productive. If, someday, we could all afford our own jet aircraft, we would still have the need to travel even faster and more efficiently. Such a benefit can only be provided by a mass transportation firm that spreads its costs over many users.

expert supervision is far more rewarding. And computer software can provide drill and other forms of practice, but the introduction of new material, adapted to each student, is still best accomplished by a live teacher.[47]

As part of the modern prepared environment, paperback books, audio-visual aids, and computers and the Internet have made it possible for students and adults alike to acquire greater amounts of knowledge in shorter periods of time. Lawrence Cremin referred to this phenomenon, especially the prevalence of television, as the "cacophony of teaching";[48] in an earlier work, he cited a televised production of Shakespeare's *Hamlet* that was watched by more people in one night than had seen the play since its opening in 1600.[49] As civilizations advance, however, the level of knowledge required to become a cultured citizen rises, necessitating, at least in essentials, a broader range and greater depth of knowledge than had been required in earlier years. It is, of course, not possible for anyone to acquire all extant knowledge, but efficiency in the delivery of essential knowledge geared to specific student purposes needs to be developed to continue the advance of civilization. The live teacher is still the one best able to communicate these fundamentals while at the same time adapting them to individual needs. Subsequently, some teachers may publish their essentializations for wider audiences to acquire.

A Lecture/Tutorial System

Efficiency, both cognitive and financial, in the mass delivery of essential knowledge that can also be adapted to each individual is the most important challenge of education today. Making money as a teacher in the free market, and financing education generally, is little understood, because the government-run model of flat fees and group learning is

---

[47] Email has improved communication between student and teacher, but nothing beats the personal contact. The Internet, astounding as it is as a colossal database, is just a convenient tool of research. The next big, perhaps revolutionary, aid to research is likely to be the digitization of the world's published works. So-called distance learning, though, is a new name for the old-fashioned correspondence course, a niche market.

[48] Lawrence A. Cremin, "The Cacophony of Teaching" in *Popular Education and Its Discontents* (New York: Harper & Row, 1989), 51–83.

[49] Lawrence A. Cremin, *The Genius of American Education* (New York: Vintage Books, 1965), 79. Cremin's source is Frank Stanton, *Mass Media and Mass Culture* (New York: Columbia Broadcasting System, 1962), 35.

assumed to be the only way education can be operated. Its rigid price fixing in particular—that is, pay a set amount for one course or for a whole year—prevents many people from thinking of alternatives. Yet, services in the private sector today often have elaborate price schedules for their various offerings. In chapter 4 it was suggested that a few mass lectures combined with many tutorials might be the best method of communicating large amounts of knowledge while at the same time catering to the individual differences of each student.[50] This system could work from secondary school on, possibly from upper elementary school (age 9 or 10) through university, if adapted carefully to age and stage of development.

The system could operate as follows. Lecturers and tutors, whether working as sole proprietors, individual contractors, or employees of entrepreneurs, will earn income according to how many students each teaches. Talented lecturers who command large audiences will earn more and their fees will be commensurate with the demand for their services. Prices of lectures would vary according to talent and demand, thereby giving students a range of choices. If the lectures were licensed for sale on audio and video devices, and the prices of recorded lectures were reduced, say, to one-half of the live price for video and one-fourth for audio, students who cannot afford the live price, or do not want to attend live lectures, now would have a lower cost alternative. Some recorded lectures could appeal to wider audiences than students of school age and students could mix live and recorded series according to their needs or whims. "Star" lecturers could become wealthy; others would have to settle for a more modest income.

There would be no entrance requirements or evaluations to determine who would be allowed to attend the lectures. Anyone who could afford the price of admission would be allowed in—just as any concert goer today, whether tone deaf or professional musician, is "allowed" to attend classical music performances. If demand outstrips supply, the incentive in a free market is either to raise prices or to produce more, not to pompously boast about waiting lists and rejection rates. Grades would not be assigned to students because examinations would not be given. Just as music teachers of private lessons today know how well each student is progressing, tutors in a free-market school would be the ones to know how well a particular student is learning. If recommendations need to be made, to a higher school or employer, for

---

[50] See pp. 126–27.

example, tutors are the ones to make them. In tutorial settings, however, grades and exams are not necessary. The constant contact, one on one, gives tutors instant feedback on the progress of each student.

To effect in-depth learning, the essential supplement to large lectures is the tutorial, to fine tune student learning by adapting the teaching to each student's interests and pace of learning. Because the number of mass lecturers in this free-market scenario probably would be small, relative to tutors, most of today's teachers who do not have the talent to become successful free-market lecturers, or do not have the desire to lecture, would be freed to become tutors. Advanced students also would likely be tutors. Thus, the number of tutors could far exceed the number of lecturers. Fees for tutoring, again, would be competitive depending on talent and demand and would provide a range of choices for students. Advanced students, working as tutors, would presumably have the lowest rates; "star" lecturers who also wanted to tutor presumably would have the highest rates. Tutors and students together would decide whether they make a good fit, in ability and interests; again, there would be no entrance requirements or evaluations. Full-time tutors could probably see twenty students a week, perhaps more, depending on ability and desire.

Hypothetical calculations, using dollars in 2007, illustrate the feasibility of such a system. A series of ten or fifteen lectures priced at $200 live, $100 on video, $50 on audio, make large amounts of knowledge affordable to virtually anyone who wants it. (Video and audio lectures may be sold or rented). A more highly demanded series might be priced at $500 live, $250 on video, $125 on audio, or, for a "star" lecturer, perhaps, $1000 live, with corresponding reductions for video and audio. Size of audience? Whatever the market will bear: perhaps 100 students, perhaps 500, perhaps thousands. And therein lies the potential for lecturers to earn high incomes. For tutorials advanced students may charge as little as $20 or $25 per session, again making education highly affordable. Full-time tutors may charge anywhere from $50 to $100, depending on reputation and demand. "Star" lecturers may demand and get $200 or $300 per session.

Affordable education under this system, when compared to the two-semester, four courses per semester system of today, could cost less than $3000 a year, plus books and other materials. This is based on eight lecture series per year and four tutorials per week.[51] There is no reason to think four tutorials a week are necessary. Students may choose only one or two, or six or seven. The important point is that they will be free to choose and they and their parents may select any price level. The $8700 per student (excluding capital outlay) that governments today spend on K–12 education,[52] it must be remembered, will be available in a free market to parents and adult students in the form of lower taxes;[53] state-run undergraduate universities spend over $11,000 per student, graduate and specialized institutions well over that amount.[54] Private K–12 schools today spend about half of their state-run counterparts;[55] private universities spend considerably more.[56] Whatever the level of prices in a free market in education, the costs to low-income parents and students should easily be less than the expenditures of the current bureaucratic system, perhaps as low as the example above, perhaps not greater than the private K–12 expenditures of today.[57]

---

[51] Eight courses x $50 for audio-recorded lectures = $400. Four tutorials per week x 32 weeks x $20 for student tutors = $2560. The total is $2960. This would make aristocratic tutorial education available to the masses.

[52] National Center for Education Statistics (NCES), "Common Core of Data," Table 3, http://nces.ed.gov/pubs2007/expenditures/tables/table_3.asp.

[53] But see below, p. 181.

[54] NCES, "Digest of Education Statistics: 2005," Table 341, http://nces.ed.gov/programs/digest/d05/tables/dt05_341.asp?referer=list.

[55] Michael Garet, Tsze H. Chan, and Joel D. Sherman, *Estimates of Expenditures for Private K–12 Schools*, (Washington, D.C.: U.S. Department of Education, 1995), working paper no. 95–17. Available at National Center for Education Statistics, NCES Electronic Catalog, http://nces.ed.gov/pubsearch/pubsinfo.asp?pubid=9517.

[56] "Digest of Education Statistics," Table 346, http://nces.ed.gov/programs/digest/d05/tables/dt05_346.asp?referer=list.

[57] The American Federation of Teachers (AFT) disputes the claim that private schools spend less than their public counterparts. Extra services, such as special education, transportation, and school lunches, paid for out of public school expenditures are not covered by private school spending. When subtracted out, the AFT concludes that expenditures are about the same. American Federation of Teachers, "AFT Press Center, Speeches and Columns, Where We Stand, 1998, May: No Bargain," http://www.aft.org/presscenter/speeches-columns/wws/1998/0598.htm. Some of these services are provided by private schools at extra charge. Most, however, would not exist or be attached to a regular school in a free market. Special education, much of which is remediation, is the largest of the extra services subtracted out (17%). A good free-market education system would eliminate the need for the remediation; for those truly in need of special education, the market would provide its own schools.

What about buildings and land, libraries, laboratories, and computers? Capital expenditures must be paid for out of the fees of students, but as a Protestant clergyman once said about the need for a cathedral, "A good shade tree to protect us from the elements is all we need." So it is with education, because most of what is communicated to students is abstract. Tutoring can be accomplished either in the tutor's home or in the student's (there would be no zoning laws to restrict running a business out of one's home); lectures can be given in leased space in office buildings. In a free market scientific research will be conducted by large businesses, as it was in Thomas Edison's day.

Independent libraries will be for-profit rental operations, probably not unlike today's video rental centers; successful educational entrepreneurs probably would make libraries one of their first investments after lecture halls and offices—although the Internet may make this capital outlay superfluous in a decade or two. The more successful the educational service, the more capital goods it will make available to students (perhaps at higher fees, although perhaps not, since market leaders have the uncanny ability of providing higher quality products at lower prices). Today's schools, especially universities, are considerably overbuilt and over-equipped for the services they provide.

The lecture/tutorial suggestion described here must not be confused with those systems that have existed for centuries in European countries, particularly England and Germany.[58] All such systems are run by the government and Adam Smith properly upbraided the bureaucratic mentality for having "given up altogether even the pretence of teaching."[59] In a free market lecturers who read from a boring text and tutors who relate poorly to their students and fail to give them value for the money are not likely to remain in business for long. Indeed, students in a free market will be motivated to listen to good lecturers and to produce work for tutors, because doing so will be the students' choice, not the state's, to study what and with whom they want to study. And it will be their (or their parent's) money that is being spent. Consumers do not need to be coerced into buying shoes and food. Why should they be forced into buying knowledge? Coercion kills motivation—for both teachers and students.

---

[58] Or the lecture/section system of some American universities.

[59] Adam Smith, *An Inquiry in the Nature and Causes of the Wealth of Nations*, 2 vols. in one, ed. Edwin Cannan (Chicago: University Chicago Press, 1976), vol. 2, 284. See the first epigraph to chapter 1 of the present work for full quotation.

Unsolved Problems of Education

In chapter 1 the unsolved problems of education were described as "how to provide mass, in-depth, economical education that cultivates individual differences and produces independence."[60] Mass education today has been achieved, but at the point of a gun. The free-market challenge is how to reduce the price of education such that the lowest income families could still afford to send their children to school. The lecture/tutorial system suggested above proposes to accomplish just that. The lecture communicates mass knowledge to the masses; the tutorial adapts it to individual differences and achieves in-depth learning. The voluntariness of the system, above all, along with practice of the theory of concentrated attention, especially the nurturing warmth of tutors and their ability to teach the skills of concentrated attention, will encourage the development of independence and purpose in life.

The lecture/tutorial system is suggested for upper elementary school at the earliest. This leaves the problem of how economically to produce education for the earlier ages. Montessori's classes typically were large, 35 to 40 students, with one directress and an assistant.[61] The materials and older students are relied on to assist in teaching. Peer teaching is an old technique for economizing on education that enhances learning for all participants and increases confidence. In 1791 Scotsman Andrew Bell developed a system he called "mutual instruction," which Englishman Joseph Lancaster adapted; it became known more widely as the "monitorial system." Monitors were older students who were responsible for various tasks of managing the schoolhouse. Some taught younger students, typically ten each. If one teacher supervises 25 teaching monitors, 250 students can be taught. The privately-run system was popular until the 1840's when governments took over and turned it into a scheme of common schools.[62] Clearly, a free-market adaptation

---

[60] See p. 23.

[61] Regulations today limit the size of most preschool classes. In California, a class size over 28 requires two teachers and one aide. "California State Code of Regulation, Title 22, Summary of Regulations for Child Care Centers—'Preschool,' Infant Centers, School Age Centers, and/or Combination Centers," http://i.b5z.net/i/u/696577/f/Child_Care_Centers.pdf.

[62] John Chodes, "State Subsidy to Private Schools: A Case History of Destruction," *The Freeman*, March 1991. The complaint against the monitorial system was that it was regimented, focusing on drill and memorization and preventing the development of creative thinking and initiative. This need not be the case. In England

of peer teaching could reduce the cost of elementary education dramatically; in the absence of child labor laws, the peer teachers might even be paid a modest sum.

The lecture/tutorial and peer-teaching systems are not the only models to be expected in a free market in education. Montessori's suggestions for secondary school, for example, might be implemented. Montessori did not develop or sanction a secondary school based on her ideas. However, she did briefly discuss the needs of adolescents and what she thought would be required to satisfy them. The fundamental need of this period of development is to strengthen self-confidence. Creative work, recognition for it, and economic independence are what adolescents crave. Montessori's suggestion was to move secondary schools to the country and organize them as working farms, perhaps also with hotels attached to the farms and stores in town to serve as outlets for the farms' produce. Students would then work and study in these institutions, away from the strains of family life, and earn money for the schooling and for personal independence. They would learn about nature and civilization, as well as commerce and exchange.[63]

While Montessori's suggestion is probably impractical for mass education, she does identify the essential needs of adolescents: self-confidence and independence, not parental or teacher manipulations and control; acknowledgment of and help identifying their emotions and desires, not denial and ridicule; and opportunities for self-expression in preparation for adult life, not abandonment or micromanagement.[64]

---

government edict replaced monitors with older "pupil-teachers," apprentice teachers aged 13–18; the next step after this was to eliminate the pupil-teachers and replace them with "properly" credentialed instructors from government-run teacher training schools. The government-mandated "simultaneous method" of teaching, that is, the modern group lesson of limited class size, brought the monitorial system to a practical end. The underlying motive for government takeover of education was to ensure that certain moral and religious values were taught. James Bowen, *A History of Western Education*, vol. 3, *The Modern West* (New York: St. Martin's Press, 1981), 298–301, 307–14.

[63] Maria Montessori, "Erdkinder," in *From Childhood to Adolescence* (1948; repr., New York: Schocken Books, 1976), 97–109. Montessori also suggested that schooling in the country would be healthier for adolescents than in the city; for example, it would help reduce the chance of catching tuberculosis, which obviously is not a problem today.

[64] An important work on the needs of adolescent girls is Mary Pipher, *Reviving Ophelia: Saving the Selves of Adolescent Girls* (New York: Putnam, 1994). For the emotional needs of boys of all ages, see Daniel Kindlon and Michael Thompson, *Raising Cain: Protecting the Emotional Life of Boys* (New York: Ballantine Books,

It may happen under capitalism, in the absence of compulsory schooling and child labor laws, that adolescents choose for a time to engage in full-time, paid employment, just as some college students now do.[65] The break from studies combined with real-world work could sharpen their thoughts about life and their goals in life. It would advance their ambitions for independence.

The deregulation and privatization of education would open up a new era of experimentation, not unlike, and probably greater than, the experimentation that took place in the late nineteenth and early twentieth centuries. This time, however, the experiments would take place entirely outside of the bureaucracy and be tested by the market.

PRIVATIZATION

The establishment of a free market in education will probably be one of the last reforms made in efforts to deregulate and privatize present-day governments by lobby. Education is the means by which special interests maintain control over the minds of the young, and it is a sacred cow among the intellectual and political elite. From Martin Luther to the Enlightenment to today's social liberals and religious conservatives, universal education means compulsory and government-controlled. Privatization of social security and the abolition of welfare will likely occur long before freedom of choice in education by parents and students will be taken seriously. Suggestions that follow are just that: suggestions awaiting a time when the intellectual climate becomes more conducive to the deregulation and privatization of education.

Vouchers, however, are one idea that I do not support.[66] Because the atmosphere today is not one of deregulation, privatization, and, generally, acceptance of the notion of laissez-faire capitalism, payments

---

1999). Both works are somewhat shallow psychologically, by not acknowledging the role of the subconscious in framing personality, and Pipher blames advertising too much, but both raise serious questions about how the needs of girls and boys are not now being met.

[65] This also assumes the absence of a military draft, which is involuntary servitude, regardless of what the Supreme Court has declared in the past.

[66] The origin of the notion of vouchers is attributed to economist Milton Friedman, "The Role of Government in Education," in Robert Solow, ed. *Education and the Public Interest* (New Brunswick, NJ: Rutgers University Press, 1955). Friedman modeled his idea on the G.I. Bill, the government program of giving money to returning World War II veterans; they could then spend the money at any college of their choice.

by the government of one to several thousand dollars to parents, so they may spend the money at any school they choose, is an invitation for more government control over education, particularly over private schools. If intellectual and political leaders openly advocated a free market in education, then there might be some argument that vouchers would lead not to more control over education, but to an undermining of the government monopoly; the goal of vouchers would ultimately be to remove government from education. That the voucher itself is government money makes this unlikely ever to happen.

There is another reason to oppose vouchers, this time on moral grounds. Vouchers redistribute wealth as much as does "free" public schooling. Money is coerced from taxpayers in the community, including most who have no children in the system, and given to the neighborhood school or, in the case of vouchers, to the few who do have school-age children. Either way an injustice is done to the majority for the sake of the few.

In contrast to vouchers, economist George Reisman suggests the following approach to the privatization of education. Pass a law, stating that after the seventh year of its enactment the "state and its localities will no longer be responsible for the financing of the first-grade education of any student; that a year after that, they will no longer be responsible for the financing of the second-grade education of any student; and so on, through all the elementary, secondary, and college grades." Thus, in a generation, says Reisman, the government would be out of the education business. The purpose of the seven-year grace period is to enable parents to prepare for the first year of transition and to allow them, if they so desire, to keep existing school-age children in the system. Reisman's proposal is presented in a context of much additional deregulation and abolition of government involvement in the economy. The most significant deregulations for education would be the elimination of all educational licensing requirements and other hindrances to the rights of parents to educate their own children, as well as the barring of public education from teaching controversial subjects, such as religion, history, economics, civics, and biology.[67]

---

[67] Reisman, *Capitalism*, 986. Teaching controversial subjects in the public education system "necessarily entails forcing at least some taxpayers to violate their convictions, by providing funds for the dissemination of ideas which they consider to be false and possibly vicious." Ibid.

In addition to the above, continues Reisman, the following de-bureaucratizations of society must either precede or accompany the privatization of education: the sale of all publicly owned property to private investors, which includes school buildings and land; the elimination of all government violations of the freedom of production and trade, including, but not limited to, minimum-wage laws and pro-union legislation; the abolition of the welfare state, including the elimination of government unemployment insurance, welfare legislation, social security, medicare, food stamps, and rent subsidies and controls; the elimination of income and inheritance taxes; the establishment of gold as money and formation of a completely private, 100-percent reserve banking system; a pro-capitalist foreign policy, which includes freedom of immigration; the separation of government and science; and the separation of government and church.[68]

De-bureaucratizing society to this extent is necessary before establishing a free-market in education because of the enormous burden bureaucracy imposes on the pocket books of average citizens. One can point out that education today is financed by state income, sales, and property taxes (about equal amounts income and sales, on the one hand, and property, on the other—a small percentage paid by the federal government) and that if privatized the citizen would enjoy lower taxes, close to fifty per cent lower for state income, sales, and property. However, low income people do not pay property taxes and their tax savings (as probably would also be the case of property-owning middle income people) likely would not be sufficient to pay for a private, free-market education. The true cost that prevents low income people from being able to afford a higher quality of life is not just taxes but the unseen consequences of regulations, licenses, subsidies, public ownerships, and the like, that restrict supply, prevent innovation, inhibit access, freeze out other options, lower the productivity of labor, and, generally, beat down citizens, especially low income citizens, with higher prices, lower quality and fewer quantities of goods and services, and lower incomes than they would otherwise experience under laissez-faire capitalism.

One estimate of the annual cost of government per person, calculated as federal and state spending plus cost of federal and state

---

[68] Ibid., 972–88.

regulation divided by population size, is put at nearly $19,000.[1] Whatever the actual cost may be, any significant rollback of government would put a sizeable chunk of change in everyone's pocket.

So, in a free market who will pay for the education of the poor? Why, the poor, of course!

The poor will pay for their own education, just as most of them now pay for their own food, shelter, and clothing. Education is a staple that everyone who has children must budget for. And under capitalism, they will budget for it, because the poor will enjoy higher incomes, lower prices, and better quality and greater quantities of goods and services than they now have.

---

[1] American Tax Reform Foundation, "2005 Cost of Government Day: By the Numbers," http://www.atr.org/content/pdf/2005/jul/070705COGD-by%20the%20 numbers.pdf.

6

Independent Judgment

The fundamental problem in education is not an educational problem at all; it is a social one. It consists in the establishment of a new and better relationship between the two great sections of society—children and adults.

—Maria Montessori[2]

THROUGHOUT HISTORY, the relationship of child to adult has been one of obedience to authority. However, a healthy disrespect of authority is what children need to learn.

This includes a disrespect of authority based on expertise, especially when the expertise has no basis in fact and the label is retained as cover for intimidation and coercion of the unbelieving. Authority based on coercive power, of course, should always be scorned and opposed, when safely possible. The scientific revolution of the seventeenth century is an example of a healthy disrespect of authority based on sham expertise and the American revolution of the eighteenth century represents the self-confident discarding of coercive power. The young need desperately to be taught how to differentiate true expertise from the specious varieties and how to react to all forms of adult thoughtlessness, intimidation, and coercion. For the world we live in today is a culture of coercion—less coercive, to be sure, than in previous

---

[2] Quoted in E. M. Standing, *Maria Montessori: Her Life and Work* (1957; repr. New York: Plume/Penguin, 1984), 251.

centuries but still oppressive nonetheless and more subtle than in earlier times.[3]

The devastating consequence of adult insensitivity and demands for obedience to authority is mental passivity. Not social passivity or shyness in relation to other people, although that may occur in some, but a resignation and lack of confidence about how to use one's mind effectively. The result is a lack of ability and willingness to make first-hand judgments about the world, other people, and oneself and, more importantly, a lack of ability and willingness to stand by and act on the judgments that are made. The result, even though the mature adult may be gregarious and articulate in social situations, is intellectual shyness that manifests itself as an inability to think conceptually or in principles. It is a syndrome that Ayn Rand calls the anti-conceptual mentality, but this epithet is too moralistic.[4] It is a defensive maneuver that children adopt in the face of adult-induced anxiety. More than anything else, it is this syndrome that defeats the educational goal of independence.

MENTAL PASSIVITY

Education in its generic sense is a process of developing the mind to achieve a particular purpose. The purpose itself may be general, as in a preparation for adult life, or specific, as in training to become a lifeguard or learning through accumulated experience how to run a successful business. Instruction and experience are the means by which development of the mind is achieved, with instruction being more prominent in our early years. The educational process is ongoing and does not or, rather, should not, stop at the ages of eighteen or twenty-two. Although learning in adulthood varies widely, unfortunately for many it seems to shut down completely. In some cases, conceptual learning much beyond directly perceivable concretes seems never to have gotten started, even in the formative years of schooling, and psychological self-awareness is unheard of or, if known, is condescendingly—and defensively—dismissed as voodoo science or only for the weak willed.

---

[3] The Holocaust and other genocides of the twentieth and twenty-first centuries might cast doubt on the qualification of this statement, but among the educated the trend seems to be away from coercion as a means of dealing with others. Then again, the Holocaust might not have occurred had educated people had the courage to speak up and oppose the rise of modern racism, that is, had they exhibited independence, the subject of this chapter.

[4] Ayn Rand, "The Missing Link," in *Philosophy: Who Needs It* (Indianapolis: Bobbs-Merrill, 1982), 42–55.

What Rand means by the anti-conceptual mentality is a mind that is passive "in regard to the process of conceptualization and, therefore, in regard to fundamental principles. It is a mentality which decided, at a certain point of development, that it knows enough and does not care to look further."[5] Psychologically, however, this type of mental passivity is not always self-caused in the culpable way that Rand so adamantly asserts, for mental passivity is the inability (and only sometimes the unwillingness) to look inward to examine and, if necessary, change the premises that determine one's beliefs, evaluations, emotions, and behavior. Mental passivity is the unquestioning acceptance of part or all of one's psychology. Many people never perform the needed introspection, either because they have not been taught to do so or because, if they do know something about the process, fear what they might find. Some perform partial examinations, leaving other areas of their subconscious untouched. Very few, if any, given the state of psychology today and of the knowledge of how to perform such actions, can monitor their inner realities continually.

Awareness of one's premises is essential to concept formation and the understanding of broad principles because all thought, as stated in chapter 3, is a process of conscious differentiation and subconscious integration—differentiation of something new from the already known and integration of the new with the already known. Significant effort, therefore, to identify what one already knows is required for advanced learning. Knowledge of one's premises is required in order to maintain a well-organized subconscious and to make the existing knowledge stored in the subconscious readily accessible. The reason for studying logic, after all, is to enable us to maintain order in our thinking. What most people today do not realize is that this includes, in addition, applying logic to our evaluations, emotions, and behavior. Disagreeing with a particular person or idea solely because that person or idea makes us angry—or anxious—is an obvious fallacy that is all too prevalent even among the highly educated. Conceptual thinking presupposes a mentally active mind; the "pro-conceptual" mentality is skilled in introspection.

Unfortunately, mental activity and mental growth in children and youth are hampered and sometimes silenced completely by a barrage of adult rules and commands that add up to thoughtlessness, intimidation, and coercion. Some talented children who are subjected to these

---

[5] Ibid., 45.

assaults and consequently suffer psychological scars can still go on as adults to achieve high goals, but not as high as they might have, had they been properly nurtured. Only a rare few can avoid the self-doubt and anxiety that result from such treatment by parents and teachers. That the educational system itself is founded on and operated by coercion against the young magnifies and compounds the problem.

Children are not born mentally inactive or uninterested. The steps to resignation and passivity proceed as follows. Physical punishment and the language of unacceptance (as discussed in chapter 4) create an atmosphere of rejection, which produces self-doubt. The emotional expression of self-doubt is anxiety, a fear that seems to have no object. Anxiety so paralyzes children that they will do anything to alleviate the unpleasant feelings. A variety of coping methods thus develops, along with a split focus: one eye on reality—conceptual learning and work—the other on fighting anxiety. The more anxiety, the less effort will be spent on conceptual development. At a certain point in life, later for some, earlier for others, the decision is made to stop learning, or at least to slow down the learning, and concentrate efforts on relieving anxiety. The decision is made by each individual, often subconsciously as an emotional generalization, about one's ability to learn; given the lack of knowledge of and teaching about introspection, such a decision cannot be considered a moral breach.

Foremost among coping methods, besides repression, is the defense value, major destroyer of independent judgment. A defense value, once again, as stated in chapter 3, is any value, rational or not, pursued for the purpose of relieving anxiety. Defense values cannot succeed in removing the anxiety, but they do temporarily blunt it by making one feel special in the eyes of significant others. Like a drug high, though, the feeling wears off quickly and the pursuit of specialness must continue, a boaster being the more obvious example. Because of the emphasis on feeling special in the eyes of others, one consequence of defense values is group conformity. This can produce a provincial or even tribal personality that cannot or will not go beyond—or against—its group of significant others to grasp new concepts or to understand fundamental principles. This is the form of anti-conceptual mentality that Rand is talking about. Such a personality, however, is not found only in the provinces or in primitive tribes; it can be found at the highest levels of business, academia, and government.

To be sure, this personality exists on a continuum that ranges from small-town skilled or unskilled laborers whose values and dreams go no further than their extended families to big-city professors who uncritically mouth the slogans of their leftist (or rightist) colleagues. In essence, this personality is the conventional person who has no purpose in life other than to get along with or to impress the group. And the group may be a family, social class, or race, one's ethnic peers or fellow workers, or a social, political, religious, or philosophical affiliation, or some combination. To be sure, also, this personality exists on a continuum from one person who is largely independent, but suffers areas of conformity caused by anxiety-induced defensiveness, to one who is largely consumed by desires to conform. The latter in literature is eloquently portrayed by Sinclair Lewis' Babbitt, from the novel of the same name, and Ayn Rand's own Peter Keating in *The Fountainhead.* Unconventional, but not less dependent, persons who define themselves by being opposed to the ideas and values of a specific group constitute a variant of this personality, such as rebellious teenagers who deliberately but aimlessly go against the tastes and principles of their families.

Defense values destroy independent judgment because attention is turned away from reality—from the development of one's own mind, on one's own terms—to the judgments of others. Defense values, however, are not the only coping method that can create mental passivity and therefore destroy independence. All defense mechanisms, whether repression, rationalization, denial, projection, hostility, withdrawal, compulsion, and so on, turn attention away from the task at hand to the management of anxiety. Nor are defense mechanisms and defense values the only things that work against independence. The morality of altruism, which has preached self-sacrifice for millennia, is a prescription for passivity of all kinds, especially the mental type; it also is a prescription for authoritarianism, because someone must collect the sacrifices.[6] This has given us the belief in an omnipotent government to which we must give up our independent judgment, especially about how to educate children. The notion of an omnipotent being, for similar reasons, also deters the development of independence.

INDEPENDENCE

The desire of many parents and teachers is that the young, when they become mature adults, should possess sound, not independent,

---

[6] Parents and teachers oblige the young both by encouraging them to sacrifice and by collecting their sacrifices.

judgment. Sound judgment is the ability to perceive facts correctly and evaluate them appropriately for one's chosen purpose. Wisdom and common sense are other terms that might be used here, but the former is a little too grandiose and the latter too often means conformity to the ideas and values of whoever is describing something as common sense.[7] Sound judgment means sensible decision making. While correct perception and evaluation of the facts, strictly speaking, mean doing so entirely on one's own without regard for what others say or do, among laypersons, and even among the highly educated, sound judgment still often means doing so only within a narrow range of what is conventionally accepted.

Understood as an abstract personality trait, rather than as the commonplace ability to pay one's own expenses, independence is not well tolerated as a goal of mature adulthood by those who themselves are not independent. Independent judgment and independent action clash directly with the obedience to authority that many parents and teachers demand of their charges until they are eighteen or twenty-two. Extreme frustration and even anger, for example, can be seen on the faces of parents who suddenly realize—when, say, a son or daughter turns twenty-one—they can no longer be dictators over their children; some parents never stop trying. After reaching adulthood and entering society, the young are then confronted with more demands for obedience to authority by the interventionist policies of government bureaucrats. The only way to protect and encourage the development of independence in the young is to rid their lives of all forms of authoritarianism—parental, educational, and societal.[8]

---

[7] J. Glenn Gray in *The Promise of Wisdom* (New York: J. P. Lippincott, 1968), 17–25, argues that theoretical and practical wisdom, not just the accumulation of information or knowledge, are the proper aims of education.

[8] To combat one of the more subtle forms of authoritarianism, Robert Fuller, former president of Oberlin College, coined the word "rankism," meaning the abuse of rank, to describe a concept similar to, but broader than, racism, sexism, bullying in general, and other forms of attempted or real domination. "Rankism insults the dignity of subordinates by treating them as invisible, as nobodies. Nobody is another n-word and, like the original, it is used to justify denigration and inequity." Robert Fuller, *Somebodies and Nobodies: Overcoming the Abuse of Rank* (Gabriola Island, BC, Canada: New Society Publishers, 2003), 5. The concept is psychological and clearly derives from defense values and the necessity of setting oneself up as special in the eyes of others or as superior to them. Rankism, says Fuller, is the last "vestige of aristocratic class" that must be eliminated from the home, workplace, and society before we can achieve a just society based on equal dignity. Ibid., 10. Fuller, however, believes that social, rather than market, liberalism, is the means of achieving this equality.

The personality trait of independence has two components, one mental, one behavioral. The mental act of asserting something as fact and doing so entirely on one's own is independent judgment. The willingness to act on what one has judged to be right, in the face of disapproval and opposition, is independent action. The former precedes and is required for the latter; independent action is impossible without independent thought. Volition and, therefore, morality enter most clearly in the decision to act on what one knows to be right, which means that the full expression of independence requires integrity and courage. In contrast, it is not so clear that the failure to develop independent thought is a moral flaw, considering the influence of psychology on thinking and lack of teaching about the proper use of the mind. Ignorance also is a major influence on one's judgments, which is why content in education is equal in importance, not secondary, to method. Refusal to look at one's own psychology, though, after being taught the skill of introspection and the proper use of the mind, or the refusal to become informed about a topic, can be viewed as a moral deficiency.

A key fact about independent judgment is that no one can get inside our heads to do our thinking for us or to make us accept certain ideas; we are the proverbial horse at water's edge that must decide on its own whether or not to drink. We can, however, fake the process of thought through memorization and imitation.[9] Memorizing the conclusions of others and imitating the way they talk or act are hallmarks of dependence. Independence means observing, concluding, and saying that a chair is a chair, regardless of what anyone else calls it. Sometimes, independence means enduring great personal expense. Galileo's condemnation and Socrates' execution are only two dramatic examples from history. In literature, Henrik Ibsen's Dr. Stockmann in *An Enemy of the People* stood steadfastly to his judgment while one by one losing nearly all who were supposedly his friends. On a more contemporary but no less personally expensive level, independence may mean standing up to one's parents and becoming an artist, despite the parents' insistence that a legal or computer programming career would be more lucrative or respectable (to the parents' significant others). It may mean telling a professor that recycling, as a waste of labor, reduces the economic well-being of everyone or that a few cells in a woman's body do not constitute a separate life.

---

[9] Rand, "Missing Link," 46.

Independence means first saying to oneself, then aloud to anyone who can hear, that the Emperor has no clothes. When agreeing with the ideas of others, independent judgment requires additional effort to avoid mere memorization or imitation; it requires, in effect, a mental reinventing of the wheel. That is, to maintain independent judgment, we must recreate the thinking behind the ideas that are accepted, retracing and digesting the steps of the arguments. This insures that we have understood the conclusions with our own minds and not just parroted them. It is a skill, like introspection, that most students today in our bureaucratic educational system do not possess, or if they do possess the skill, do not use it, because they are too busy chasing grades and degrees. Disagreeing with others thoughtfully, as opposed to hastily dismissing the ideas, requires an equivalent or greater effort. It may also require great tact, if the consequence of disagreement is punishment by the initiation of physical force.

In a civilized world, using a civilized code of ethics, there is no moral obligation to die or suffer for one's independent judgment. Galileo capitulated to the Inquisition and was condemned anyway to house arrest for the remainder of his life.[10] Socrates was offered a chance to escape but refused it, remaining steadfast to his death. Moral guidance here derives from the principle of self-defense; "morality ends where a gun begins" is the way Ayn Rand describes it.[11] If confronted with an unprovoked physical attack, the victim may fight or flee, that is, the alternatives are morally equivalent. When the attack is on one's independent judgment, such as threatened punishment through censorship, imprisonment, or a lower grade in a coercively bureaucratic educational system, going along as a pretense is a third option.

The threat, however, must unmistakably be an initiation of physical force, not just the prospect of disagreement, disapproval, or a voluntary refusal to cooperate. Private businesses that forbid employees from discussing their political views on television talk shows are enforcing a voluntary contract; they are not imposing censorship. Freedom of speech presupposes voluntary cooperation between property own-

---

[10] On Galileo's supposed defiance about the earth's movement around the sun: "There is no evidence that at this time he whispered, 'Eppur si muove' ('And yet it moves')." *Encyclopædia Britannica Online*, s.v. "Galileo," http://o-search.eb.com.opac.library.csupomona.edu:80/eb/article-8441 (accessed April 24, 2007).

[11] Ayn Rand, *Atlas Shrugged* (New York: Random House, 1957), 1023. The full statement, spoken by Rand's hero, John Galt, reads: "Force and mind are opposites; morality ends where a gun begins."

ers and speakers, whereas censorship is the government's initiation of physical force against both to prevent the free flow of ideas. Censorship, fundamentally, is always an action by the government. Private businesses exercise censorship only to the extent that they hold government-granted privileges, which means to the extent that they have become bureaus of the state. This includes today's private schools. State-run schools are already agents of the government and, therefore, function as censors of state-approved speech.

This is why teachers, as discussed in chapter 5, can brandish their red ink pens as bureaucratically issued guns; the education monopoly gives them political power that they otherwise would not have under capitalism. Marking down students for their views in any system of education is unfair, but in a free market in education students might respond to the injustice by demanding the return of their money or by taking their business elsewhere, or both. Under the current monopoly there is no elsewhere to go, so students must endure and try somehow to preserve their autonomy and self-respect.[12] College students who dare to ask for their money back are usually greeted with contemptuous disdain (and given stern sermons about how higher education is a privilege, not a right).[13]

The challenge of going along as a pretense is to maintain one's independent judgment without actually believing the pretense and succumbing to abject conformism. "Going along" means giving teachers what they want, a mission at which students today, regardless of the fairness or unfairness of teachers, have become expert. The unfortunate double task required to maintain independence in the present bureaucratic establishment is to work extra hard at clarifying one's own thoughts while, at the same time, writing papers and taking examinations on topics that one disagrees with or is not interested in to earn the grades and degrees necessary to move ahead in life. This extra-effort double task is not unlike that of the few citizens of authoritarian political regimes

---

[12] Name-calling today such as marking down students for their "simplistic"—meaning capitalistic—ideas, is not the prerogative of leftist teachers. Conservatives seem to have made sarcasm and parody into an archetype of intellectual argument. Bureaucracy breeds insensitivity even in teachers who are fair, because in bureaucracy there is no marketplace accountability.

[13] The implication, if not stated explicitly, is that the students should shut up and obey. The right of voluntary cooperation between teacher and student, however, is precisely what is being denied by the privileged elite of bureaucrats (the teachers and administrators).

who, working underground, manage to survive with their independent judgment intact; most take the easier path of compliance, never questioning, even silently in their own minds, what is said.

PSYCHOLOGICAL SELF-AWARENESS

The goal of education in a free society is to prepare the young for adult life as independent human beings. Most significantly, what adults in a capitalist society need to possess are the knowledge, value, and skill of how to make independent judgments. What educational theory to date, however, has least focused on and needs urgently to address is psychological self-awareness, the ability to recognize and admit the influence of subconsciously held premises on conscious perceptions. This is the essential first step in achieving mental control, prerequisite of self-esteem and independence.

The influence of subconsciously held premises on conscious perceptions means that content of consciousness determines awareness and interpretation of newly encountered facts. Some facts are not even noticed, because of the mental set we have programmed in our minds over the years. Others can be distorted by the knowledge we do or do not possess.[14] Supporters of minimum wage laws, for example, fail to see the unemployment that the laws cause; they also assume that opposition to the laws is mean-spirited. Engineers and salespersons often do not see or understand the detailed and creative work that each do; this sometimes leads to abrasive friction within companies. And a husband may fail to notice his wife's new dress or hair style; the wife may then conclude that her husband does not love her. These are all examples of subconscious premises influencing conscious perceptions; they also exhibit a lack of psychological self-awareness on the part of each protagonist, for the premises motivating each are not recognized or acknowledged.

The claim that knowledge determines behavior is not controversial; educators have been making it for centuries, which is why they have placed so much emphasis on education as the shaper of personality. Narrowing the claim to assert that knowledge determines other knowledge is more likely to raise eyebrows, especially when the former is said to be held subconsciously. Awareness and acceptance of the notion of a subconscious mind and the need to introspect it is thwarted today by

---

[14] Intense concentration can also cause failure to notice a fact and emotional stress can cause both failure to notice facts and distortion of the facts that are perceived.

several factors. Most people do not stop long enough to question where their thoughts and emotions come from; both are taken as givens. On a more sophisticated level, two opposing beliefs prevent or minimize acknowledgment of the subconscious.

On the one hand, many people act as if the acquisition of knowledge is nearly automatic, provided teaching and learning are handled in the right way, because the mind is said to be a mirror of nature (as discussed in chapter 3), that is, because of the doctrine of intrinsicism. Learning just requires the ability and willingness, so to speak, to position the mirror in the right place in order to reflect the intrinsic essences; the effort required is the ability and willingness to separate form from matter, using Aristotle's terminology, to identify the essences, and to memorize them. Broad abstractions may require additional effort, but the process of positioning and memorizing is essentially the same. There is no need to look inward to become psychologically aware, because there is no inward place to look; there is no subconscious mind, according to this view. Therefore, only one legitimate perspective is possible; all others are erroneous and must have been acquired through faulty, probably less than moral, means. This is the viewpoint of most educational and political conservatives.

On the other hand, there are those who recognize that the acquisition of knowledge is not automatic and does take considerable effort, but that the very act of processing perceptual material produces different perspectives. And, they conclude, all such perspectives are equally valid. The mind is not a mirror of nature, but a processor that distorts nature. Introspection might make people feel better about the conclusions they draw, but it will not make an idea better or more true than any other. Disputes are resolved through democratic voting and negotiation to achieve a mutually acceptable solution. This is the doctrine of subjectivism, which is running rampant today, and is the viewpoint of most social liberals.[15] However, it is difficult to take subjectivism seriously, because it suffers so many contradictions, the self-excepting fallacy being most prominent.[16]

In art the invention of artificial perspective did not render the object being reproduced on a flat surface false or distorted; it provided more information about the object and a more accurate representation

---

[15] Subjectivism, once again, is "the view that essences and values are entirely dependent on the contents of consciousness and, as a result, have no connection to or basis in reality." See chap. 3, p. 72.

[16] See chap. 3, p. 80.

at that. The same can be said about differing perspectives on any subject of knowledge. Some perspectives may ultimately be shown to be false but the variety available enriches our understanding of the world. Indeed, through psychological self-awareness we may notice how our own perspective on things differs from that of someone else, but defensiveness can cause us to stop at this point, not appreciating the enrichment that can result, and remain aware only of the fact the two perspectives differ. Or defensiveness may lead us to condemn the other viewpoint as wrong and assume that it derives from an inappropriate motivation.

Perspectives, however, may differ because of misinformation, which may or may not contain a volitional element worthy of condemnation, or because of differing amounts and quality of information that constitute the conclusions that have been drawn. Defensiveness will cause this last to be missed entirely because reduction of anxiety is the focus of a such a psychology, not perception of the facts. Psychological self-awareness is required not just to provide insight into one's own motivation, and to change premises that need changing, but also to give one a sense of patience and openness toward different ideas and to those who espouse them. Knowledge of one's inner self and the consequent tolerance of the ideas of others that follows from that knowledge produce mental control and self-confidence.

Control of mental processes means the ability to regulate one's thoughts and emotions, not by repressing them, but by knowing the premises that lie behind the thoughts and emotions and by applying logic to the premises to assess their soundness. Applying logic to one's awareness of inner reality is as important as applying logic to one's awareness of outer reality, but the application of logic to inner mental processes is what assures us of having a correct relationship to the outer world. Mental control produces self-confidence and self-esteem. This in turn enables us to assert something as fact without regard for the disapproval or opposition of others, that is, it enables us to exercise independent judgment. Psychological self-awareness is required not just to know true from false perspectives in our own minds, but also to give us the strength and resolve to assert outwardly what we know to be true. Introspection is precondition of independence.

THE WORK AHEAD

Much work in the philosophy of education remains to be done, especially as it applies to a capitalist society. One required area of work is theoretical, the other practical. The rehabilitation of introspection as a legitimate, scientific method of acquiring knowledge is essential to advancement in the fields of psychology and educational psychology. The ability to perceive inwardly is crucial for both teachers and students. While self-report questionnaires may have their place in data collection, they are not the sine qua non of scientific research that positivists, behaviorists, and even cognitivists of the twentieth century have promoted. Universal principles concerning the operation of the mind, which includes the interactions between the mind's conscious and subconscious components, need to be identified. Conceptualization of mental processes and the relation between mental processes and behavior, especially between independent judgment and independent action, is the next step in developing the philosophy of education for a free market in education.

On the practical side of establishing a free market in education, parents and teachers must genuinely want their children and students to learn and exercise independent judgment; they must genuinely want their children and students to be freed from the servility of having to obey authority. Today, it is not obvious that this is what parents and teachers want. On a more fundamental level, adults must learn not to feel threatened when the young assert their independence and adults must reject doctrines that encourage obedience to authority, such as altruism, the worship of government as dispenser of justice, and religion. For these reasons, the development of a free market in education is not likely to occur in the near future. A major cultural change will be required first and the fields of philosophy, economics, and psychology must lead the way.

Bibliography

American Federation of Teachers. "AFT Press Center, Speeches and Columns, Where We Stand, 1998, May: No Bargain." http://www.aft.org/presscenter/speeches-columns/wws/1998/0598.htm.

American Tax Reform Foundation. "2005 Cost of Government Day: By the Numbers." http://www.atr.org/content/pdf/2005/jul/070705COGD-by%20the%20numbers.pdf.

Anderson, William P. "Mises versus Weber on Bureaucracy and Sociological Method." *Journal of Libertarian Studies* 18, no. 1 (Winter 2004): 1–29.

Ariès, Philippe. *Centuries of Childhood: A Social History of Family Life.* Translated by Robert Baldick. New York: Vintage Books, 1962.

Arieti, Silvano. *Creativity: The Magic Synthesis.* New York: Basic Books, 1976.

———. *Interpretation of Schizophrenia.* 2nd ed. New York: Basic Books, 1974.

Aristotle. *Nicomachean Ethics.* In *The Basic Works of Aristotle.* Richard McKeon, ed. New York: Random House, 1941.

Barzun, Jacques. *Teacher in America.* Garden City, NY: Doubleday Anchor Books, 1954.

Bear, Harry. "The Theoretical Ethics of the Brentano School: A Psycho-Epistemological Approach." Ph.D. diss. Columbia University, 1954.

Becker, Gary S. "If You Want to Cut Corruption, Cut Government." *Business Week.* December 11, 1995, 26.

Bishop, Morris. *The Middle Ages.* 1968. Reprint, Boston: Houghton Mifflin, 1987.

Blumenfeld, Samuel L. *How to Tutor.* Milford, MI: Mott Media, 1977.

Boaz, David, and Edward H. Crane, eds. *Market Liberalism: A Paradigm for the 21st Century.* Washington, DC: Cato Institute, 1993.

Boisvert, Raymond D. *Dewey's Metaphysics.* New York: Fordham University Press, 1988.

Bowen, James. *A History of Western Education.* 3 vols. New York: St. Martin's Press, 1972–81.

Boyd, William. *The History of Western Education*. 6th ed. London: Adam and Charles Black: 1952.

Branden, Barbara. *The Passion of Ayn Rand*. New York: Doubleday, 1986.

Branden, Nathaniel. "The Contradiction of Determinism." *The Objectivist Newsletter*. May 1963, 17, 19.

———. "Intellectual Ammunition Department: What is the Difference Between the Objectivist Concept of Free Will and the Traditional Concepts?" *The Objectivist Newsletter*. January 1964, 3.

———. *The Psychology of Self-Esteem*. New York: Bantam Books, 1971.

Brozen, Yale. *Is Government the Source of Monopoly? And Other Essays*. San Francisco: Cato Institute, 1980.

California State Code of Regulation, Title 22, Summary of Regulations for Child Care Centers—Preschool, Infant Centers, School Age Centers, and/or Combination Centers. http://i.b5z.net/i/u/696577/f/Child_Care_Centers.pdf.

Cameron, Rondo. *A Concise Economic History of the World*. New York and Oxford: Oxford University Press, 1989.

Chall, Jeanne S. *Learning to Read: The Great Debate*, 3rd ed. Ft. Worth, TX: Harcourt Brace, 1996.

Chodes, John. "State Subsidy to Private Schools: A Case History of Destruction." *The Freeman*. March 1991.

Comenius, John Amos. *The Great Didactic*. 1632. Translated by M. W. Keatinge. New York: Russell & Russell, 1910.

———. *Orbis Sensualium Pictus, English and Latin*. 1659. Reprint, London: Oxford University Press, 1968.

Compayré, Gabriel. *Abelard and the Origin and Early History of Universities*. 1893. Reprint, New York: Greenwood Press, 1969.

Conant, James B. *The American High School Today*. New York: McGraw-Hill, 1959.

Cooper, Lane, ed. *Louis Agassiz as a Teacher: Illustrative Extracts on His Method of Instruction*. Ithaca, NY: Comstock Publishing, 1917.

Copleston, Frederick. *A History of Philosophy*. Vol. 8, *Bentham to Russell*. Garden City, NY: Doubleday, Image Books, 1985.

Coulson, Andrew J. *Market Education: The Unknown History*. New Brunswick, NJ: Transaction Publishers, 1999.

Cremin, Lawrence A. *The Genius of American Education*. New York: Vintage Books, 1965.

———. *Popular Education and Its Discontents*. New York: Harper & Row, 1989.

———. *The Transformation of the School*. New York: Vintage Books, 1961

Csikszentmihalyi, Mihaly. *Flow: The Psychology of Optimal Experience*. New York: Harper & Row, 1990.

Dewey, John. *Democracy in Education: An Introduction to the Philosophy of Education*. New York: Free Press, 1916.

———. *Essays in Experimental Logic*. New York: Dover Publications, 1916.

———. *Experience and Education*. 1938. Reprint, New York: Collier Books, 1963.

———. *Experience and Nature*. 2nd ed. Chicago: Open Court, 1929.

———. *How We Think*. 1910. Reprint, Buffalo, NY: Prometheus Books, 1991.

——. "Individuality and Experience." 1926. Reprint, in John Dewey et al. *Art and Education*. The Barnes Foundation Press, 1929.

——. *Interest and Effort in Education*. Boston: Houghton Mifflin Co., 1913.

——. "Interest in Relation to the Training of the Will." In *Second Supplement of the Herbart Year Book for 1895*. 1896. Reprint, in John J. McDermott, ed. *The Philosophy of John Dewey: Two Volumes in One*. Chicago: University of Chicago Press, 1981, 421–42.

——. *Liberalism and Social Action*. New York: G. P. Putnam's Sons, 1935.

——. *The President's Report: July, 1898—July, 1899*. 1900. Reprint, in John Dewey, *The Middle Works, 1899—1924*, vol. 1, *1899—1901*. Jo Ann Boydston, ed. Carbondale, IL: Southern Illinois University Press, 1976.

——. "Progressive Education and the Science of Education." *Progressive Education*. July-August-September, 1928.

——. "Propositions, Warranted Assertibility, and Truth." *Journal of Philosophy* 38, no. 7 (March 27, 1941): 169–86.

——. *The Quest for Certainty*. 1929. Reprint, in *The Later Works, 1925–1953*, vol. 4, *1929: The Quest for Certainty*. Jo Ann Boydston, ed. Carbondale and Edwardsville: Southern Illinois University Press, 1984.

——. *The School and Society*. 1900. Reprint, Chicago: University of Chicago Press, 1990.

Domarus, E. von. "The Specific Laws of Thought in Schizophrenia." In J. S. Kasanin, ed., *Language and Thought in Schizophrenia*. Berkeley and Los Angeles: University California Press, 1944, 104–14

Drucker, Peter. *The Effective Executive*. New York: Harper & Row, 1966.

Farrell, Allan P. *The Jesuit Code of Liberal Education: Development and Scope of the Ratio Studiorum*. Milwaukee, WI: The Bruce Publishing Co., 1938.

Folsom, Jr., Burton. *Entrepreneurs vs. the State: A New Look at the Rise of Big Business in America, 1840–1920*. Reston, VA: Young America's Foundation, 1987.

Freud, Sigmund. *The Interpretation of Dreams*. Translated by James Strachey. 1900. Reprint, New York: Avon Books, 1965.

Friedman, Milton. "The Role of Government in Education." In Robert Solow, ed. *Education and the Public Interest*. New Brunswick, NJ: Rutgers University Press, 1955.

Froebel, Friedrich. *The Education of Man*. Translated by W. N. Hailmann. New York: D. Appleton and Company, 1895.

Fuller, Robert. *Somebodies and Nobodies: Overcoming the Abuse of Rank*. Gabriola Island, BC, Canada: New Society Publishers, 2003.

Garet, Michael, Tsze H. Chan, and Joel D. Sherman. *Estimates of Expenditures for Private K–12 Schools*. Washington, D.C.: U.S. Department of Education, 1995. Working paper no. 95–17. http://nces.ed.gov/pubsearch/pubsinfo.asp?pubid=9517.

Gay, Peter. *The Enlightenment*. 2 vols. New York: Alfred A. Knopf, 1969.

Gibson, James J. *Reasons for Realism: Selected Essays of James J. Gibson*. Hillsdale, NJ: Lawrence Erlbaum Associates, 1982.

Ginott, Haim G. *Between Parent & Child*. New York, Avon Books, 1965.

——. *Teacher & Child*. New York: Collier Books, 1972.

Glenn, Jr., Charles Leslie. *The Myth of the Common School.* Amherst, MA: University of Massachusetts Press, 1987.

Global Initiative to End All Corporal Punishment of Children. "End All Corporal Punishment of Children." http://endcorporalpunishment.org/pages/frame.html.

Goertz, Donna Bryant. *Children Who Are Not Yet Peaceful: Preventing Exclusion in the Early Elementary Classroom.* Berkeley, CA: Frog, Ltd., 2001.

Gordon, Thomas. *Discipline That Works.* New York: Penguin Putnam, 1991.

———. *Parent Effectiveness Training,* rev. ed. New York: Three Rivers Press, 2000.

———. *Teacher Effectiveness Training.* New York: Peter H. Wyden, Inc., 1974.

Gray, J. Glenn. *The Promise of Wisdom.* New York: J. P. Lippincott, 1968.

Green, T. H. "Lectures on the Principles of Political Obligation." In *Lectures on the Principles of Political Obligation and Other Writings.* Paul Harris and John Morrow, ed. Cambridge: Cambridge University Press, 1986, 13–193. Originally published posthumously in 1895.

Greenberg, Daniel. *Free at Last: The Sudbury Valley School.* Framingham, MA: Sudbury Valley School Press, 1995.

Haney, Craig, and Phillip Zimbardo. "It's Tough to Tell a High School from a Prison." *Psychology Today,* June 1975.

Haskins, Charles Homer. *The Rise of Universities.* 1923. Reprint, Ithaca, NY: Cornell University Press, 1957.

Hayek, Friedrich A. *The Counter-Revolution of Science: Studies on the Abuse of Reason.* Glencoe, IL: The Free Press, 1952.

———. *The Road to Serfdom.* Chicago: University of Chicago Press, 1944.

Herbart, Johann Friedrich. *Outlines of Educational Doctrine.* Translated by Alexis F. Lange. New York: Macmillan, 1901.

Herndon, James. *How to Survive in Your Native Land.* New York: Bantam Books, 1972.

Highet, Gilbert. *The Art of Teaching.* New York: Vintage Books, 1950.

Hobhouse, L. T. *Liberalism.* 1911. Reprint, Westport, CT: Greenwood Press, 1964.

Holmes, Paul. *Brahms: His Life and Times.* Southborough, England: Baton Press, 1984.

Holt, John. *How Children Fail.* Rev. ed. Reading, MA: Perseus Books, 1982.

Horney, Karen. *Neurosis and Human Growth: The Struggle toward Self-Realization.* New York: W. W. Norton, 1950.

James, William. *The Principles of Psychology.* 1890. Reprint, Cambridge, MA: Harvard University Press, 1983.

The Jesuit Ratio Studiorum of 1599. Translated by Allan P. Farrell. Washington, DC: Conference of the Major Superiors of Jesuits, 1970.

Johnson, Thomas L. *The Real Academic Community and the Rational Alternative.* Fredericksburg, VA: Lee Editions, 1980.

Kant, Immanuel. *Prolegomena to Any Future Metaphysics.* Translated by Lewis White Beck. 1783. Reprint, Indianapolis, IN: Bobbs-Merrill, 1950.

Kelley, David. *The Art of Reasoning.* New York: W. W. Norton, 1988.

———. *The Evidence of the Senses: A Realist Theory of Perception.* Baton Rouge, LA: Louisiana State University Press, 1986.

Kierstead, Janet. "Montessori and Dewey: The Best from Both." In M. P. Douglass, ed. *Claremont Reading Conference, 45th Yearbook.* Claremont, CA: Claremont Graduate School, 1981, 88–95.

Kilpatrick, William Heard. *Froebel's Kindergarten Principles Critically Examined.* New York: The Macmillan Co., 1916.

———. *The Montessori System Examined.* Boston: Houghton Mifflin Company, 1914)

Kindlon, Daniel, and Michael Thompson. *Raising Cain: Protecting the Emotional Life of Boys.* New York: Ballantine Books, 1999.

Kirkpatrick, Jerry. *In Defense of Advertising: Arguments from Reason, Ethical Egoism, and Laissez-Faire Capitalism.* 1994. Reprint, Claremont, CA: TLJ Books, 2007.

———. "In Defense of Lecturing, or: It's Time to Cut Down on TV in the Classroom." In Jeffrey T. Doutt and Gary F. McKinnon, eds. *Marketing Education: Exploring New Directions.* Proceedings of the Western Marketing Educators' Association Conference, April 1990, 80–85.

Kohn, Alfie. "The Dangerous Myth of Grade Inflation," *The Chronicle of Higher Education,* November 8, 2002. Also available online at http://www.alfiekohn.org/teaching/gi.htm.

———. *No Contest: The Case Against Competition.* Rev. ed. New York: Houghton Mifflin, 1992.

———. *Punished by Rewards: The Trouble with Gold Stars, Incentive Plans, A's, Praise, and Other Bribes.* Boston: Houghton Mifflin, 1993.

———. *Unconditional Parenting: Moving from Rewards and Punishments to Love and Reason.* New York: Atria Books, 2005.

Lave, Jean, Michael Murtaugh, and Olivia de la Rocha. "The Dialectic of Arithmetic in Grocery Shopping." In Barbara Rogoff and Jean Lave, eds. *Everyday Cognition: Its Development in Social Context.* Cambridge, MA: Harvard University Press, 1984, 67–94.

Leach, Penelope. *Your Baby and Child: From Birth to Age Five,* 3rd ed. New York: Alfred A. Knopf, 1997.

Lenin, V. I. *State and Revolution.* 1917. Reprint, New York: International Publishers, 1988.

Lillard, Paula Polk. *Montessori Today.* New York: Schocken Books, 1996.

Locke, John. *An Essay Concerning Human Understanding.* 1689. Reprint, Oxford: Oxford University Press, 1975.

———. *Some Thoughts Concerning Education.* 1690. Reprint, Ruth W. Grant and Nathan Tarcov, eds. Indianapolis: Hackett Publishing, 1996.

Love, Robert. *How to Start Your Own School.* Ottawa, IL: Green Hill Publishers, 1973

Mandelbaum, Maurice. "Some Instances of the Self-Excepting Fallacy." *Psychologishe Beiträge* 6 (1962): 383–86.

Marrou, H. I. *A History of Education in Antiquity.* Translated by George Lamb. 1956. Reprint, New York: Mentor Books, 1964.

Mayhew, Katherine Camp, and Anna Camp Edwards. *The Dewey School: The Laboratory School of the University of Chicago 1896—1903.* New York: D. Appleton-Century Company, 1936.

McMurry, Charles and Frank. *The Method of the Recitation.* New York: Macmillan, 1897.

Mises, Ludwig von. *Bureaucracy.* 1944. Reprint, Cedar Falls, IA: Center for
Futures Education, 1983.

——. "Economic Calculation in the Socialist Commonwealth." 1920. Reprint,
in F. A. Hayek, ed. *Collectivist Economic Planning: Critical Studies on the
Possibilities of Socialism.* Clifton, NJ: Augustus M. Kelley, 1975.

——. *Human Action.* 3rd rev. ed. Chicago: Henry Regnery Company, 1966.

——. *Liberalism: A Socio-Economic Exposition.* Translated by Ralph Raico.
Kansas City: Sheed Andrews & McMeel, 1978.

——. *Socialism.* Translated by J. Kahane. 1936. Reprint, Indianapolis, IN: Liberty Classics, 1981.

Montessori, Maria. *The Absorbent Mind.* 1949. Reprint, New York: Henry Holt,
1995.

——. *From Childhood to Adolescence.* 1948. 2nd ed. Reprint, New York: Schocken
Books, 1976.

——. *The Montessori Elementary Material.* Translated by Arthur Livingston.
1917. Reprint, Cambridge, MA: Robert Bentley, Inc., 1971.

——. *The Montessori Method.* Translated by Anne E. George. 1912. Reprint,
New York: Schocken Books, 1964.

——. *The Secret of Childhood.* Translated by M. Joseph Castelloe. 1936. Reprint,
New York: Ballantine Books, 1972.

——. *Spontaneous Activity in Education.* Translated by Florence Simmonds.
1917. Reprint, Cambridge, MA: Robert Bentley, 1971.

——. *To Educate the Human Potential.* 1948. Reprint, Oxford: Clio Press, 1989.

Montessori, Jr., Mario M. *Education for Human Development: Understanding
Montessori.* 1976. Reprint, Oxford: Clio Books, 1992.

Murray, Gilbert. *Five Stages of Greek Religion.* Garden City, NY: Doubleday &
Co., 1955.

National Center for Education Statistics (NCES). "Home, Digest of Education
Statistics Tables and Figures." http://nces.ed.gov/programs/digest/.

Neill, A. S. *Summerhill: A Radical Approach to Child Rearing.* New York, Hart
Publishing, 1960.

Nicholson, Eleanor. "An Analysis of Dewey and Montessori—Philosophers with
Many Similar Concepts." *The Constructive Triangle* 6 (1979): 12–21.

Oppenheimer, Franz. *The State.* Translated by John M. Gitterman. 1914. Reprint,
New York: Free-Life Editions, 1975.

Packer, Edith. "The Art of Introspection." *The Objectivist Forum.* December
1985.

——. "An Interview with Edith Packer on Psychotherapy." By Jerry Kirkpatrick.
The Intellectual Activist. March and May 1994.

——. *The Obsessive-Compulsive Syndrome.* Pamphlet. Laguna Hills, CA: The
Jefferson School of Philosophy, Economics, and Psychology, 1988.

——. *The Role of Philosophy in Psychotherapy.* Pamphlet. Laguna Hills, CA: The
Jefferson School of Philosophy, Economics, and Psychology, 1987.

——. "Understanding the Subconscious." *The Objectivist Forum.* February
and April 1985.

Passmore, J. A. "The Malleability of Man in Eighteenth-Century Thought." In Earl R. Wasserman, ed. *Aspects of the Eighteenth Century*. Baltimore: Johns-Hopkins Press, 1965.

Pestalozzi, Johann Heinrich. *How Gertrude Teaches Her Children: An Attempt to Help Mothers to Teach Their Own Children*. Translated by Lucy E. Holland & Frances C. Turner. Syracuse, NY: C. W. Bardeen, 1898.

———. *Letters on Early Education, Addressed to J. P. Greaves, Esq.* London: Sherwood, Gilbert, and Piper, 1827.

Piaget, Jean. *The Growth of Logical Thinking: From Childhood to Adolescence*. Translated by Anne Parsons and Stanley Milgram. New York: Basic Books, 1958.

———. *Science of Education and the Psychology of the Child*. Translated by Derek Coltman. New York: Orion Press, 1970.

Pipher, Mary. *Reviving Ophelia: Saving the Selves of Adolescent Girls*. New York: Putnam, 1994.

Plato. *Laws*. In *The Collected Dialogues of Plato Including the Letters*. Edith Hamilton and Huntington Cairns, eds. Princeton, NJ: Princeton University Press, 1961.

———. *The Republic of Plato*. Translated with introduction and notes by Francis MacDonald Cornford. New York: Oxford University Press, 1941.

Quintilian on Education. Translated by William M. Smail. New York: Teachers College Press, 1938.

Rand, Ayn. *Atlas Shrugged*. New York: Random House, 1957.

———. *Capitalism: The Unknown Ideal*. New York: New American Library, 1966.

———. *For the New Intellectual*. New York: Signet Book, New American Library, 1961.

———. *Introduction to Objectivist Epistemology*, expanded 2nd ed. New York: NAL Books, 1990.

———. *The New Left: The Anti-Industrial Revolution*. New York: Signet Book, New American Library, 1971.

———. *Philosophy: Who Needs It*. New York: Bobbs-Merrill, 1982.

———. *The Romantic Manifesto: A Philosophy of Literature*. New York: Signet Book, New American Library, 1971.

———. *The Virtue of Selfishness: A New Concept of Egoism*. New York: New American Library, 1964.

Ravitch, Diane. *Left Back: A Century of Failed School Reforms*. New York: Simon & Schuster, 2000.

———. *The Schools We Deserve*. New York: Basic Books, 1985.

Reardan, Linda. "Emotions as Pleasure/Pain Responses to Evaluative Judgments: A Modern, Aristotelian View." Ph.D. diss. Claremont Graduate University, 1999.

Reisman, George. *Capitalism: A Treatise on Economics*. Ottawa, IL: Jameson Books, 1996.

Rorty, Richard. *Philosophy and the Mirror of Nature*. Princeton, NJ: Princeton University Press, 1979.

Rothbard, Murray. "Bureaucracy and the Civil Service in the United States." *Journal of Libertarian Studies* 11, no. 2 (Summer 1995): 3–75.

———. *Man, Economy, and State: A Treatise on Economic Principles.* 1962. Reprint, 2 vols. in 1. Los Angeles: Nash Publishing, 1970.

Rousseau, Jean-Jacques. *Considerations on the Government of Poland.* Translated by Willmoore Kendall. Minneapolis: Minneapolis Book Store, 1947.

———. *Émile.* Translated by Barbara Foxley. London: J. M. Dent & Sons, 1911.

Royce, Joseph R. *The Encapsulated Man: An Interdisciplinary Essay on the Search for Meaning.* Princeton, NJ: D. Van Nostrand, 1964.

Rusk, Robert R. *The Doctrines of the Great Educators.* 2nd ed. London: Macmillan and Company, 1954.

Searle, John R. *Mind, Language, and Society: Philosophy in the Real World.* New York: Basic Books, 1998.

———. *Minds, Brains, and Science.* Cambridge, MA: Harvard University Press, 1984.

———. "Reality Principles: An Interview with John R. Searle." By Edward Feser and Steven Postrel. *Reason.* February 2000, 42–50.

Silberman, Charles. *Crisis in the Classroom.* New York: Random House, 1970.

Smith, Adam. *An Inquiry in the Nature and Causes of the Wealth of Nations.* 1776. Reprint, 2 vols. in 1. Edwin Cannan, ed. Chicago: University Chicago Press, 1976.

Smith, William A. *Ancient Education.* New York: Philosophical Library, 1955.

Spencer, Herbert. *Education: Intellectual, Moral and Physical.* New York: D. Appleton and Company, 1896.

———. *The Man Versus the State.* 1884. Reprint, Indianapolis: Liberty Classics, 1981.

Standing, E. M. *Maria Montessori: Her Life and Work.* 1957. Reprint, New York: Plume/Penguin, 1984.

Stanton, Frank. *Mass Media and Mass Culture.* New York: Columbia Broadcasting System, 1962.

Stoner, Winnifred Sackville. *Natural Education.* Indianapolis: Bobbs-Merrill, 1914.

Swafford, Jan. *Johannes Brahms: A Biography.* New York: Random House, 1997.

Teng, Ssu-Yu. "China's Examination System and the West." In Harley Farnsworth MacNair, ed. *China.* Berkeley and Los Angeles: University of California Press, 1951, 441–51.

Terman, Lewis. "An Experiment in Infant Education." *Journal of Applied Psychology* 2 (1918): 219–28.

Veazie, Walter B. "John Dewey and the Revival of Greek Philosophy." In *University of Colorado Studies, Series in Philosophy,* No. 2. 1961.

Wallas, Graham. *The Art of Thought.* New York: Harcourt, Brace & Co., 1926.

WASC Accreditation Handbook. Alameda, CA, 2001. Also available online at http://www.wascsenior.org/wasc/Doc_Lib/2001%20Handbook.pdf.

Watson, Robert I. *The Great Psychologists.* 4th ed. New York: J. B. Lippincott, 1978.

Weber, Max. "Bureaucracy." Translated by H. H. Gerth and C. Wright Mills. In *Max Weber on Charisma and Institution Building.* Edited by S. N. Eisenstadt. Chicago: University of Chicago Press, 1968, 66–77.

Whyte, Lancelote Law. *The Unconscious Before Freud*. New York: Basic Books, 1960.

Young, S. David. *The Rule of Experts: Occupational Licensing in America*. Washington, D.C.: Cato Institute, 1987.

Zilversmit, Arthur. *Changing Schools: Progressive Education Theory and Practice, 1930–1960*. Chicago: University of Chicago Press.

Index